A NEW ENGLAND PRISON DIARY

In the winter of 1812, the New Hampshire shopkeeper Timothy M. Joy abandoned his young family, fleeing the creditors who threatened to imprison him. Within days, he found himself in the Ipswich, Massachusetts, jailhouse, charged with defamation of a prominent politician. During the months of his incarceration, Joy kept the remarkable journal that forms the centerpiece of the microhistory presented in this book.

Martin J. Hershock situates Joy's account in the context of the political, cultural, and economic revolutions of the early nineteenth century. First and foremost, Joy's journal recounts a personal, anguished path toward spiritual redemption. It offers a vista into the pugnacious politics of the early American republic and illustrates a common citizen's perspective on partisanship. Significantly, it also sketches a profile of an unfortunate shopkeeper swept along in the transition to market capitalism. Hershock provides close-up views not only of an ordinary person's experience of a transformative period but also of a historian at work. In the final chapter, he discusses the value of diaries as historical sources, the choices he made in telling Joy's story, alternative interpretations of the diary, and other contexts in which he might have placed Joy's experiences. The appendix reproduces Joy's original journal so that readers can develop their own skills using a primary source.

MARTIN J. HERSHOCK is Associate Provost and Associate Professor of History at the University of Michigan–Dearborn.

A NEW ENGLAND PRISON DIARY

*Slander, Religion, and Markets
in Early America*

Martin J. Hershock

THE UNIVERSITY OF MICHIGAN PRESS
Ann Arbor

Published in the United States of America by
The University of Michigan Press
Manufactured in the United States of America
⊗ Printed on acid-free paper

2015   2014   2013   2012   4   3   2   1

A CIP catalog record for this book is available from the British Library.

Library of Congress Cataloging-in-Publication Data

Hershock, Martin J., 1962–
    A New England prison diary : slander, religion, and markets in early
America / Martin J. Hershock.
        p.   cm
    Includes bibliographical references and index.
    ISBN 978-0-472-07181-4 (cloth : alk. paper) —
    ISBN 978-0-472-05181-6 (pbk. : alk. paper) —
    ISBN 978-0-472-02852-8 (e-book)
    1. Joy, Timothy Meander, 1789–1813.   2. Joy, Timothy Meander, 1789–
1813—Diaries.   3. Prisoners—Massachusetts—Biography.   4. Prisoners—
Massachusetts—Diaries.   5. Massachusetts—Social conditions—19th
century.   6. Libel and slander—Massachusetts—History—19th century.
7. Pickering, Timothy, 1745–1829—Adversaries.   I. Title.
HV9468.J69H47   2012
364.9744'5—dc23
[B]   2012011071

CONTENTS

Illustrations following page 108

ACKNOWLEDGMENTS

The amount of time that has passed between the moment that I first conceived of this project and its culmination ensures that I have a great many people to thank for helping me at various stages along the way. Most obviously, I am grateful to the Bentley Historical Library at the University of Michigan for permission to reprint Timothy Joy's prison journal as well as for financial assistance, in the form of a Mark C. Stevens Research Fellowship in 1998, in support of the project. More important still, I am forever indebted to the staff of the library for their always amiable and efficient help. I never tire of visiting the library and of seeing my many friends there.

Additional funding sources have been critical to this project as well. In particular, a Faculty Research Grant from Hobart and William Smith Colleges for the academic year 1998–99 enabled me to hire a student assistant to help in verifying an extant transcription of the manuscript and in funding a return visit to the Bentley Library to finish up my research there. Likewise, a Rackham Faculty Research Grant and Fellowship from the University of Michigan in Ann Arbor and Research Grants obtained through the Provost's Office, the Office of Sponsored Research, and the Office of the Dean of the College of Arts, Sciences, and Letters at the University of Michigan–Dearborn, as well as a Research Fellowship granted by the Phillips Library at the Peabody Essex Museum in Salem, Massachusetts, supported me in my numerous trips east in search of the contextual evidence necessary to reconstruct Timothy Meader Joy's life and to tell his story. Without this support, this project would not have been possible.

I have also had the good fortune of working with a number of wonderful people at the various archives, libraries, and government offices that I visited while trying to track down relevant information. The staff at the Baker Library at Harvard University found a way to make my hurried trip to their cramped temporary facility (the main building was under renovation) both enjoyable and productive. I was also the beneficiary of the exceptional level of service extended by the staff of the Probate and Deeds Offices at the Strafford County, New Hampshire, county building; by the librarians at the New Hampshire Historical Society in Concord; and by the archivists at the American Antiquarian Society. The bulk of the research for this book, however, took place at the New Hampshire State Archives, in the Milne Special Collections at the Dimond Library on the campus of the University of New Hampshire in Durham, and in the Phillips Library (a truly underappreciated gem) at the Peabody Essex Museum in Salem, Massachusetts. I cannot say enough about the wonderful staffs of these fine institutions or about how welcome they all made me feel. I would also be remiss if I did not mention the assistance of the volunteer staff at the Durham Historic Association who gladly made their collection available to me and who not as gladly, I am certain, shared a very hot afternoon in a museum temporarily bereft of air-conditioning, answering my many questions. Thank you all.

A huge thank-you is also due to Melody Herr of the University of Michigan Press. Your belief in this project and in my scholarship has been unwavering, and I am most appreciative of your patience and unflagging support. Like far too many authors, I have taken advantage of your kind generosity and tolerance. I can only hope that the final product is what you hoped it might be. I remain forever in your debt for all that you have done for me.

A great many others deserve recognition for their part in this work. Dr. Claudia Walters eagerly took on the job of creating the accompanying maps. Lisa Fasolo Frishman diligently worked to transcribe the text of the journal and, perhaps even more important, provided a new and rather uncertain professor with unceasing encouragement and support. I will never forget what she did for me, and I remain eternally grateful for her continued friendship. I also owe tremendous debts to Elizabeth Zellner and Jennifer Huff, both former students at the University of Michigan–Dearborn, for their assistance in untangling Joy's complex religious thinking. Your insightful suggestions and comments were most helpful. Others, such as Jennifer Reid-Lamb, a truly gifted history teacher, read early drafts of the work and offered very useful suggestions. Any errors that made their way into the final manuscript are by no means a fault of theirs.

Thanks go as well to Jamie and Mark Labelle, for their gracious hosting and their interest in my work and for (with the assistance of Jack, their dog) providing me with a story for the ages. I am so pleased that we are family. Dr. Sean Kesterson is owed a thank-you and a cold beer for his assistance in deciphering Timothy Joy's illness. Additional thanks are due to the students and faculty at Fitchburg State College, where I spoke about an early draft of the book, and to the students—especially Emily Shafer—in my fall 2007 senior seminar on microhistory at the University of Michigan–Dearborn, for their thoughtful comments on this work and on my approach to Joy. I hope the final project reflects the imprint that you all made on the work.

I am especially thankful to the many friends and colleagues who read various drafts of this material, who listened patiently while I talked incessantly about Timothy Joy, and who offered wonderful company and release when I became too consumed with my work. No one could ask for a better set of colleagues than I have at the University of Michigan–Dearborn. Cam Amin, Pam Pennock, Gerry Moran, Elaine Clark, Liz Rohan, and Ron Stockton all took an early interest in the project and offered very useful suggestions and advice. Georgina Hickey graciously agreed to fill in for me as department chair so that I could take a sabbatical to write the book. I am truly fortunate to have such a wonderful group of colleagues and friends.

I have also been blessed, over the course of my professional life, to have a close circle of personal friends who serve as a constant source of sage advice and personal support: Kevin Thornton, Paul Finkelman, John Quist, Cara Shelly, and Mills Thornton. While you may not recognize your imprint on this work, all of you have shaped it (and me) in important ways. One of my greatest pleasures over the last few years has been my friendship with Christine Dee. Beyond her astute eye for a good historical hook and her astonishing historical knowledge, she is also an incredible friend. Your unflagging support of my work (and our ongoing hockey dialogue) means the world to me. If not for my dear friend Kevin Boyle, this book would look much different than it does. His masterful work *Arc of Justice* and lots of hand-holding helped me to find a new voice and led me to a number of new insights about the craft of history. Beyond his professional guidance, I am grateful for yet another opportunity to thank him for being such a tremendous friend for so many years. Words cannot even begin to express my gratitude for the blessing that is my friend Bil Kerrigan. We have shared much over the course of more than two decades of friendship, and I treasure every moment of it. With each passing day, I become more aware of how incredibly fortunate I am to call you friend.

My greatest debt, however, is owed to my family: my wife, Kathy, and my daughters, Rebecca and Rachel. They have lived with Timothy Joy for well over a decade now and with a myopic spouse/father who has been consumed with him. Your patience and understanding, even in those many moments when it was not at all deserved, were duly noted and very much appreciated. I cherish our life together much more than any of you could know. It is to the three of you that this work is dedicated.

INTRODUCTION

In late March of 1812, an obscure, indebted, twenty-two-year-old trader by the name of Timothy Meader Joy found himself suddenly and unexpectedly, if only momentarily, thrust into the national limelight. Hard pressed by his creditors and thrown into a heightened state of confusion by an early morning raid on his crossroads store by local officials acting on these creditors' behalf and threatening to return and arrest him, the young man had, just days before, frantically fled his home in Middleton—a struggling town only recently hewn from the New Hampshire frontier—leaving behind his pregnant wife, Mary, and two infant children, Alfred Timothy and Mary. Setting his sights on the bustling seaport of Salem, Massachusetts, where he hoped to find employment, Joy, fearing impending arrest at every turn, wandered frenetically through the frozen New Hampshire countryside for two days. Finally making his way into Massachusetts, Joy stopped at a Haverhill tavern for a bite to eat and some liquid refreshment. There he became involved in an animated political debate. Partisan to his Democratic-Republican core and under the influence of too much drink, the young man, finding himself surrounded by convivial company, spun a tale of treason and deceit involving the prominent national symbol of Federalism and local denizen Timothy Pickering. Coming as they did in the midst of the nation's intensely partisan build-up toward war with Great Britain and on the eve of a closely contested gubernatorial election in Massachusetts, Joy's allegations sparked an immediate furor and led to his arrest in Salem the following day for defamation. Dragged before a local magistrate at an arraignment hearing and confronted with the allegations he had made,

Joy owned up to his fabrication. Joy's scandalous behavior earned the young man the early nineteenth century's equivalent of fifteen minutes of fame (or, more appropriately, infamy) and jail time (initially in Salem and then at the new stone prison in nearby Ipswich) while he awaited his May trial date in the Massachusetts Supreme Judicial Court. While incarcerated, the unlucky Joy kept a detailed diary of his prison experience.

Beginning the prison journal that stands at the core of this book and that serves as the primary foundation for what we know of his life story, Timothy Meader Joy wrote, "I have thought proper to commit to paper while in my rational moments the most extraordinary circumstances which have happened to my Imprisonment." Certainly, elements of the "extraordinary" are evident in Joy's story—notably, his widely publicized arrest in the aftermath of a scandalous public slander (albeit in a rather inconspicuous place) of one of the nation's best-known politicians and the intense partisan rancor that his allegations initiated. It is also certainly doubtful that any other word but *extraordinary* could even begin to describe the feelings of this young man who found himself in the unfamiliar circumstance of being the focus of public attention and incarcerated for the first time in his life, and Joy was undeniably aware of the turn of events—which must have seemed extraordinary to him—that had precipitated his flight from New Hampshire and his rapid and surprising fall from respectability. In the end, however, there was apparently too little of the extraordinary in Joy's story to suit the broader public: he quickly faded, if he had even ever registered, from the public consciousness and returned, after his release in June of 1812, to his life in relative obscurity. After a brief and unremarkable stint in the United States Army during the War of 1812, Joy contracted illness and returned to his boyhood home in Durham. There, in July of 1813, he succumbed to his illness and passed from this world, with no obituary marking his passing and with nothing more than a simple white headstone to mark his final resting place in the Joy family plot.[1]

Compiling and sorting through the minutiae of the twenty-three years that constitute Timothy Meader Joy's ephemeral life and then weaving those details into the narrative that constitutes this book has taken me nearly as long as it did for the young man to live out his all-too-brief life. For over eighteen years, Timothy Joy has been part of my professional and personal life, sometimes as an all-consuming passion (shaping family trips and dinner-table discussion), but more often than not as a lingering puzzle and collection of questions turning constantly and persistently in my mind. What was this young man's life like? How typical were he and his plight? What did the Durham of his youth look like? What had driven him to abandon his wife and two small children on that cold March evening in 1812? To whom did he owe money, and how much did he owe? Why did he say such outlandish things about Timothy Pickering in Kendall's Tavern on that Friday afternoon? What ran through his mind as he stood on Derby's Wharf amid the hustle and bustle of Salem on the day of his arrest? Why did officials offer such a heavy-handed response to the utterances of a young inebriate? How can we account for the absence of Timothy's father, Deacon Samuel, from Timothy's journal writings while the young man awaited his trial date in Ipswich Prison? Did the renewed spiritualism that he discovered in prison stay with him for the remainder of his short life? What was his military experience like? What was it that finally led to the young man's untimely death? What became of his young family? These and many, many more questions have kept my mind very busy throughout the duration of this project. This book represents my effort to address some of what I believe to be the most salient of my findings in light of the questions that I have asked and to share with readers what I believe I have come to know about Timothy Joy and the many ways in which his life intertwined with the myriad threads that comprise this chapter of the American national story.

The questions that inspired and perplexed me and the ways in which the questions that I asked shaped my approach to and interpretation of the historical evidence can in no way be said to be the only approach that one could take in exploring, describing, and delineating the contours of Joy's life and its overall relevance or irrelevance. On the contrary, as any student of history knows, historical thinking and interpretation is a process, a craft, that depends equally on scrupulous investigative work, analytical rigor, and skilled inference and guesswork, all of which are colored by an individual historian's personal perspective, experiences, and point of view. More often than not, these considerations are clearly evident in the interpretation of the historical past offered by individual historians. What is generally not so clear to readers of historical literature is how this process of historical thinking unfolds and the choices confronted and decisions made by those engaged in writing the history being explored. With this in mind, my approach to my recounting of Timothy Joy's life has always been twofold: (1) to tell Timothy Joy's story and explain its broader significance and connection to contemporary historical trends as I understand them and (2) to tell this story in a way that will enable readers to see how a historian approaches a body of evidence and how that historian, in turn, mines and then employs that evidence to construct answers and explanations; that is, I want to make clear to all why my work looks and reads the way that it does.

My interest in making transparent what is all too often rendered murky and impenetrable by many working historians stems from my own experiences with my undergraduate students and their frequently expressed disinterest in what they perceive to be "history"—that is, the rote memorization of a collection of names, dates, and events—and from my extensive collaboration with K–12 history professionals through the Teaching American History Grant program. These experiences have inspired me to take stock of my own approach to teaching history and of how to better demonstrate to those being exposed to the subject that the discipline is one of inquiry and exploration, that history is a series of puzzles and conundrums waiting to be worked out in light of the available evidence. Indeed, as argued in a seminal 2007 address at the National History Center by Professor Robert Bain, one of the leading proponents of this new, more transparent approach to teaching history, teachers of history "should learn how historians frame problems, select details, and analyze and construct stories in order to present these 'invisible' structures to their students in meaningful ways." The same can also be said, of course, for general readers of historical works. Bain believes that only by pulling back the layers and revealing how historians use facts to make meaning of the world do we demonstrate the importance and relevance of history to those engaged with the discipline. With this brief discussion as a backdrop, I intend to strive to make clear to the readers of this work the "invisible" structures that serve as the foundation for my retelling of Timothy Joy's story.[2]

Why does Timothy Meader Joy or his diary matter? The answer lies in the things that made his life typical of the millions of ordinary post-Revolutionary American men whose day-to-day struggles and triumphs remain the stuff of vague generalities, speculation, and informed guesswork. In the end, it is Joy's preoccupation with the "ordinary" in the journal he kept while in prison—his struggle to make a go of it in an increasingly commercial world, his feelings about that world, his individual hopes and fears, the worry and embarrassment surrounding economic failure and the inability to live up to society's prescribed gender roles, his personal struggles over matters of faith, the partisan ruminations of an everyday citizen, and the daily rhythm of life in an early American prison—that renders the document that he created and the retelling of his story most interesting and meaningful to the modern reader. We find the human condition, in all of its complexity and immediacy, revealed in the thoughts Joy sometimes carefully and painstakingly wrote out and sometimes absentmindedly scrawled; in the heartrending tears shed by the lonely, confused, and ill young man; in the vivid descriptions of the bone-chilling cold that gripped him in his frigid stone cell; in the deeply felt outrage expressed after an insult to an aged Revolutionary War veteran whom he did not know personally; and in the intimate disclosure of his spiritual torment and search for truth. The organic nature of Joy's journal and his close attention to detail draws us into his life and allows us to almost touch the past.[3]

At the same time, as much as we might empathize with Timothy Joy and feel a bond forged in our common humanity, as much as we might shed a tear in sympathy or see something of ourselves or our own circumstances in his words and deeds, it is imperative to remember that his story is very much rooted in a specific historical context— a moment in time very different from any that we have individually known—which we must consider carefully before extracting lessons and attributing our own meaning. Born in the immediate aftermath of the Revolutionary struggle with Great Britain, Timothy Joy was one of those individuals both blessed and burdened with the responsibility for forging a new national identity and charting a new direction for the now independent United States. In this heady historical moment, custom, community, and convention frequently found themselves jostling uneasily with innovation, individualism, and modernism, especially among those, such as Timothy Joy, who had no tangible experience with the nation's colonial past and thus fewer reasons to cling to tradition. With political, economic, religious, and social orthodoxies now open questions, the first generation of Americans sought to craft a new America that blended elements of the past and the present in an effort to best embody the nation's ideals and spirit. The degree to which any one individual borrowed from these competing sets of ideals and values was, of course, an intensely personal decision dependent on a great many factors (race, religion, class, gender, ethnicity, and regional identity, to name but a few). In the end, of course, the collective process of forging an identity and of establishing new social, economic, and political boundaries within such an unsettled environment led to the creation of a more open, more democratically inclined and commercially oriented society wherein, many came to believe, one's ability to rise and succeed was limited only by their own initiative and talent. Thus, an examination of Joy's life, as revealed through his prison journal and the supporting historical evidence, offers a wonderful opportunity to examine the forging of both individual and national identities as the process played itself out at the most fundamental level—in the day-to-day life of one of the post-Revolutionary generation. Though his diary entries often raise as many questions as they answer, they explain much about Timothy Joy the individual, his neighbors and family, the early American nation, and the era in which he lived.[4]

I have organized this book in a manner that is intended to reflect what Timothy Meader Joy believed (as revealed by his journal entries) to be the most important themes influencing his own life—family, his quest for personal respectability, religion, and politics—while simultaneously striving to provide a contextual base for these themes (and thus Joy's story) within the broader history of the era. I do not attempt to deal with every facet of Joy's journal but, rather, seek to deal with its most salient themes.

I begin by exploring the long history of the Joy family in the Americas and its efforts over time to seek out opportunity, stability, and respectability. The struggle to achieve a competency (a level of success that ensured an individual's economic autonomy) among Joy's male ancestors explains why the family made its way to Durham, New Hampshire; the difficulties faced by the various generations as they worked toward and eventually succeeded in earning their success; the choices available to them in pursuing their goals; their efforts to preserve and solidify their individual and family status; and the legacy that Timothy Meader Joy desperately sought to live up to. I also examine the social, religious, and economic environment of Durham, Joy's birthplace, and how that town's post-Revolutionary growth and commercial success, along with its contested religious environment, influenced and shaped the young man's outlook and the eventual choices he made in the pursuit of his own calling in life, choices that eventually led him into the mercantile trade in Middleton, New Hampshire.

The second phase of Timothy Joy's life was that of a young head of household, which illuminates the pervasive burden of debt and contemporary attitudes regarding personal financial failure. Timothy Joy's decision to forsake the vocation of his father and brothers—that of farmer—and to become a country trader and conduit between seaboard suppliers of finished and household items and local producers of foodstuffs and other raw materials, such as lumber, was predicated on his experiences as a youth and young man coming of age in the coastal region of New Hampshire during the region's golden age of post-Revolutionary economic growth, a period of success that hinged on demand driven by the Napoleonic Wars in Europe and lubricated by an extensive and increasingly impersonal credit system. Poor timing and a tightening credit market, however, quickly doomed Joy's business venture and threatened to land him in prison for debt, thus precipitating his subsequent flight. Because Joy lived in a time and place that offered multiple and sometimes contradictory understandings of the root causes and meaning of failure and that provided few, if any, safety nets, his attempts to make sense of his situation and thus to attribute blame to some personal fault or to some external cause were necessarily difficult. He struggled to work through these various points of view and to sift through the inherent contradictions between Protestant teachings and material wealth, and his struggle and his conclusions about the meaning of failure in light of his deliberations shed much light on what the "pursuit of happiness" meant as the new nation was establishing its foundational market economy.

Religion serves as another key theme in the life of Timothy Joy. Above all else, he was a deeply spiritual person who tended to view most of what happened around him and to him through the lens of his spirituality. Though grounded in the orthodox Calvinism of his father, Joy had also, by 1812, been exposed to the more liberal doctrines of the Freewill Baptists and other Protestant reformers and to the idea that salvation, once obtained, could be lost. Uncertain about how to interpret, in a spiritual sense, his economic failure, the incident at Haverhill, and his subsequent arrest, Joy spent much of his jail time engaged in self-study and scriptural reflection. His writings reveal a man in the throes of spiritual upheaval and capture the tortured process of religious renewal, thus offering much insight into a phenomenon generally hidden from view. In the end, Joy's prison journal stands as a prime example of the tradition of the early American spiritual journal and offers a very interesting point of entry into the highly contested religious landscape of the era.

Because Joy was writing at a moment of intense party conflict between the Federalist supporters of Alexander Hamilton (who envisioned a stable, elite-led, and deference-bound commercial nation) and those favoring the more egalitarian and liberal agrarian ideals of Thomas Jefferson and James Madison (who called themselves Democratic-Republicans), his journal stands as a uniquely personal account of the hard-fought world of partisan politics in the nation's formative period. Joy's actions in Haverhill (both symbolic and actual) and the subsequent publicity surrounding his arrest and incarceration were, first and foremost, political events. Shorn of that context, they are incomprehensible and meaningless. Infused with Calvinism's stern morality and believing that his Democratic principles (typical of many in New Hampshire's Great Bay region) were those best suited for promoting the nation's overall good and, conversely, that those of his Federalist opponents were a threat to that good, Timothy Joy, not surprisingly, viewed the world as a place of stark contrasts and of constant struggle between right and wrong. Because his writing explores his personal understanding of and the meaning that he attached to the political ideologies put forth by the Federalist and Democratic-Republican parties—ideologies that he clearly conflates with his own class and religious identities—Joy's journal is able to move the reader beyond the traditional focus on party formation and party operation during the years of the first American party system and begins to recover the more complex and compelling story of what this political tension reveals about how Americans understood the meaning of their Revolution and newfound freedom and how these politics and political symbols were interpreted by individual partisans at the personal level.

In chapter 5, I examine Timothy Joy's brief and tragic postprison life: his response to his economic difficulties, his service in the War of 1812, his untimely death in July 1813, and the fate of his family. Though he was not able to achieve the personal success and respectability that he so desperately sought for himself, his children were able to achieve a measure of success.

The book's final chapter represents my attempt to make visible my own approach to the study of Joy's life. I there present the decisions I made about the structure of the book, the questions I asked of the evidence, and a discussion of the merits of the microhistorical method of inquiry. In the appendix, I include a version of the entire journal penned by Timothy Meader Joy between late March and early June 1812, slightly edited and annotated to eliminate minor repetition from page to page and to make the material more accessible to the modern reader.

My aim in this book is to reconstruct the world of Timothy Meader Joy as fully as possible, in the hope of better understanding a young man coming of age in the turbulent period that was post-Revolutionary America. Despite the advantages of being born into a successful Durham family and into a new nation now freed of British control, Joy, like the many thousands of others of his generation, found himself endeavoring to carve out a life for himself and his family in the context of a changing national and international economy, a nascent American political culture, and the growing threat of international war. Finding himself with one foot planted solidly in the ever-contested religious, economic, social, and cultural ethos of the tradition-bound antebellum past yet simultaneously drawn to a rapidly evolving and constantly shifting modern sensibility, Joy struggled mightily to chart his own course toward respectability and security. Sadly, but also consistent with the experiences of many of his peers, Joy's struggles to establish his place in the world did not result in immediate success but, rather, led to debt, failure, self-doubt, and, in his particular case, imprisonment and ridicule. While one might be tempted to dismiss Joy's story as insignificant or unimportant, it is anything but. Because many of Joy's life experiences were widely shared by many ordinary Americans at the time and because we know so much about his own personal feelings about these experiences, his story is all the more important. It stands as a microcosm of the stories of many others. The rich details about his life, his thoughts, and his actions make his story a truly compelling one that reveals to the reader the complexity, the nuance, and the extraordinariness of an ordinary life lived in an "extraordinary" moment in the nation's history.[5]

Chapter 1

"A STRANGER OF GOOD ADDRESS AND PERSONAL APPEARANCE"

On a spring day in late April of 1806, the Reverend Curtis Coe, minister of the Congregational Church in Durham, New Hampshire, took to the pulpit to deliver his valedictory address. Among those who undoubtedly assembled to bid farewell to their pastor were church deacon Samuel Joy (elected to his post in 1791, though he did not accept it until 1792); his wife, Hannah Meader Joy; and the couple's youngest sons, twenty-year-old Ebenezer and sixteen-year-old Timothy.

The atmosphere in the fourteen-year-old meetinghouse that day was certainly charged as the Joy family assumed their places in their pew (number 42, at the rear of the meetinghouse and to the left of the main entrance). The congregation was unsettled due to recent events. Confusion and anxiety lined many faces. After nearly twenty-six years of dedicated service to his flock and to the community, the fifty-six-year-old Coe, an old-line, Brown University–educated, orthodox Congregationalist, was leaving his post, forced out by a combination of Baptist and "Liberal" dissenters and a growing body of Durham residents who rejected the idea of an established church and embraced the rapidly expanding Revolutionary principle of separation of church and state. Mounted behind his pulpit, the six-foot-tall Coe faced his congregation. Such a paragon of dignity and strength must have cut an impressive figure. "More than twenty-eight years have elapsed since, in compliance with your request, I first visited you; and more than twenty five years, since my life was solemnly consecrated to your service," Coe began in an emotional voice. "It was expected," he continued, "that the remainder of mortal life would have been spent in arduous labors for the endless salvation of a friendly people." "But the unfriendly conduct of some has," Coe continued, "for a number of years, interrupted our general harmony, served to encourage dissipation, and eclipsed my once fair prospects of usefulness." "Hence," the pastor lamented, "my public labors, among you, must now discontinue."[1]

Not one to miss a final opportunity to preach his brand of Calvinist orthodoxy to an attentive audience, Coe seized the moment and proceeded to deliver a cautionary jeremiad from the pulpit. Unleashing a continuous barrage of Calvinist doctrine (a discussion of the depraved state of humankind; a review of the doctrine of unconditional election; a discourse on the unmerited favor of God's mercy, the perfection of God, etc.), the embattled minister returned to his favorite theme—the doctrine of "free, sovereign, and special Grace." In full stride now, Coe warned,

> Such is the evil of hard and impenitent hearts, that they ever continue unwilling to accept everlasting mercy, unless sovereign grace inclines them. Nothing, indeed, is required of the sinner, in order to acceptance [*sic*], but repentance toward God, and faith toward our Lord Jesus Christ. But still they choose rather to die in their sins, than to turn, unless an almighty power shall make them willing. Hence, no truth is more evident from the bible, and from observation, than that special grace is given to some, while others are left to their own evil courses.

Despite his best efforts, this message had not resonated with the residents of Durham, he claimed. As a result, "sorrow, grief and lamentation become us, that so few appear cordially to love the religion of Christ, the source of all real happiness and true pleasure in time and eternity."[2]

Embedded within Coe's familiar discourse on Calvinist theology was a biting critique of contemporary Durham and American society writ large. "The pleasures of sin, or the deceitful charms of this vain world, have alas," Coe deplored, "gained more attention, than endless good and life everlasting." Greatly disturbed by what he perceived to be the selfishness and greed of the times—traits inimical to his understanding of Protestantism—Coe queried his audience, "Is not the land defiled by falsehood, profanity, and blasphemy of the present age?" "Has not self," he asked, "often had the ascendancy, and more inconsiderable motives gained general attention?" Emphasizing the point further, Coe warned, "In these last days perilous times have come.

Men have become lovers of their owne [*sic*] selves, and lovers of pleasures, more than lovers of God." "You were born to live in a day of uncommon temptation," he admonished, "a spirit of slumber has come
upon this generation, eyes that do not see, and ears that do not hear
unto this day." Most troubling of all, the departing Coe pointedly
noted, particularly in light of the sad state of contemporary society,
was the spiritual condition of Durham's youth, young men and women
such as Ebenezer and Timothy Joy and their peers. "Little encouragement have I received to catechize and instruct rising plants in society,"
he declared, "in the great things which concern their everlasting
peace." The tragic result of this circumstance, Coe stated, was that,
"having little privilege of instruction, many in this hour of temptation,
which has come on the world, learn to despise that being, in whose
hands is their breath, and all his holy and good commands." With his
words reverberating through the meetinghouse and through the
minds of his congregants, Reverend Coe bid his church peace and
somberly left his pulpit.[3]

Seated among the emotional congregants, Timothy Joy must certainly have been moved by what had just transpired. Like his own father, Samuel, the Reverend Coe had been a constant in Timothy's
young life. Coe was the only minister he had ever known and had been
his primary source, along with his father, for religious training. He had
baptized all of the Joy children, including Timothy himself (in September of 1789), and had married Timothy's brother Samuel and his
sisters Sally and Polly. Moreover, as the father of one of Timothy Joy's
closest childhood friends (also named Curtis, born 1787), Coe had had
ample opportunity to interact with and influence Timothy outside of
the village meetinghouse as well. As the prison journal that Timothy
penned a mere six years later (itself an unwitting valedictory) makes
clear, the theology preached by the Reverend Curtis Coe and the
broader message of his final sermon definitely struck a chord with
Timothy Joy. The outgoing pastor's warnings about the perils of contemporary life were undoubtedly made all the more prescient for Joy
by the rapidly shifting socioeconomic environment and tumultuous
political and ideological climate of the day. The conflicted Durham
described by Coe was hardly a fiction of the disgruntled pastor's imagination. On the contrary, a great many of the trends described by Coe
were very much in evidence in turn-of-the-century Durham and
throughout the nation at large. Coming of age in an era of pronounced, dramatic, and, for many, unsettling change, Joy, who wit-

nessed firsthand the ambiguous effects of this transformation on Durham and how his beloved village minister had been cast aside as a relic, could not have helped but to have taken Coe's sermon to heart.[4]

Timothy Meader Joy was born on July 16, 1789, into a Durham community that was in the throes of redefining and reordering itself in the aftermath of the recent upheaval of the Revolutionary struggle and the attendant efforts to decipher its meaning and ramifications and in the face of an embryonic and rapidly expanding market capitalism. First settled by Europeans around 1640, the Oyster River Plantation (as Durham was originally known) sat on a point of land jutting out into New Hampshire's Great Bay and initially stood as a remote outpost of Dover (originally named Northam), a larger settlement established by a group of Puritan merchants and led by Captain Thomas Wiggins nearly a decade before on the Piscataqua River's Dover Neck. Hoping to mirror the compact, corporate, ordered, Puritan town model established in the Massachusetts Bay Colony to the south, Wiggins and his compatriots quickly built a meetinghouse (though finding a permanent minister to serve in it proved to be much more difficult) and began the process of allocating land to Dover's settlers, the best lands going to those at the top of the new settlement's pecking order. With the land immediately surrounding the small settlement quickly distributed, the town's founders began assigning parcels of outlying land more distant from the town center but still accessible via the many tributary rivers and creeks that drained into the Piscataqua River basin, among them the Oyster River (known to the area's native Newichawannock inhabitants as the Shankhassick).[5]

Though linked directly to Dover via the Great Bay, the Oyster River settlement rapidly established an identity of its own. Situated in the midst of an incredibly rich tidal estuary, the Oyster River settlers had little difficulty extracting a competency from their new home. Fish, shellfish, eels, waterfowl, and wild game were readily available to the settlers, and their free-ranging livestock grew fat on the bay's luxuriant marsh grasses, or "salt hay," as it was known locally. An abundance of fertile soil yielded bountiful grain and root crops, and vast tracts of virgin timber lined the river's banks, a fact not unnoticed by the Oyster River settlers or by ordnance officers in the British navy. A mere nine years after initial settlement, a Boston merchant named Valentine Hill, along with a partner, Thomas Beard, obtained a grant on the falls just upstream from the river's mouth and the main point of settlement and established a sawmill. Overnight, a new knot of settlement sprang up around Hill's and Beard's mill at the falls, vying with and eventually surpassing the older Durham Point community for local dominance. Of equal consequence, the Oyster River and other nearby streams also quickly rose to prominence as the center of the Atlantic mast trade. Direct access to the Piscataqua Basin and coastal Portsmouth, only twelve miles distant yet intimately connected to the burgeoning Atlantic economy and the lucrative West Indies trade and British trade in naval stores, guaranteed a ready market for area pine and for Hill's and Beard's lumber and ensured sustained growth for the infant community. The mushrooming lumber trade, especially the transport needs of the sawmills and lumber/mast merchants, also encouraged a thriving ship-building industry in the bay region and gave rise to a locally distinctive watercraft known as the Piscataqua gundalow (a name derived from the term *gondola*), designed to navigate the region's peculiar currents and tidal patterns.[6]

The insatiable local and West Indian demand for lumber, coupled with the British navy's incessant need for mast timber, along with a bounty of fine natural pastures, also enticed settlement and development along another of the bay's major tributaries, the Lamprey, roughly two miles south of the Oyster River settlements. Socially and economically linked to the Oyster River community, the Lamprey River settlements (Lubberland, on the river's northern bank along the shore of the Great Bay, and the Packer's Falls area, upstream from the river's mouth) were contested entities in the seventeenth century, claimed simultaneously by the established towns of Dover to the north and Exeter to the south. Moreover, like their immediate northern neighbors on the Oyster River, the Lamprey River settlers, existing as they did in relative isolation on the extreme periphery of their more established and more densely settled metropolitan communities, were the frequent target for devastating attacks by local bands of aggrieved Native Americans (who still laid claim to the area) and their French allies (who feared that English homesteaders would negate their own claim to northern New England and who also coveted the area's stands of mast pine). The combination of years of neglect by their host communities, a shared experience as embattled frontier Puritan settlements, a common economic orientation, and very real mutual needs proved to be powerful forces that drew the area's settlers together, promoting a collective identity and resulting in efforts (both in 1669 and 1695) to set Durham apart from Dover. Though these initial attempts failed, the Durham community continued to assert its autonomy, successfully petitioning to establish a separate church in 1717 and finally incorporating as an independent township in 1732.[7]

Among those drawn to the area and the opportunities it provided was Timothy Joy's grandfather, Samuel. Born in the northeastern Massachusetts town of Salisbury in 1706, Samuel Joy descended from an already long line, by that date, of American Joys. The story of this family and its movement to the New Hampshire frontier provides us with important clues about the broad economic, cultural, political, and religious forces that shaped the life of Timothy Meader Joy and his Durham peers.

Samuel Joy's great-grandfather, Thomas Joy, was the first of the family to settle in the New World, arriving in Boston in the mid-1630s. A master builder and carpenter by trade, Thomas Joy was responsible for the construction of many buildings in Boston, including, in 1658, Boston Town Hall, which served as the first seat of government in the Massachusetts Bay Colony. A political foe of powerful governor John Winthrop, Joy, along with his wife, Joan Gallop Joy, and their four small sons, removed, in 1648, to nearby Hingham, twelve miles southeast of Boston, where he took up farming and built a gristmill. It was there that the couple raised and expanded their family, though Thomas continued to do business in the bustling colonial capital of Boston. The oldest of the Joy children, their son Samuel, born on February 26, 1639, seems to have followed in his father's footsteps, pursuing the carpenter's trade in Boston and amassing property in both Boston and Hingham. In 1668, Samuel married Ann Pitts of Hingham. Roughly two years later, on October 22, 1670, Ann gave birth to a son, also named Samuel. Unfortunately, the young family was rent asunder when the senior Samuel Joy perished early the next year. Though apparently not left destitute, Ann and young Samuel most certainly had a rough time making a go of it in the patriarchal world of Puritan New England. It is possible that Ann returned to her parents' Hingham home as a way of coping with her new situation. It is undeniable that she relied heavily on her family for assistance and advice. Ann's widowhood came to an end in 1678 when she married Benjamin Eastman and relocated, along with eight-year-old Samuel, to Eastman's home in the remote northern settlement of Salisbury.[8]

Joy family history relates that Eastman was a tanner by trade. Given what we know about seventeenth-century New England and Samuel's later life, it is unlikely that Eastman made his livelihood exclusively through this line of work. More probably, Eastman followed the norm among New England artisans of the time and combined his tanning trade with farming in order to ensure his family's subsistence. Eastman's stepson, Samuel, a farmer in his adult life, thus undoubtedly learned the requisite skills for his vocation from Benjamin Eastman. Just as important, Samuel learned to complement his farming with a collateral trade—in his particular case, as a ship caulker. With Salisbury's proximity to the Merrimack River and the Atlantic Ocean, especially via the busy port town of Newburyport, the combination of agricultural and maritime skills was far from incongruous and represented a well-devised, balanced, economic strategy that provided opportunities for year-round employment. Samuel was certainly close with Eastman and his relations, as attested to by his marriage to Marah Eastman, Benjamin's niece, in 1696. Together, Samuel and Marah had seven children, among them Timothy Joy's grandfather, Samuel (b. 1706), their fifth child and third son.[9]

Like his father and namesake, Samuel learned the trades of farming and ship caulking. The latter trade apparently led the young man, in early adulthood, northward to the volatile yet promising New Hampshire frontier. Samuel's move would not have been an easy one. The region had, in the not-too-distant past, been wracked by spasms of brutal violence, including a number of bloody massacres of women and children, associated with the conflict known as Queen Anne's War, and, more recently (or perhaps even simultaneously—we do not know when Samuel arrived in New Hampshire), by the carnage of Dummer's, or Lovewell's, War (1722–25). Despite the risks, the prospect of new opportunities (and perhaps the lure of adventure) led Joy, following the pattern cast by his ancestors before him, to leave the relative safety of a more established community (in this case, Salisbury) and begin anew on the frontier. Once there, Samuel found employment on the banks of the Lamprey River, in Captain John Burley's shipyard in present-day Newmarket, New Hampshire (then part of the town of Exeter). Joy clearly made a good impression on Burley, as the captain permitted the young man to wed his daughter Mary around 1730. Sometime soon after their marriage, John Burley died. The young couple used proceeds derived from cashing out the bulk of Mary's share of the inheritance from her father's estate to move to the neighboring Oyster River Parish. There, in 1732, Samuel became one of the signatories to the successful petition requesting the incorporation of the Oyster and Lamprey River settlements into the autonomous town of Durham. Joy's status in the community was further solidified by his service in Captain John Smith's military company, which saw frequent action during the ongoing hostilities with area natives. In 1740, with his prospects rising, Samuel Joy gave John Gilman of Exeter £295 for an eighty-eight and one-half acre farm in the Packer's Falls district of Durham (named after Thomas Packer, who constructed a mill at the site in the 1660s), just a short distance north of what became the Newmarket town line and in close proximity to the Lamprey River. Here on the Joy farm, Samuel and Mary raised five children, Samuel (b. November 1738), Hannah and Sarah (birth years unknown), Jacob (b. 1749), and Susanna (b. 1750). The farm provided well for Samuel and Mary and would remain in the Joy family for four generations.[10]

That Joy's rise to respectability was both hard won and fortuitous cannot be overstated. Undeniably, hard work and perseverance played a crucial role in Joy's successful rise. At the same time, however, Joy was the beneficiary of the chaos associated with a fluid, unsettled, frontier socioeconomic order and of the patronage (both in life and in death) of one of Newmarket's most successful and influential early residents. Indeed, the historical record reaffirms this and attests to the fact that Samuel Joy's life and business dealings in New Hampshire were conducted along a very fine and permeable line separating success from failure. Between the time of his marriage to Mary in 1730 and the purchase of the Joy farm in 1740 (a period that also encompasses the birth of Deacon Samuel, Timothy's father, in 1738), Joy was involved in at least eight court cases in the New Hampshire Court of Common Pleas, all related to debt. In three of the cases, Joy sued for a debt owed, and in five of them, he was sued for money due. Over the next five years, Samuel's interactions with the court system remained relatively constant, with six more cases, though his condition seems to have improved, as he appears in the records as plaintiff in four of the six cases (at least two of these were filed in York County in neighboring Maine, then part of Massachusetts). Joy then disappears from the court record until 1748, when Stephen Greenleaf of Portsmouth brought suit against him for a debt of eight pounds. Nonetheless, the trailing off of suits filed against Joy for debt during the 1740s suggests that Samuel and Mary Joy's situation was stable, if not improving. It may also indicate that Samuel Joy's personal reputation (he was, after all, a relative newcomer to Durham in the 1730s) was growing. Bringing suit for debt was always a dangerous action—both for the plaintiff (who risked the debtor's flight, a protracted legal battle, or the total loss of their assets) and to the defendant (who, beyond the possibility of incarceration and the loss of material assets, also risked damage to one's personal reputation and thus to future business relationships and much-needed credit). Negotiation and forbearance were always the more prudent course in debt cases, and this privilege was much more likely to be extended to those who had a proven record for reliability and personal diligence. The trailing off of suits brought against Joy implies that this might just have been the case, that is, that Joy had crossed the threshold into a position of relative respectability.[11]

The evidence that this was indeed the case for Samuel, that he had achieved a modicum of respectability, is bolstered by the fact that he (clearly intent on establishing a patrimony for his growing family) was among the sixty-three men of the Durham area who signed their names to a petition sent to Royal Governor Benning Wentworth in 1749 requesting the grant of a new township, forty-five miles square, north of Rochester (the area that eventually became the town of New Durham in 1762). The request was granted, and the township, named Cochecho, was surveyed and auctioned off in 1750. The record is incomplete as to whether or not Joy was one of the original proprietors. His estate of 2,833.70 (inventoried in 1752, though the actual inventory has not been located) suggests significant landholdings beyond the eighty-eight-acre farm purchased back in 1740. Moreover, his son Samuel's later pursuit of land in the township could be construed as an effort to build on or improve the family's holdings there. Conversely, Joy's name does not appear in John Scales's published history of the county, which includes a listing of the New Durham proprietors. Though it is certainly possible that the name was overlooked or that handwriting was improperly read, it is also curious that Joy's name, though documented elsewhere, is missing. Other evidence also raises questions about Joy's involvement as a New Durham proprietor. The fact that his youngest child, Jacob, was apprenticed as a young boy and became a blacksmith could be taken as an indication that Joy lacked the requisite real estate assets to establish his son as a freeholder. This choice of vocation, of course, might just as easily be explained by interest on the part of Jacob, in which case, any New Durham assets that existed might have been used to help defray the cost of the apprenticeship. In the end, it seems unlikely that we will ever know the full truth about this petitionary incident in Samuel's life. Nonetheless, such a request, if made as reported, speaks volumes about Samuel Joy's elevated position in Durham. In a society that recognized achievement and power as both a sign of masculine proficiency and of God's favor, Joy stood unquestioned as a respected and successful townsman.[12]

Tragically, the young family's stable existence was short lived. In 1752, the senior Samuel drowned while crossing the Exeter River (also known as the Squamscott River) a mere five miles from his home. The burden of running the family farm (which Timothy Joy's father, Samuel, eventually inherited) and of providing for the family fell to the eleven-year-old boy and his widowed mother, Mary.[13]

The historical record is silent about Samuel and Mary's struggles to make the farm a going concern, but one can readily imagine the many difficulties faced by mother and son. Mary remarried (the year is uncertain; her new husband's surname was Monroe), but where the couple resided is unclear (though it seems likely that the couple resided in the Joy house, given Mary's position as administrator of Samuel's estate), as are the exact arrangements regarding the Joy farm. Ironically, Mary's second husband also drowned (the date is unknown) in the Squamscott River. According to family history, the tragedy occurred very near the spot where her first husband, Samuel, had died. The obstacles confronting Mary and young Samuel were daunting, but together they managed to hold on to the Joy farm.[14]

The known details of Samuel's youth and early adult life are few and disjointed. An account book from the period 1813–24 and numerous deeds, Durham town receipts, and court records demonstrate that Samuel was literate. Thus he presumably spent at least a portion of his early years in school or learning to read, write, and cipher under the tutelage of his mother, father/stepfather, and/or neighbors. As the deeds attest, Joy also began to expand his landholdings during this period. In 1761, at age twenty-three, he purchased two large tracts of land (proprietors' grants) for 235 in what was soon to become the town of New Durham. In 1765 and 1766, he added to his estate two smaller plots adjoining his Durham holdings.[15]

Little is known about Samuel's early religious training. The Durham of Samuel Joy's childhood was a community rife with religious division and discord. Months after Samuel's birth, an ecclesiastical council dismissed the long-serving Reverend Hugh Adams from his post with the Durham Congregational Church, censuring the outgoing minister for "his great presumption in pretending to imprecate the divine vengeance and that the calamities that had befallen sundry persons were the effect of his prayers." Despite such serious allegations, a large number of Durham parishioners forwarded a petition to the town's officials requesting that Adams be allowed to continue preaching at Durham Point. The petition was denied, but its existence is indicative of the deep-seated religious tensions within Durham. These tensions became all the more evident during the ministry of Adams's successor, the Reverend Nicholas Gilman.[16]

The scion of one of New Hampshire's most powerful families, the Harvard-trained Gilman began his ministerial duties in Durham in September of 1739, the year following Samuel's birth. Deeply pious, Gilman eagerly followed the spread of evangelicalism (known as the Great Awakening) coursing through contemporary New England and was among the many thousands who gathered on the village green in nearby Hampton, New Hampshire, in October of 1740 to listen to the preaching of George Whitefield, the most famous revivalist of the day. Touched to his core by Whitefield's impassioned oration, Gilman fervently worked to produce a similar manifestation of the Holy Spirit within his own church. In November of 1741, Gilman's efforts began to bear fruit, and within a month's time, he was preaching daily sermons to a packed house. Sadly, in the midst of his long-awaited success, Gilman suffered the loss of two of his five sons to throat distemper (diphtheria). Despondent, the young minister dealt with his grief by recommitting himself to his pastoral duties. In January of 1742, Gilman's long-standing effort to provoke a revival in Durham finally paid off. Irked by his congregation's eagerness to leave the church after service, Gilman was "movd to tell em that if I coud See them flocking to Heaven as they were from Meeting it woud Make My Heart leap within me." The chagrined congregation shuffled back to their pews and heard a spirited nightlong exhortation from their minister. Over the next few weeks, with Gilman's active encouragement, the Durham church became the scene of all manner of religious visions and agitation. Gilman's "New Light" preaching rapidly alienated many, more conservative members of the Durham parish and quickly drew the critical attention of the more tradition-bound "Old Light" ministers from surrounding churches. In response to reports of religious "enthusiasm" in the Durham congregation, a 1747 convocation of New Hampshire ministers appointed a committee to investigate the goings-on in Gilman's church. Their findings, not surprisingly, were damning. Before any official action could be taken, however, Gilman died of consumption in April of 1748. His replacement, the Reverend John Adams, though a polarizing figure himself (he was the nephew of the town's dismissed former minister, Hugh Adams), finally managed to bring some stability to the church, serving for thirty years until his own dismissal in 1778, the result of alleged impropriety with a female resident of Durham.[17]

There is no way of knowing for certain whether young Samuel was directly exposed to any of the Gilman controversy or to what degree he, as a young boy, understood the parameters of the dispute. Given the unusual nature of the affair and the highly charged and controversial atmosphere, Samuel was, at a minimum, aware of the tempest. Certainly, he would have heard local gossip about what was going on. It seems probable, in light of his subsequent position as deacon in Coe's orthodox church and his commitment to that congregation's embattled minister, that Samuel (or, perhaps more likely, his father and/or mother or others whom he trusted) would not have approved of Gilman or his evangelicalism. It is suggestive that no record of church participation exists for the elder Samuel Joy, Mary Joy, or their children during this time period. The family does once again appear in church records in January 1754, when Mary (then a widow) had her children Sarah, Jacob, and Susanna baptized by the more orthodox John Adams. While this prolonged absence in the official records of the church is by no means definitive proof of her or her husband's disapproval of Gilman and his message/approach, it certainly hints at a conscious decision to disassociate the family from the divided congregation and to stand apart from the fray (Sarah, after all, had been born during Gilman's pastorate). Needless to say, the Joy family's absence from the formal church record should also not be construed as evidence that the family eschewed religion during Samuel's formative years. On the contrary, the family may well have chosen to attend Pastor John Moody's church in nearby Newmarket (Mary's hometown) or perhaps, after 1765 (as the Reverend John Adams' pastorate descended into ignominy), the newly established church in neighboring Lee (where Samuel's son Timothy would eventually be married). It is certain that, at a minimum, young Samuel learned that religion, at least as it was practiced in Durham, could be a very contested affair, a lesson that he would later see play out yet again during his tenure as church deacon.[18]

The historical record makes clearer that Samuel's business and personal prospects improved during this period of his life, as the Packer's Falls neighborhood was integrated more directly into the social, political, and economic pulse of the region through the construction of roads linking the falls district to the adjoining town of Lee in 1758 and to the main coastal road to Durham in 1768. Of particular consequence to Joy was the construction of a new road in 1763 that passed directly by his homestead (cutting his farm in two), linking the Lamprey River and Lee to his north and the Newmarket/Durham town line to his south. It was certainly along these roads that Samuel traveled to court his future wife, Hannah Meader (b. June 22, 1749), whose father, Samuel Meader, owned property straddling the road to Lee north of the Lamprey River bridge. Surely, it was along these same roads that the young couple journeyed, after their marriage in January of 1767, to set up their household (which most certainly included Samuel's fifty-two-year-old mother, Mary, who would not pass away until 1805) on Samuel Joy's land.[19]

Later that same year, Hannah gave birth to twin sons, who the couple named Jacob and Samuel. Unfortunately, the young parents' joy was fleeting, as both infants soon died—Jacob after one day and Samuel after three—a not uncommon experience for eighteenth-century American parents. The daily demands of farm and home left the young couple little time to grieve, however. The rigors of extracting a competency from the land forced their lives back into motion. One can assume that the couple put the tragedy behind them rather quickly and that things returned to a more or less normal rhythm, for within one year's time, Hannah was once again with child. In February of 1769, she delivered another baby boy, who the couple also named Samuel. Additional children followed in a regular cycle of two to three years apart, a common postpartum spacing for nursing mothers. In all, Samuel and Hannah welcomed seven more children into the world—Sally in 1771, Susannah in 1774, Elizabeth in 1777, Polly in 1780, Jacob in 1783, Ebenezer in 1785, and Timothy Meader Joy (most likely named in honor of his mother's older brother) in 1789—all of whom, save Elizabeth and Jacob, lived to reach adulthood.[20]

It appears, given the birth dates of his children, that Samuel Joy devoted most of his energy and time to domestic and farm affairs during America's critical Revolutionary era. There is no real evidence of how the pre-Revolutionary crisis and subsequent armed struggle affected Joy and his family on a personal level. The story of the Durham community during this era has not been well documented by historians, making even broad generalizations difficult at best. Existing accounts would have us believe that devotion to the Revolutionary cause was near universal in the town and its surrounding area. Certainly, solid evidence exists to suggest that local commitment to the Patriot cause was widespread. In the aftermath of the British closure of the port of Boston in retaliation for the Boston Tea Party, for instance, the Reverend John Adams penned an eloquent letter of support for the beleaguered city on behalf of the residents of Durham. One month later, Durham became the hiding place for the gunpowder and arms seized in the December 1774 raids on Fort William and Mary, the British fort guarding the mouth of the Piscataqua River—the pilfered armaments were initially sequestered in Pastor Adams's church (some accounts say under the pulpit). In addition, the town, which counted roughly twelve hundred residents in 1775, and neighboring Lee (with a population of roughly nine hundred), contributed at least 226 soldiers to the Revolutionary struggle, including one of the Revolutionaries' most noted military leaders, General John Sullivan. Nonetheless, participation in the conflict was far from universal. Samuel Joy, for one, did not, as best we can tell, serve in any branch of the military during the war. As the preceding figures reveal, many of his contemporaries made the same decision. Joy's decision to remain at home, however, should not necessarily be interpreted as opposition to the cause. Equally, the one scanty piece of documentary evidence that we do have relative to Joy during this period—his signature on a 1779 resolution pledging that he would refrain from charging more for commodities enumerated on the document than the price set by a special committee established to consider price gouging and currency depreciation—cannot be construed as compelling evidence of firm support for the Revolution, as we have no way of knowing whether the signature was freely given, induced by peer pressure, or coerced. While it is unlikely that Joy was a Loyalist (he did stay in Durham and seems to have faced no hostility), it is impossible to say whether he belonged to that segment of the American population that actively supported the Revolution or to that comparably large group who tried to remain neutral in the conflict.[21]

The tumult of the Revolutionary era most certainly left an indelible imprint on the Durham region and its people. Though no systematic treatment of the subject yet exists, studies of other communities make clear the myriad and sometimes contradictory forces unleashed by the chaos and disorder that characterized the struggle. For some, resistance to British tyranny offered a ready symbol and rallying point for preexisting social and political grievances. In the minds of these participants, the Revolution's democratic rhetoric and politics of the street offered a tangible vehicle for making their hopes and fears evident and held the promise of expanded opportunities vis-à-vis existing social, economic, and political hierarchies. Others saw the conflict in conservative terms, as a struggle to preserve the established order—for some, through the continuation of crown rule; for others, under self-rule—and to maintain things as they currently stood. Though many Americans found their individual hopes and desires fulfilled, many more confronted the sobering reality that little, if anything, was changed by the Revolution, that opportunities that eluded them in the period before the war remained closed to them after its conclusion. Indeed, for many Americans, their particular circumstances actually deteriorated after the war. Conversely, many conservatives bristled at the leveling forces unleashed by the war and fought tooth and nail to constrain incipient democracy and to stay the course, often with great success. While one can but hazard a guess about how Samuel and Hannah Joy and their children interpreted the Revolutionary crisis and its broader significance, it seems clear that the conflict did not diminish in any discernible way the family's economic situation or its social standing within the Durham community.[22]

Much clearer are the local economic consequences of the war. At first blush, one might expect that the Piscataqua region would have been devastated by the war. Beyond the wartime depredations on local shipping, Americans along the Great Bay now found their economic lifeblood—the West Indies trade—choked off, and the ships that they sent out to sea to engage in the Atlantic trade now did so without the protection of the Royal Navy. Moreover, British manufacturers actively sought to dump trade goods onto the now fully accessible American market (one such incident occurred in Portsmouth in the summer of 1785, when two British ships were turned away after trying to avoid a state-mandated duty on British imports and attempting to sell their cargoes directly to American consumers), and British merchants and banks pressed American debtors for payment of debts that had been difficult, if not impossible, to collect during the war. When combined with the inefficiencies and untenable fiscal condition of the new government under the Articles of Confederation and the lack of stable and reliable local currency, Durham residents might well have anticipated a precipitous economic decline for their town and its surrounding area. In reality, however, despite such obstacles and the sharp downturn prompted by the embargo put in place during the Jefferson administration, the Piscataqua region experienced what one historian calls "thirty thriving years" following the Revolutionary War. The Great Bay's lumbering and shipbuilding industries regained their legs, and a thriving trade in area-made bricks, formed from the thick clay taken along the banks of local rivers, helped to lead the way.[23]

The French Revolution and subsequent European conflict dramatically accelerated this trend and ushered in a period of unprecedented prosperity for the Piscataqua region, as Durhamites and their neighbors rushed into the void left by the wartime destruction of France's and Britain's merchant fleets. Indeed, Durham and other Great Bay communities experienced an economic golden era in the period between 1789 and 1809, an era unlike anything the town had ever before known. It was also the era into which Timothy Joy was born. The scope of the boom was impressive. Within the ten years between 1791 and 1801, for instance, the value of New Hampshire exports rose from $142,859 to $555,055. That figure continued to rise in the years following, peaking at $680,000 in 1807. Among these exports could be counted nearly one billion feet of boards and planks; tens of millions of staves, headings, and shingles; hay, beef, cattle, sheep, and barrels of dried fish and maple sugar; and bricks. The registered tonnage of Portsmouth ships engaged in foreign trade climbed from 12,521 in 1793 to 18,379 in 1801. In the meantime, the registered tonnage of ships engaged in the coastal trade remained constant at 1,200. New wharves, docks, and warehouses sprang up along the Portsmouth waterfront and within the towns of the Great Bay, and money made through expanding trade financed the construction of new stores and grand residences for the area's merchant elite.[24]

The Durham of Timothy Joy's childhood, though a secondary port on the Great Bay, nonetheless shared in this prosperity. Durham timber joined the green tide flowing through the Piscataqua to the sea. Likewise, the products of the town's farms (barley, wheat, cattle, corn, hay, potatoes, etc.) made their way to markets both near and far. Shipbuilding, long a profitable enterprise on the Oyster and Lamprey Rivers, intensified during this period, and Durham launched some seventy-eight ships between 1777 and 1829. While the overwhelming bulk of the town's economic activity was fixated on the Great Bay and the transatlantic and Atlantic coastal trade, Durham's access to the New Hampshire interior and to the town's own hinterlands also markedly improved during this time, with the completion of a half-mile-long bridge over the Piscataqua River in 1794 (considered the engineering marvel of its time, the bridge boasted the nation's longest arch, at 244 feet), followed by the completion, in 1796, of a state-funded turnpike that ran on an east-west course through the town to

Concord. Readily accessible by both land and sea, Durham emerged as a supply post for east-west travel and a market center for the towns in its immediate environs. As one early twentieth-century historian of the region phrased it,

> [Durham] was a good place for general trade; the store keepers waxed rich and some of their descendants are enjoying the benefits of the fruit of their labor. When the turnpike road was in full swing the tavern keepers were kept busy in supplying the wants of the teamsters, and in caring for their teams that had come to market from the up-country towns . . . No dull times then; everybody was busy, and Durham by men grew rich.[25]

Typical of those who profited from Durham's new economic climate was George Ffrost II. A second-generation merchant, Ffrost (b. 1765) commenced storekeeping in Barrington, a small town north of Durham, in 1789. Three years later, he broadened his operations and opened a second store in nearby Northwood. Real success, however, came when Ffrost, following his father's death, relocated to Durham with his wife, Margaret Burleigh Ffrost (Deacon Samuel Joy's cousin), and commenced business on a small rise of land adjacent to the Newmarket/Durham Road and overlooking the town landing on the Oyster River, in 1804. Heavily engaged in the trade of lumber and wood products, Ffrost, like most country merchants of his day, also necessarily dabbled in provisions and agricultural goods, which he accepted in trade and/or as payment from neighboring farmers. His many commodities (as well as those, such as bricks, commissioned for transport by him on behalf of others) were then shipped from Ffrost's own wharf at the landing and aboard his own small fleet of gundalows and packet boats to market along the Great Bay, to nearby towns, and to Portsmouth and the world beyond the Piscataqua. Ffrost's success enabled him to provide well for his family and was replicated by other Durhamites, including two of Timothy Joy's contemporaries, the sons of the Reverend Curtis Coe: Ebenezer Coe (b. 1785), who was apprenticed to George Ffrost in 1803 and purchased Ffrost's Northwood shop in 1804, and even more successfully by his older brother, Joseph Coe (b. 1782). The elder Coe brother began his business career as a saddler and dealer in saddlery and harnesses. With profits from this business, Coe entered the shipbuilding business in Durham (apparently with other members of his family) and participated intermittently in the

European trade. His main income, however, was derived from his mercantile enterprises. Indeed, Coe's two stores and shipping interests gained him the title of Durham's largest employer in the early nineteenth century. The successful mercantile establishments of Ffrost and Coe (and others like them), along with the grand estates these businesses built and supported, were regular fixtures in the day-to-day lives of Durhamites such as Samuel Joy and his son Timothy. The diversified economic activities that these merchants engaged in and the opportunity that they represented could not have escaped the consciousness of the impressionable young boy.[26]

Tucked away in his Packer's Falls household, Timothy's father, Deacon Samuel Joy, mirroring the well-entrenched social and cultural traditions of masculinity so deeply embedded in New England for middle-aged family men, chose to solidify his own respectability and social and economic stability (and thus that of his family) by pursuing a more established path to competency, that of faith, land acquisition, and farming. By all accounts, he (with the assistance of the rest of his household) succeeded in doing so admirably. In 1786, Samuel Joy formally petitioned for membership in the Durham church led by the Reverend Curtis Coe. On July 6, a group of church members "assembled at the meeting house" agreed to "admit him as a member." Joy took his commitment seriously, baptizing all of his children and, as best as we can tell, actively participating in church sacraments. In recognition of his devotion, Joy's fellow church members turned to him when they looked to elect a new church deacon a mere five years after he joined their church.[27]

Deacon Samuel's post-Revolutionary religious respectability paralleled the concurrent solidification of Joy's personal and economic standing in the Durham community. Between the Revolution's end and the commencement of the War of 1812, Samuel bought and sold scores of acres of land in Durham, adding nearly one hundred acres to the Joy homestead. Likewise, the deacon engaged in a brisk trade in New Durham lands, mainly adding to his already extensive holdings, but also selling land in that new town (incorporated in 1762). It was there that Joy planned to establish his eldest son, Samuel (who married and started a family in 1797 and shortly thereafter relocated to New Durham), and, most likely, either Ebenezer or Timothy, with the other inheriting the family homestead in Durham. Beyond general farming, Deacon Samuel also, like a great many of his neighbors, engaged in the timber and wood trade (e.g., he provided "plank" to the town of Durham on a number of occasions for repairs on the "Lampreel" [Lamprey] River bridge and, in 1803, for a bridge over the Piscassic River, a tributary of the Lamprey). His account books, though maintained primarily for the years beyond the scope of this study, show that Joy's commercial contacts were many and widely dispersed and that his livelihood was dependent on a great many commodities and mediums of exchange.[28]

In the end, the legacy left to Samuel by his father, a legacy doggedly maintained and expanded in the face of the uncertainty and upheaval of the Revolutionary crisis, along with the deacon's pluck and persistence, served him and his family very well. Lists of Durham tax rates and tax inventories from the period clearly show that Joy was successful. In the town's 1784 inventory, Joy is listed as owning one-half acre of orchard land, one-half acre of tillage, six acres of mowing land, sixteen acres of pasture, one horse, two oxen, one cow, four horses and cattle aged one to three years, and 40 worth of buildings and unimproved land. His tax rate of 2 3s. 11d. placed him in the upper one-quarter of the town's taxpayers. Six years later, Joy had risen into the top fifth of Durham taxpayers, and his estate, then listed at 54 5s., was valued 87 percent higher than the mean estate value of 29 1s. for the town as a whole. Despite the early loss of his father (and thus his father's assistance and tutelage in building the necessary foundation to prepare young Samuel for a life as an independent householder), Deacon Samuel Joy had clearly made his mark on the town. When his life had run its course and he died in October 1824, at the age of eighty-six, Joy left behind an estate valued at approximately four thousand dollars.[29]

The Durham household in which Timothy Joy grew up undoubtedly provided the young man a great many opportunities unavailable to many of his peers. His father's place in Durham society was secure. In recognition of his achievements and his indisputable respectability, the elder Joy, as mentioned before, was named a deacon in the Durham church in 1791 and was chosen fence viewer at the Durham town meeting in April 1800. Surely, Timothy was aware, even as a young boy, of the respect afforded his father by the people of Durham and of his father's never-ending effort to better himself and his family. Economic stability certainly enabled the Joy family to enjoy the minimal creature comforts available at the time: hired help, a church pew, tinware, furniture, a looking glass, linen blankets, pictures, imported spices and tea, and books—the Bible, of course, foremost among them. Indeed, the record is clear that education was strongly emphasized by Deacon Samuel and his wife, Hannah. All of the couple's sons were literate, and one could reasonably presume that the same was true of the Joy daughters. Whether they were taught at home or in the nearby Packer's Falls schoolhouse (situated north of the Joy farm, near the intersection of the roads to Lee and to Durham) cannot be determined. We do, however, know that both Timothy and his brother Ebenezer worked as teachers at one point or another in their lives: Ebenezer in Durham's South District, at the town's Packer's Falls school, in nearby Milton, and privately for the children of neighbors Edmund Pendergast and Thomas Chesley; Timothy in some undetermined, though likely similar, scenarios. Beyond the sound educational foundation provided for his children, Deacon Samuel also, as clearly demonstrated, worked hard to ensure a solid economic footing for each as they set off to make their way in the world—protecting his name and status to help attract suitable marriage proposals for his daughters, bequeathing household goods and small amounts of money to his daughters, and purchasing land on which his sons could carve out a competency for themselves and their own families. From the perspective of any reasonable contemporary observer, Timothy Meader Joy's future seemed unquestionably assured. He was, by any measure, "of good address."[30]

As with his father before him, the details of Timothy's early life are sketchy. Still, given what we do know about contemporary life in New England and about his brother Eben, whose account book offers some insight into his activities as a young man, some elements of this life might be pieced together. With his eldest brother, Samuel, available to help with the heavy work on the family farm, young Timothy, though certainly required to perform numerous chores such as weeding, tending to livestock, milking, gathering firewood, mending fences, fetching water, and the like, certainly also had sufficient time to pursue his education and, as his later ruminations on the Bible make clear, his religious training. Undoubtedly, the young boy accompanied his father on his trips to local mills to have the family's grain ground or its timber sawn into lumber. Likewise, Timothy would have journeyed with his father to town to attend church services and church business meetings (where, perhaps, he was free to play with his friend Curtis Coe, son of the village minister) or to the stores owned by George Ffrost, Joseph Coe (his playmate's older sibling), or some other local merchant, to purchase needed items or to barter/sell the products produced on the family farm.

The nearby towns of Newmarket and Lee were also likely destinations for young Joy. Newmarket, because of the tremendous power-generating potential of the Lamprey River, quickly eclipsed its neighbor Durham in terms of population and commercial importance. Given its proximity to the Joy farm and the existence of a plethora of Burleigh relatives and, after the departure of the Reverend Curtis Coe from Durham, an established Congregational church (though the Reverend James Thurber left his post shortly after Coe, in 1808), Timothy was certainly no stranger to Newmarket (indeed, his future wife, Mary French, was a resident of the town). Timothy also seems to have had some early connection with the town of Lee, to the northwest of the Joy farm and a brief distance beyond his maternal grandparents' home. It is possible that this connection had to do with his father's determination to practice his faith after the Durham church lost Coe. Perhaps Lee's minister, the Reverend John Osborne, made a favorable impression on the deacon (though it is reported that Osborne, who began his career as a Congregationalist, embraced Freewill Baptist teachings later in his life), and perhaps Samuel and his family became regular visitors to the Lee church. Timothy might also have been introduced to the church through the family of his future wife, Mary. French family history relates that Reuben French, Mary's father, "was active in church affairs, and a member of Elder Osborne's Conference, 1800." While it cannot be definitively stated which of these two scenarios, if either, are accurate, Timothy's connections to Lee and to the Lee church—he and Mary would later be married by Reverend Osborne—are indisputable.[31]

It is also very likely that Timothy, like his brother Eben, spent some portion of his time performing paid work on neighboring farms. Farm labor, though subject to the ebb and flow of the seasons, was never ending, and the need for extra hands on surrounding farms was undoubtedly acute, for any number of reasons. It is therefore very likely that Timothy earned some money performing odd jobs—ploughing, clearing land, chopping wood, mending fences, lending a hand at harvesttime, felling trees, butchering livestock, and so on—not to mention the money he earned while engaged in some form of private or public teaching.[32]

We do not know when Timothy Meader Joy first met Mary French, nor are the details of their courtship available for recounting. Given the era's social mores, however, we can be confident that Joy likely initiated the courtship and that it involved ritualized, chaperoned visitations and perhaps an exchange of letters and flirtatious notes. We can be certain that the young man, given his father's social standing and the well-documented shortage of marriageable men vis-à-vis women existing in New England at the time, was perceived as a very good catch and thus that the courtship unquestionably gained the approval of Mary's family. Such a circumstance would have paved the way for the couple's marriage, undeniably easing the doubt and fear of rejection that would naturally have arisen in Joy given the public nature of courting and the vagaries associated with affairs of the heart. Beyond the most rudimentary details, little is known about Mary's family. The records do reveal that she was the second daughter and third of twelve children born to Reuben French and Lydia Churchill French and that she was born in Stratham, New Hampshire, just south of Newmarket, on February 13, 1790. The contours of Mary's childhood are unknown, though it is clear from documentary evidence that, somewhere along the way, she did learn to at least sign her name. She also certainly spent untold hours learning the necessary skills— sewing, cooking, weaving, washing, and so on—to prepare her to someday manage a household of her own. On September 13, 1807, Mary, not yet eighteen, and Timothy, all of eighteen, exchanged marriage vows before the Reverend John Osborne in the Lee church.[33]

Soon after their marriage, the newlyweds, carting their meager possessions (a bed and bedding, a cooking pot, perhaps a chest, some spoons and knives, and a family Bible), departed for New Durham to take up "housekeeping" on land owned by Deacon Samuel and in close proximity to Timothy's older brother Samuel. The nature of their dwelling place is uncertain, though it was in all likelihood small and simply built. There, on September 5, 1808, the young couple welcomed their first child, Alfred Timothy, into the world. The new family remained at New Durham until some time after April 1811. In that month, Timothy's father sold one hundred and thirty-five acres of his New Durham land to Josiah Hannaford of Newmarket. In the description of the property included in the registered deed, Samuel notes that he is selling to Hannaford "one whole lot of land in New Durham . . . upon which my son Timothy M. Joy now resides." Whether the sale forced Timothy's hand or whether he had already made up his mind to move on cannot be determined. But soon after the sale, Timothy and Mary could be found living in nearby Middleton, where they were blessed, on June 22, 1811, with a second child, a daughter who they named Mary.[34]

Timothy's decision to move his family to Middleton and his subsequent course of action there strongly suggest that he had determined (or that his physical condition dictated) that farm life was not for him. Certainly, his friendship with the Coe family, as well as his early life in the flourishing commercial entrepôt of Durham, had exposed him to a world beyond the farm and to a level of material comfort and success that surpassed anything that his father, even through dint of hard work and diligence, had been able to attain. Or perhaps, as historian Joyce Appleby contends, Joy, like many of his "first-generation" American peers, embraced the liberal, democratic legacy of the Revolution and cast his eyes forward, toward a new social and economic reality, one that no longer limited an individual's choice or constrained their actions through the dead weight of tradition. Mary's mind, of course, is even more difficult to gauge, and it would not have occurred to many at the time to even bother to consult her. In the patriarchal world of post-Revolutionary New England, life-altering decisions, such as the one that Timothy Joy was about to make, remained entirely within the masculine sphere.[35]

It is very much an open question as to why Joy chose Middleton as the place for his new life. Only recently settled in the years immediately preceding the Revolution, the town's earliest residents had migrated chiefly from Somersworth, Rochester, and Lee to establish new farms for themselves and/or their children. Unlike in his native Durham, the prevailing religious sentiment in Middleton leaned in the direction of the Freewill Baptist Church (which adhered to the principle of universal atonement—rather than the Calvinist doctrine of election—and to the Arminian principle that one's salvation could be lost as a result of an individual's conscious actions), as did the town's only established minister, the Reverend William Buzzell. This did not seem to deter Joy: he hints in his later journal that he attended Baptist service with his neighbors, and as previously mentioned, he may have already been exposed to such teachings in the church of the Reverend John Osborne of Lee. Small in size (only 7,154 acres) as New Hampshire towns went, Middleton, while bisected by the main highway that connected the colonial capital of Exeter with the colonial governor's summer residence at Wolfboro, remained very much an isolated frontier settlement in 1811, totaling a mere 439 souls (less than half that of neighboring New Durham and only one-third of his place of birth, Durham) in 1810. A small knot of buildings, a church, a hotel, and a couple of stores, standing at a small crossroads, was what passed for the town's center.[36]

A quick comparison of Middleton and Durham's tax inventories for 1811 further illustrates the primitive state of Timothy's new home. Durham's 1811 inventory listed 103 acres of orchard, 257.25 acres of arable land, 1,173.73 acres of mowing land, and 2,770.67 acres of pasture, as opposed to 6 acres, 63 acres, 277 acres, and 513 acres, respectively, for Middleton. Middleton's soil, a visitor to the town in July of 1814 noted, "is rocky" and "unfavorable to fruit." The totals for livestock divided in a similar manner, and the sum total value for all buildings for the two towns stood at $36,372 for Durham and a mere $1,800 for Middleton. Durham also reported $3,700 worth of stock-in-trade and $7,100 worth of currency and interest- or dividend-bearing securities. Middleton had no reported assets in the latter two classes. Despite its obvious shortcomings, in December of 1811, Timothy Joy, perhaps buoyed by his personal recollections of Durham's boom and the potential for growth in the new town or drawn by his Lee connections, purchased from William Buzzell, Jr., for seventy-five dollars, "a certain building in Middleton aforesaid now standing on the Parsonage lot, so called, it being the store lately occupied by Reuben Ellis and is the same wherein the said Timothy M. Joy now lives." It was in this small store on the New Hampshire frontier that Timothy, with his young family and his father's status at his side, would attempt to build his own reputation and success as a trader and Middleton townsman and thus stake his personal claim to respectability.[37]

Chapter 2

"THE DISTRACTED STATE
OF MY AFFAIRS"

The dawn broke cold and gray in the village of Middleton on Tuesday, March 17, 1812. Timothy Joy and his wife, Mary, rose as normal and busily went about the numerous daily chores necessary for the operation of their small general goods store. Mary, who was in the early stages of her third pregnancy (though unbeknownst to her husband—he never mentions this in his diary—and perhaps to herself as well), also carried the extra burden of attending to the needs of the couple's young children, Alfred Timothy, age three and a half, and Mary, nine months old. Though in business for a mere three months, the young "trader" found himself struggling in a tightening economy and undoubtedly spent no little time worrying about how he would meet his financial obligations and provide for his young family. Stretched to his financial limit, Joy's fortunes had plummeted sharply during the winter of 1812 (the diarist E. A. Holyoke called the winter of 1812 "the coldest and wettest ever known since the country was settled"). Though certainly aware of his deteriorating situation, Joy and his family were unprepared for what happened later that day.[1]

A nearly imperceptible strand in an expansive web of credit and exchange that transcended his immediate neighborhood and that stretched back to the Atlantic coast and across that ocean to the massive wholesale mercantile houses of Britain, Joy's small store relied extensively on the credit of the numerous middling firms that comprised the essential links between Europe and America in the Atlantic economy. With tensions mounting between the United States and Britain in response to British efforts—most notably, the Orders in Council—to prevent American trade with Napoleonic France and to the retaliatory measures adopted by the Jefferson and Madison administrations (the Non-Importation Act, the Embargo Act of 1807, and the Non-Intercourse Act) to force European recognition of American neutrality and freedom of the seas, this inchoate mercantile system sputtered and limped along in the years between 1806 and 1812, raising fears among British suppliers that their American accounts might soon become irrecoverable. As demand for immediate payment rose, coastal American merchants, in turn, squeezed their own debtors in a desperate attempt to remain solvent in an atmosphere of diminished credit and risk aversion. Responding to such pressure and with their backs to the proverbial wall, Joy's immediate suppliers, who undoubtedly feared the worst from the inexperienced trader, "broke upon" the young family and claimed every article at hand except for a few household goods that the hapless Joy had, in desperation, recently sold to his older brother Samuel in neighboring New Durham. Dissatisfied with their haul, Joy's creditors threatened to return with local law officials and to arrest the young shopkeeper as a debtor.[2]

Disconsolate and confused over his failure and his precipitous fall from respectability and with his mind muddled by the unexpected turn of events of the day, Joy sought advice from nearby friends who encouraged him to take flight. As the daylight hours gave way to darkness, Joy's anxiety increased, as did his inclination to leave. Determined to put up a brave front, Mary Joy attended to her daily routine and, as Joy's diary makes clear, busied herself putting her children down to sleep. Returning to her agitated husband's side, her own anxiety naturally mounted. In the end, despite her worries about going it alone, she relented, giving her support to her husband's rapidly evolving plan. Casting a last glance at his sleeping children, Joy kissed his sobbing wife and rushed out into the cold night air, hastily grabbing what money he had, his long coat, a small number of notes, and a pocket pistol. After quietly hitching his horse to his sleigh, he set off for the bustling seaport of Salem, Massachusetts, some eighty miles to the southeast, where he hoped to find work enough to pay off his debt. Fearful of being caught or of providing any clues as to his whereabouts, the frantic and desperate Joy guided his sleigh erratically down a series of lesser-traveled country lanes, initially heading north and west and later making his way south and east.[3]

After wandering aimlessly through the New Hampshire countryside for the better part of two days, Joy found himself in Haverhill, Massachusetts, as the midday bell sounded on Friday, March 20. Fam-

ished, tired, and chilled to the bone, Joy stopped at a tavern run by Asaph Kendall, located on Elm Corner, at the junction of Main and Water Streets. Noteworthy only for what was to transpire there, the small
tavern was likely very typical of the numerous public houses that dot-
ted the New England landscape at the time. A large, open fire would
have beckoned to Joy as he entered the smoky, dimly lit room. Small
knots of locals would have been scattered across the common space,
eating, drinking, and lost in conversation. One group of local men engaged in a rather boisterous political discussion—Francis Eaton, a
Democratic-Republican attorney and Haverhill's postmaster; Stephen
Crooker, an aspiring lawyer; and Dr. Moses Elliott—attracted Joy's attention. After "having drank a considerable quantity of spiritous
liquor," Joy joined the party at their corner table and became "a disputant" in the discussion, making a number of allegations that immediately drew "the atention of the [assembled] gentlemen."[4]

Enmeshed in a closely fought gubernatorial campaign between
Democratic-Republican Elbridge Gerry, the incumbent, and Federalist Caleb Strong, as well as the acerbic partisan buildup that would
eventually precipitate war with Great Britain, political emotions ran
extremely high in Massachusetts and throughout New England in the
early months of 1812. Indeed, the region was still very much abuzz over
the recent, highly publicized allegations of Federalist and British collusion connected to the so-called Henry Affair, which had broken just
two weeks before, on March 9. Suggestions of Federalist disloyalty
were nothing new in the region by March of 1812. Tensions nevertheless reached a new level of intensity after President James Madison's
pronouncement to Congress that documents provided to him (purchased for the sum of fifty thousand dollars) by John Henry—an An-
glo-Irish immigrant to Canada who claimed to be operating as a
British agent and who carried a letter of introduction to the president
from Massachusetts governor Elbridge Gerry—proved the existence
of a British plot to promote and facilitate New England's secession
and the destruction of the fragile new republic. Despite the subsequent discrediting of Henry and the realization that the "evidence"
provided by him had been drawn largely from the opposition press in
New England, the region's partisan fault line continued to rumble
mightily. The behavior of Timothy Joy, an ardent Democratic-Republican partisan, in Kendall's Tavern on that March day very much
reflected the intensity of this political environment and threatened to
unravel any semblance of calm then existing in Massachusetts.[5]

Emboldened by his libations and clearly influenced by the ongoing press coverage of the Henry Affair, Joy launched into a political character assassination of the prominent arch-Federalist and former senator and member of George Washington's cabinet Timothy Pickering (ironically, the son of a deacon himself), of nearby Salem. Pickering, as discussed elsewhere, was a long-standing target of Democratic-Republican attacks. Partisans like Joy had long harbored suspicions about the loyalty of this embodiment of Federalism, the chief architect of a failed New England separation movement in 1803–4, the author of a widely publicized 1808 letter denouncing Jefferson's Embargo Act of 1807, and, more recently, the recipient of a censure vote by the United States Senate for breach of confidence in 1811. Claiming to be "a Brittish subject by the name of Nathaniel Emery," a lieutenant in the Sixty-Seventh Regiment of Light Dragoons, Joy alleged to have knowledge of "a correspondence being carried on between Timo[thy] Pickering & a Brittish Officer in Canada" concerning "measures for the separation of the United States." Stunned by the assertions of treason against their sworn political foe and only three days away from their town's local election, the three men, now joined by Moses Wingate, Haverhill's Democratic-Republican town clerk, a justice of the peace, and a relative of Timothy Pickering, accompanied the young man to Eaton's law office (which also served as the town's post office), above the Haverhill Bridge. Here, Wingate deposed Joy. After documenting the allegations made, the assembled men asked Joy (alias Emery) "to swear to" his claims by signing an oath. Much to Joy's relief, however, God "kept [him] from sealing [his] destruction in that manner" (he claimed to be "unacquainted with the nature of an oath" but did "call God and these witnesses to evidence the truth of these facts"), and the indebted merchant beat a hasty departure from Haverhill.[6]

News of Joy's allegations, "a circumstance, which has greatly alarmed our good people," as one Haverhill Federalist put it, spread like wildfire. It rapidly made its way to Salem, even in advance of Joy himself, and to the ears of the city's large and very powerful Federalist community, the Pickering family being prominent among them. Needless to say, this news was not well received.[7]

Arriving in Salem late in the evening of the twentieth, Joy, now using his true name, took a room at the Salem Hotel, on the corner of Crombie and Essex Streets (also known as Main Street), to the south and west of the city's lively harbor. Exhausted, humiliated, and still in his cups (Joy purchased more wine somewhere between Haverhill and

Salem), Joy slept deeply. A night's rest did little to assuage Joy's guilt, however. Waking with an ominous feeling of despair, Joy took a moment to pray for divine guidance before mounting his horse (he abandoned his sleigh at the tavern where he purchased the additional wine) and riding through the chilly Salem morning to survey the bustling port city and to secure employment.[8]

Boasting a population of nearly thirteen thousand, Salem, the nation's ninth largest city, had risen to national and international fame as one of the most important ports in the lucrative East Asia trade. Indeed, in the latter years of the eighteenth century and in the years before the Embargo Act of 1807, Salem prospered, and merchants such as Elias Hasket Derby, Nathaniel Bowditch, John Crowninshield, Joseph Peabody, William Gray, and Jerathmiel Pierce and his partner Aaron Waite, among others, amassed huge fortunes. While intense regional and national competition and the disruptions associated with the recent embargo and the ongoing conflict in Europe had dampened the city's immediate prospects, Salemites continued to look to the future with great hope, optimism, and anticipation. Undoubtedly impressed and awed by all that he was seeing, Joy, after first visiting Fort Lee on Salem Neck (where, at least one news account alleges, he repeated his claims about Timothy Pickering), made his way onto one of the city's many bustling wharfs, Derby's (pronounced "Darby's") Wharf.[9]

The crown jewel in Elias Hasket Derby's worldwide trade empire, the wharf bearing his name was the longest and busiest in Salem, extending nearly one-half mile out into the bustling harbor. As Joy strolled along the wharf on that chilly morning, he would have been treated to a menagerie of unfamiliar sights, sounds, and smells. Colorful silks, exotic vases, wooden wares, and luxury items carved from ivory, jade, tortoiseshell, and mother-of-pearl, recently arrived from Asian ports, would have filled the windows of the businesses and warehouses lining the wharf and adjoining street. The fragrant aroma of tea, coffee, and spices (especially Sumatran pepper) would have mixed with the brisk, salty sea air; with clouds of thick, acrid tobacco smoke; and with the pungent smell of fresh fish. The creaking and strained vibrations of pulleys and ropes would have risen above the gentle lapping of the waves; the shouts of warehousemen, stevedores, teamsters, and sailors; the calls of seagulls; and the din and bustle of the scores of people and animals moving along the wharf and nearby city streets. While Joy does not reveal his thoughts at that precise moment, it is easy to imagine his spirits buoyed by the enterprise, commotion, and wealth surrounding him at that place and time—by a feeling that perhaps anything was possible.[10]

Taking everything in, Joy made his way to the end of the wharf, where he stood admiring a "fine new ship" laying at anchor. It was there that "a gentleman," who Joy later learned was John Pickering, son of Timothy Pickering, approached him, engaging him "in conversation untill a Constable [Seth Saltmarsh], with about three hundred men & boys at his heels, came up and made [him] a prisoner in the name of the Commonwealth of Massachusetts." Shocked and in panicked disbelief, Joy asked Saltmarsh to explain the nature of his offense. "Defaming the caracter of Timothy Pickering at Haverhill," was the simple reply. "Delivering [him]self up without the least resistance," Joy was promised good usage by the arresting officer. News of Joy's arrest spread quickly, and the crowd on the wharf continued to swell as a "big belly'd" deputy sheriff arrived. The officer, Joy angrily remembered, "caut hold of me, riffled my pocket of my pocket pistol, pocket book & money & paper." Apparently not content with this cursory search, the deputy sheriff, who Joy labeled a "cowardly wretch," hastened the detainee into a nearby store, where, as Joy tells it, he was "obliged . . . to strip every rag of my clothes off except my shirt." Before having time to collect his thoughts (much less the possessions—a great coat, mittens, and extra clothing—that he had left in his hotel room), the stunned Joy was dragged out into Derby Street at the foot of the wharf, in sight of the mansions of Derby's rival George Crowninshield (ironically situated across from Derby's Wharf), Captain Henry Prince, and the shipbuilder Benjamin Hawkes, and paraded northwesterly, perhaps up one of the nearby residential streets—Orange, Hodges Court, Herbert, or Union Street, where the procession would have passed the gambrel-roofed home (number 21) of eight-year-old Nathaniel Hawthorne—most likely on their way to Essex (Main) Street. There, Joy, now a very potent political symbol due to what had transpired in Haverhill the day before and the intense partisan buildup in advance of the pending election, would have been directed westward past the Customs House (on the corner of Newbury Street), past the stately homes of the city's well-to-do (including the grand estate of the late Elias Hasket Derby, which occupied an entire city block between Essex and Front Streets, east of Market Street), and on through the heart of the city, past the East India Marine Society's home in the old Salem Bank building and the assorted other commercial and residential buildings lining the way. After having reached Salem's First Church, where Joy would likely have been able to catch a glimpse of his hotel just a block further along Essex Street, he would have rounded a corner and would have found himself hastened northward on toward the Essex County Court Building on Washington Street, the city's main north-south thoroughfare, for examination.[11]

He was, as he relates, "escorted to the Courthouse by thousands." Many in the crowd hurled insults; others shouted that he "ought to be hanged"; still others stared curiously in silence, perhaps with sympathy, perhaps in disapproval. The courthouse, designed by Salem's master builder Samuel McIntire and built in 1785–86 by Daniel Bancroft, sat toward the north end of the thoroughfare, on a small rise, in the middle of Washington Street, its front facing Essex Street. The two-story, Romanesque, red brick building, topped by a cupola, was a point of pride for the flourishing city. From its balustrade, framed by Tuscan pillars, President George Washington had been presented to the citizens of Salem when he visited the city in October of 1789 (the year of Timothy Joy's birth). Hastened through the building's entrance and up the stone staircase, Joy was brought into the large courtroom on the second floor. The room contained seats on every side and was notable for its handsome ventilated ceiling and for the Venetian window— "highly finished in the Ionick [*sic*] order" and affording "a beautiful prospect of a fine river, extensive well cultivated fields and groves"— positioned directly behind the judge's seat. Joy undoubtedly had little time to appreciate the beauty of McIntire's and Bancroft's work as he stood, heart fluttering, in the courtroom awaiting arraignment before a local magistrate, the Federalist justice (and Salem town clerk) John Prince, Jr.[12]

The scene unfolding before him in the room only served to amplify his fear. A large throng of Salemites had crowded into the courtroom. In the tightly packed room, the smell of oil lamps mingled with the heavy stench of unwashed bodies and that of damp woolen clothing. The din of the excited crowd heightened Joy's unease. His mind raced a mile a minute as the charges against him were read: What had he done? Why had he been so foolish? How had he fallen so far? Why had he squandered his family's good name and his personal reputation? What would his family and friends think? What would become of Mary, Alfred, and his baby girl, Mary? How could he extricate himself from this mess with as little difficulty and embarrassment as possible? Asked to enter a plea of guilty or not guilty, Joy composed himself, rose, and told Prince and the packed court gallery how he "was oblidged to flee from home," that "misfortunes had overcome my reason & if I had done or said wrong it must be attributed to a disordered brain," that he "meant nobody any harm," and how he "had hardly any recollection of what had happened to me" since leaving home. Throwing himself on the mercy of the court, Joy stood silent among the audible murmuring of the gallery. After further pointed examination by the council for the government, Federalist Samuel Putnam, which continued on for another two hours (and which was designed to induce Joy to implicate Eaton, Wingate, and the other Democratic-Republicans of Haverhill as the masterminds behind his allegations), Justice Prince set bail at five hundred dollars. Unable to turn over the necessary funds to secure his release, Timothy Joy was led away and "committed to Salem Jail on Saturday, 21st of March 1812, about two oclock in the afternoon, destitute of everything except life," to await his April hearing before the Massachusetts Supreme Judicial Court. For Timothy Meader Joy, this series of unbelievable events had to have been almost surreal and represented a stunning and embarrassing reversal of fortune. In the course of just over three short months, he had gone from being a promising and respectable young trader, a man of "good address and appearance," a man "by no means used to misfortunes," to a fugitive debtor, a failure, a lying imposter, a "vagrant" (in the words of the *Portland Eastern Argus*), and, even worse, an incarcerated criminal. His fall from respectability and the ruin of his personal reputation was, as he understandably saw things at that moment, complete.[13]

Though Joy's indebtedness was not the direct cause of his incarceration, other than it having served as the precipitant for his flight and thus setting the stage for his subsequent barroom bravado, his plight as a hard-pressed debtor was an extremely common one at the time and weighed heavily on the young man's mind as he sat in his jail cell. It thus merits further consideration, along with his assessment of what had happened to him.

For the generation of New Englanders who came of age in the immediate post-Revolutionary years, expansion of markets—both domestic and international—and a shift away from household production, subsistence living, and localized trade was a growing reality, a trend scholars have come to call the "market revolution." Unfolding at varying rates of speed in any part of the region at a given moment, this revolution eventually enveloped much of the rest of the nation in the years leading up to the Civil War. The effects of the transition were far reaching and profound. Beyond the growing emphasis on enhanced transportation capabilities, profit margin, lines of credit, monetary instruments, new legal structures, and specialized production to meet market demand, the revolution also entailed a dramatic reordering of traditional life throughout the region. Many artisans, for instance, intent on tapping into broader markets made increasingly accessible to them, sought out ways of increasing production of goods, eventually abandoning traditional craft modes of production and embracing factory production. Farmers, like Samuel Joy, found their lives similarly changed as they watched, with great suspicion, the rise of a new urban/commercial world and the declining influence of rural America and as they sought to determine to what degree they should abandon their older subsistence/barter ethic and focus on producing for market. Likewise, traders such as Timothy Joy came to occupy a tricky, unpredictable, and relatively unexplored middle ground in the emerging economic order, often finding themselves operating with one foot planted squarely in both the old and the new worlds. While markets and commercial exchange might seem obvious and desirable to the modern reader, the transition Timothy Joy and his contemporaries were experiencing was often bewildering to them and spawned a great deal of anxiety and tension. Unaccustomed as many were to relying exclusively on the market to meet family needs and fully aware of the very real possibility of failing in an economic order over which the individual exercised no direct control, many entered the marketplace reluctantly or did their best to avoid its entanglements altogether, while others forged ahead intrepidly, confident of their success. With the outcome of such change yet to be determined and with the pace of the change unrelenting, many individuals desperately sought direction and stability. For some, political participation and partisan fealty offered answers. For many others, the church and the related reform/benevolence activities it generated gave voice to their hopes and concerns. It was within this shifting and tumultuous environment that Timothy Joy set out to make his mark.[14]

Certainly, Timothy Joy and the thousands of other ambitious men who, like him, ran into financial difficulties during this era never expected their business ventures to fail. While Joy undoubtedly knew many who had been ruined in business, the post-Revolutionary atmosphere of prosperity and expansion that characterized the New Hampshire seacoast region of his birth and maturity, along with his own family's steadily improving fortunes, unwittingly anesthetized Joy

43

to the very real risks facing prospective businessmen in this early stage
of the nation's commercial development. As historian Bruce Mann
phrases it,

> The increasingly commercial economies . . . created new oppor-
> tunities for success. They also multiplied the risk of failure . . .
> The lure of greater local trade opportunities induced people to
> enter the lists as small traders, just as the production of agricul-
> tural surpluses and the growing demand for manufactured goods
> encouraged merchants to become exporters and importers. With
> the kind of optimism possible in an atmosphere of prosperity
> and expansion, ambitious men launched their ventures with
> large aspirations and little capital. Credit bridged the gap.

Mann reminds us that this commercial surge (which Timothy Joy actively embraced) "rode the crest of a rising tide of indebtedness, a tide
that reflected the confidence of prosperity as farmers and planters, artisans and shopkeepers, traders and merchants borrowed against anticipated profit to finance the undertakings that they knew—not hoped,
but knew—would create them." It was this faith that would, very
quickly, lead Timothy Joy into trouble, for as Mann also points out, "[I]n
highly leveraged, largely uninsured economies, even single misfortunes
can bring ruin. However, great the wreckage, debt always remains."[15]

The precise character of Timothy Joy's small mercantile business is,
unfortunately, lost to history. In all probability, his store did not differ
dramatically, with the likely exception of scale and scope, from the
nonspecialized, diversified operations of other local traders, such as
Durham merchants George Ffrost or Joseph Coe. Having said that, it
is important to note, however, that it is very unlikely that Joy would
have been able to replicate anything like the success achieved by either
Ffrost or Coe over the long run. For one thing, Middleton provided a
much smaller immediate market than did Durham. With only
sparsely populated and undeveloped frontier settlements on its borders
to the north and west and more well-established and geographically
advantaged towns to the south and east, Middleton's immediate market was destined to remain a small one for quite some time. More important yet, the town lacked the transportation facilities and proximity to the coast necessary to enable aspiring merchants to directly
participate in the Atlantic economy (either via the coastal or
transoceanic trade), thus circumscribing the potential scope of their

business activity and rendering Middleton's traders as distant, outlying satellites in a larger trading galaxy. Entering the field rather late in the game and with meager assets, the lack of an established reputation, and limited access to credit, Timothy Joy and others in similar situations were thus relegated to less desirable and therefore more risky fields of venture, such as Middleton. Indeed, as historian Seth Rockman reminds us in his study of the early American economy's development in Baltimore, "the early republic's economy opened up new possibilities for some Americans because it closed down opportunities for others." One final factor doomed Joy's start-up as well: terrible timing. With tensions mounting between the United States and Britain in the early months of 1812, access to trade staples, as well as to external markets for goods produced in the New Hampshire interior, was dramatically reduced, as was tolerance for lingering, unpaid debt. For a number of reasons, then, Joy's business was doomed from the start and was, in the best of circumstances, likely to provide the hopeful entrepreneur but a meager livelihood.[16]

It is clear that Joy purchased a going concern when he bought his Middleton store for seventy-five dollars in December of 1811, as the property is described as "the store lately occupied by Reuben Elles." Joy's purchase also included, beyond the physical building (which is also referred to as a house in the deed), "all its appurtenances," though the nature of those appurtenances is left to the imagination. It may be that Joy was purchasing a preexisting stock-in-trade or merely other trappings associated with the property. It is altogether certain, however, that Joy's business prospects depended on his ability to obtain additional merchandise on credit. Strafford County records also indicate that Joy quickly set out to improve his business by building a new "shop," separate from the building he had just purchased. He undoubtedly did this to provide his small family with a modicum of privacy and, most likely, to increase the space available for merchandise. It is also likely that he embarked on this construction project as a means of conveying an impression of stability and confidence, to show his potential customers and suppliers that he was a man who could be counted on and who was going places. Most certainly, Joy relied to some degree on credit for this project as well. His reliance on credit (both for merchandise and construction materials) proved to be his downfall.[17]

Among Joy's known creditors was the mercantile firm of Leigh and Ferguson of Berwick, Massachusetts (now Maine), launched sometime before the War of 1812. The firm's partners, Major Thomas Leigh (1773–1831) and Timothy Ferguson (1788–1839), despite the differences in their ages, had much in common: a sharp business acumen; a ferocious work ethic (both men were bachelors when they began their business—Ferguson married in late 1811 and Leigh not until 1813); tenacity; and an aggressive, risk-averse, go-ahead spirit. As a descendant of one of Berwick's founding families (the Chadbournes), Thomas Leigh had the good fortune of family connections to assist him in building his personal estate. In 1807, for instance, Leigh was allowed to purchase shares in the Chadbourne family's mills on the Great Works River (a tributary of the Salmon Falls River, which, in turn, emptied into the Piscataqua River). The eight-acre mill complex included a sawmill, a gristmill, a hulling mill, and a card mill. The combination of this complex, his mercantile endeavors (his partnership with Ferguson, a wharf, and property at the town's Quamphegan Landing), and his farming operations in Berwick's "Plain" neighborhood enabled Leigh to amass an estate valued at thirty thousand dollars by 1815.[18]

The background of Leigh's partner Timothy Ferguson remains a bit more elusive. Though an immediate contemporary of Timothy Joy (born one year prior to Joy), Ferguson seems to have taken the fast track to success, primarily through the shipping trade, and was, early on, recognized by the residents of Berwick as a "man of affairs" and a man of "refinement and cultivation." A member of Berwick's self-proclaimed "River Society," Ferguson's home on the road to Quamphegan Landing "was noted as one of the most hospitable homes in the village. With its wide halls, large rooms, and dancing hall in the top story it was a favorite place for all the young people of the region, and the fine garden was noted for its well-kept borders and delicious fruits."[19]

The mercantile firm of Leigh and Ferguson, because it served as both a provider of general merchandise and as a seller/consigner of farm commodities and timber (and perhaps as a direct importer of foreign goods), was necessarily a much more complex business organization than the small crossroads operation run by Timothy Joy in Middleton. The documentary evidence about the firm is meager. It is known that the copartnership of Leigh and Ferguson was dissolved "by mutual consent" in December of 1814. Prior to that time, however, it appears as though the partnership had expanded (or a new one was formed) to include Barnabas H. Palmer. The new partners ran semi-regular advertisements in Portsmouth newspapers, offering lumber, staves, and shooks for sale. It is probable that the firm of Leigh and Ferguson also engaged in this commodities trade, offering timber products to the coastal market and beyond. These shooks, staves, and boards very likely originated in Berwick's hinterlands, in places like Middleton, where local farmers would have offered these items to traders such as Timothy Joy as payment in kind for the sugar, tea, salt, coffee, needles, tobacco, and other sundries purchased at their small stores on account. Joy and his peers, in turn, would have used these commodities to settle accounts with tidal merchants, like Leigh and Ferguson, who provided them with their wares and who, more often than not, had the wherewithal to market them for cash sale to facilitate the payment of their own accounts with larger mercantile firms in Boston, Salem, Philadelphia, or London.[20]

It is important to note, however, that the creditors pressing the insolvent Joy for payment, possibly even the firm of Leigh and Ferguson, might not have had any direct personal involvement with the unfortunate trader at all. On the contrary, by the early years of the nineteenth century, formal credit instruments, fully assignable to third parties (similar to a modern mortgage, for instance), had become standard commercial tools in the maturing American economy. This expansive, formal credit web thus did not rely on the personal relationships, local circumstances, and face-to-face interaction characteristic of the pre-Revolutionary past and, increasingly, put traders like Leigh and Ferguson and Timothy Joy into a position where they stood as both debtors and creditors and where their businesses stood on the periphery of an extensive and faceless transatlantic mercantile system. Critical to this system as well was the faith that the various parties involved had in those with whom they entered into business relations. Men like Timothy Joy thus worked assiduously to establish their reputations and to maintain them, for, as historian Toby Ditz notes, "what mattered most in safeguarding reputation was the judgment of other men." Given the importance of patronage and connections in structuring market relations, Ditz continues, "defining a reputable self" was a necessity. The threat of insolvency of any link in this convoluted and often invisible chain, as well as questions about one's reputation and trustworthiness, thus represented an obvious threat to a great many individuals, whose only connection consisted of an impersonal and ethereal commercial bond and their mutual, albeit largely unrealized, fiscal dependence.[21]

In the main, during the flourishing years between 1790 and 1811,

this system worked reasonably well and proved flexible enough to generally meet the needs of all parties involved. But with rumors of impending war flying thick in the early months of 1812 (exacerbated, of
course, by revelations of the Henry Affair) and with the looming
threat of another cessation of the Atlantic trade, this house of cards
quickly began to collapse. Credit rapidly dried up (particularly transatlantic credit), ship's captains balked at embarking on transoceanic
voyages that were even riskier than normal, currency values fluctuated
daily, and creditors on both sides of the Atlantic (including those who
had extended credit to Timothy Joy or who held credit instruments
drawn in his name) began calling in outstanding debt due to their fear
of the potential loss of assets in the case of war or as a necessary means
of ensuring their own continued economic viability.[22]

It was Timothy Joy's great misfortune to have commenced his business—a business already hindered by its interior location—at precisely
this most inopportune moment. It did not help matters that Joy
launched his business as winter rolled in, thereby making it even more
difficult to obtain readily salable goods from his rural customers.
Moreover, Joy's youth, his lack of business experience, his still uncertain personal reputation, and Middleton's relatively undeveloped character and lack of immediate prospects certainly did not go far in as-
suaging the anxiety of even the creditors he might have known
personally. So, almost as soon as he had signed the deed for the Middleton store in December of 1811, Timothy Joy felt pressured by his
creditors. Compounding matters for the insolvent trader was the lack
of bankruptcy legislation in the United States. Without recourse to
the legal protections afforded by such laws (the lack of which attests to
the prevailing attitude in the country at the time about economic failure as a personal shortcoming), Joy stood alone in his struggle to stay
afloat. Unable to meet the demands made on him, Timothy Joy's situation rapidly spiraled out of control, culminating in the frightening
March 17 raid (perhaps by men representing Thomas Leigh and Timothy Ferguson) on his business and domicile.[23]

The intrusion described by Joy bears every resemblance to a formal
attachment proceeding wherein property is seized to satisfy a judgment rendered—in this case, against Joy. Under New Hampshire law,
Joy's creditors were entitled to enforce contracts by "attaching" the
property or persons of the defaulter. Attachment represented the first
stage in a formal lawsuit—though, as historian Bruce Mann reminds
us, "the decision to sue was itself more of a last resort than a begin-

ning"—and it "required the debtor to provide security sufficient to satisfy the debt, using his property, if adequate, or his body, if not." Obviously dissatisfied with the property offered up by Joy as security on
that March day, his creditors threatened to return and secure his body,
on *mesne* process, to ensure full payment of the debt owed. At first
blush, it might seem that the incarceration of debtors was intended as
a punitive measure on the part of angry creditors. In reality, however,
jailing a debtor served as a guarantee of future court attendance for the
final execution phase of the process of enforcing the contract (and thus
as a means of avoiding the very problem that Joy's creditors would
soon find themselves confronted with—the debtor's flight). The tactic
was also employed as a means of inducing friends and family members
to offer up assets in fulfillment of their incarcerated loved one's debt
obligations. Whatever its intended legal/economic purpose, Timothy
Joy, through his actions, made it clear that he wanted nothing to do
with jail.[24]

Joy's decision to abscond, of course, was not a simple one, nor was
it, as his journal attests, made without hesitation and regret. "Oh my
God," he wrote, "what were the feelings of my mind at that trying moment." While it is true that much of Joy's expressed regret and perhaps
some of his recollected hesitation can be dismissed as products of a
guilty conscience and a natural response to his failed escape and subsequent incarceration—it is, after all, easy and natural to regret a decision that leads to a poor outcome—it is equally likely that Joy, given
his upbringing and the lingering and pervasive social stigma attached
to insolvency and the knowledge that damage to his personal reputation would greatly diminish his future prospects, also sincerely regret-
ted his failure and, in part, viewed it as evidence of his personal
deficiency. Of course, Joy's tendency to interpret his condition in a decidedly personalized manner was also undoubtedly influenced by the
highly personal and tight-knit world that he had grown up in and, to
some degree, given his store's remote location, still operated in. As his
father's haphazard and imprecise account books (themselves a creation
of a changing time) make clear, farm life in early nineteenth-century
Durham was an intimate and intensely interdependent lifestyle, characterized by interwoven local families, face-to-face interaction, respect, and mutuality. It was a world where a handshake and a promise
often substituted for contracts and written receipts. Accustomed to
operating in an environment where trustworthiness and personal action were fundamental barometers of a person's character, it was a sim-

ple matter for individuals such as Timothy Joy to conclude that when their business and financial affairs went poorly (not to mention when they decided to flee rather than to pay a just debt), they had not fulfilled their personal obligations and responsibilities. The stigma that accompanied such deceitful behavior was very real. As the work of Karen Haltunnen makes clear, in an era of rapidly shifting social and economic relations, there was rampant fear that many individuals (she labels them "confidence men") were resorting to sophistry, cheating, and artifice to replicate and mirror the lifestyles of the emerging market elite in an attempt to mask their true intentions to manipulate individuals in order to advance their own personal fortunes, behavior that could readily be attributed to Timothy Joy. Accordingly, for Joy, his insolvency, his efforts to evade responsibility and to flee his creditors, his poor judgment at Kendall's Tavern, and his subsequent punishment all stood as personal badges of failure and dishonor; were all inextricably linked in his mind and, one can be quite certain, in the minds of many of those looking in from the outside; and were easily interpreted as reflections of a defective character/personality.[25]

That Joy felt the way that he did should come as little surprise to anyone. Throughout the nation's history, the meaning of failure and its personal and social consequence have been actively contested. For much of the seventeenth and early eighteenth centuries (indeed, right down to the current day), for instance, many Americans, guided by an intense Calvinistic moralism and a belief (though not supported by official Puritan doctrine) in visible signs of God's favor, readily equated economic failure with personal character flaws and moral failure. Likewise, an emerging liberal ideology, forged in the resistance to British monarchial rule and in the democratic rhetoric of the Revolution, offered up an ideal of a world of boundless possibilities for individual prosperity and opportunity, attainable for all through hard work and initiative. Failure, many thus came to believe, befell only those individuals lacking effort and enterprise, only those who did not take advantage of the opportunities provided to them or who, in some way, possessed deficient character. The upheaval surrounding the American struggle for independence further complicated the picture by infusing into the mix republican political thought, with its emphasis on independent action and civic virtue, attributes very much incompatible with the dependency engendered by economic insolvency and/or indebtedness. That is not to say, however, that alternative points of view did not exist. On the contrary, in the aftermath of the French and Indian War, as the Atlantic economy matured and the intimately personal nature of economic exchange began to give way, at least in some places, to the social sterility of the marketplace, failure was increasingly described in purely economic terms (devoid of any moral trappings), as a natural and accepted by-product of entrepreneurial risk taking. For Americans of Timothy Joy's generation, then, there were myriad and often mutually incompatible ways to construct and interpret the meaning of failure. Not surprisingly, this ambivalence was also manifest in the journal entries penned by Timothy Joy. Though, more often than not, Joy fell back on convention and blamed himself personally for the stigma that he (and, by extension, his family) now donned, he did not always do so and did, on occasion, merely cast his insolvency as a misfortune or as a temporary setback.[26]

From the historian's point of view, it is both a stroke of luck and an unfortunate circumstance that Timothy Joy's arrest for defamation and his subsequent incarceration overlapped with his struggle for fiscal solvency. On the one hand, the notoriety surrounding the Haverhill incident brought Joy's story to light and better enables us to uncover and trace the varied threads of his life story. It also, of course, stands as the raison d'être for his journal. It is, in short, the only reason that the details of this obscure and ordinary life have even come to light. At the same time, the tribulations associated with the defamation suit clearly eclipsed Joy's worry about insolvency or, oftentimes, commingled with it, thus rendering it all the more difficult for historians to discern his true feelings about and his efforts to understand the underlying cause of his economic difficulties. Nevertheless, the existing evidence and a growing body of historical writing on the subject provide the discerning reader with a glimpse of Joy's and the broader society's thinking regarding his financial distress and its larger meaning.

The prison journal kept by Timothy Joy from March to June of 1812 offers a number of tantalizing insights into Joy's deeply contested personal struggle to confer meaning on his economic failure. It also reveals the very messy ways in which the religious and the secular intertwined in the young man's mind as he attempted to navigate his daily life, and it lays bare what historians of religion might call his "lived religion." The journal's dramatic opening, for example, begins with Joy's recounting of the events leading up to his incarceration. In his retelling of his story, Joy speaks of his "circumstances being very much embarrassed at Middleton." His deliberate decision to employ the particular term *embarrassed* is telling. Rather than casting his situation in

a more detached manner—as a setback, a temporary difficulty, an unfortunate by-product of hard times, the regrettable outcome of a risk
taken, or the result of a poor business climate—Joy chose (whether in-
tentionally or subconsciously) to personalize the situation he found
himself in and to describe it in terms that strongly suggest that he believed that his condition was the result of some personal failing, of an
individual deficiency, and thus was grounds for embarrassment and
shame. While it is certainly true that embarrassment can result from
actions not of one's own doing, it is clear that in the case of Joy, his embarrassment, though unquestionably amplified by his subsequent actions and arrest, stemmed from both unwanted attention into his personal affairs and from what he perceived to be personal flaws. How Joy
would interpret the spiritual significance of these blemishes, however,
remained an open question for the young man: was God testing him,
as a saved individual, to restore his faith, or was God, as Elder Buzzell
and the Middleton Freewill Baptists would have contended, serving
notice that Joy, through his errant ways, had lost his salvation? Joy
struggled greatly with this question, which (as I make clear in chapter
4) lay at the heart of the spiritual conundrum he found himself grappling with as he sorted through the events and actions that led to his
downfall and as he struggled to assign meaning to them.[27]

Writing soon after his being jailed, for instance, Joy expressed a belief that these personal shortcomings and foibles suggested to him that
he had been "rejected of God, else he [God] would not have suffered
me to have fallen from affluence to poverty." It is unclear whether Joy
intended to imply in this passage that this "rejection" represented a re-
vocation of his salvation, as the Arminian Freewill Baptists would
have argued, or merely a temporal corrective to guide a recalcitrant
young saint back to his spiritual moorings, a view in keeping with the
Calvinist belief that once individual were saved, they were always
saved. What is clear, however, is that Joy was certain, given his confessed embarrassment, that this same view—that he had been "rejected" by God because of a personal moral failure—would be preva-
lent among those around him. That he was accurate in his assessment
is borne out in part by various newspapers' references to him as "a
vagabond," a "rascal," one who "has taken to drink," and "a sore trial to
all his friends."[28]

Reflecting back on recent events in a subsequent May journal entry, Joy returned to this theme, noting, "If I am driv'n to poverty it is
no more than I deserve, if I am separated from my dear wife & chil-

dren, it is no more than I deserve, for when I enjoyed their company & conversation, I was not thankfull enough to the great giver of such inestimable blessings." He had, lamentably, given in to the very temptations Reverend Curtis Coe had warned of when he addressed his Durham congregation for the last time on that sad April day in 1806; Joy had joined men who were, in Coe's words, "lovers of their owne selves, and lovers of pleasures, more than lovers of God." In Joy's own words, he had become a lover of "the world's false joys." Fully chastened by the recognition of his personal deficiency and of his nearly irreversible misstep, as well as in recognition of the fact that his individual flaws had been laid bare for the world to see, Joy took a moment to articulate the lesson learned by inserting Matthew 16:26 into his journal, "What shall it profit a man to gain the whole world and lose his own soul?" "God," he would add a few lines later, "is still merciful in sparing my unprofitable life."[29]

Importantly, however, as previously noted, Joy's choice to represent his insolvency as a personal moral failing, while certainly the pervasive theme of his journal, is not the only representation that can be found. Joy's overall struggle to comprehend the meaning of his plight was complex and messy and led him down a number of different paths. Indeed, the young man's tradition-bound view of his fall from respectability jostled, sometimes uneasily, alongside a host of equally viable alternative constructions of the meaning of his failure. This side of Joy's story confirms Bruce Mann's insightful contention that "debt could also be different things to the same people at different times."[30]

Beyond his perceived personal moral shortcomings, Joy also deeply lamented his failure to meet the contemporary cultural standard of masculine success, that of the independent provider and head of household. As an economic failure in a culture that equated manliness with economic and social mastery and independence for oneself and one's dependents, Joy, who found himself cast into a dependent status as a result of his debt, thus felt that his masculinity was under intense scrutiny and that his claim to virtuous manhood was very much an open question. Historian Toby Ditz's work on late eighteenth-century Philadelphia merchants reveals similar concerns. "Uncertainty about the bases of manly character and reputation," she argues, "apparently led to an insistent association of disparaged conduct and personal characteristics with femininity." This was certainly the case for Joy. The young man expressed serious reservations about whether he was up to the task of meeting such standards. His decision to leave his family and the message that it conveyed to the wider world about his ability to fulfill his role as head of the household obviously suggested to him as well as to others that he was not up to the task. That the decision to flee was not entirely a spontaneous one is clear from his journal; even before the March attachment proceeding, Joy had already determined to strike out for Salem to seek employment. Still, he regretfully recollects in his journal that even at his moment of truth, he doubted his resolve to carry out his plan and questioned whether he could detach himself from his family emotionally as a real man must, given the circumstances and his obligations, to ensure their economic security. The uncertainties that he harbored about his manhood were amplified, of course, by his subsequent flight—resorted to, as he indicates, when "misfortunes had overcome my reason"—and by his arrest. Incarcerated and powerless, Joy fixated on his inability, during this moment of tremendous need by his family, to "grant them . . . assistance" and to assume his proper role as both provider and protector. Sinking into deep despair, the young man wallowed in self-pity and berated himself for being "the unhappy cause" of his wife's misfortune. It could not have helped Joy's mental state any to know that, unlike his own father, Deacon Samuel—who had begun life as a young man bereft of his father and who had, through hard work, rational deliberation, measured risk, and manly exertion, carved out a competency for his family as well as resources for his children's future lives—he had, thus far, failed miserably.[31]

Elsewhere in the journal, Joy further fleshes out the era's gendered dynamics of failure by opting to personify, in female form, the new world of risk that he was engaged in, conjuring up the figure of "Dame Fortune" in a piece of doggerel inscribed in his April 17 entry. By casting himself as the "sport of Dame Fortune," Timothy Joy alluded to the captivating, alluring, seductive, and yet fickle nature of the marketplace and to his own equating of what historian J. G. A. Pocock contends was an oft-employed metaphor that rendered "the changeable, the unpredictable, and the imaginative as feminine." Furthering the allegory, Joy refers to his frustration at having been "Given up to the passions a prey" and of allowing reason to lose its seat and "phrenzy [to seize] the reigns." The references to "passions" and "phrenzy," as well as the previously mentioned passage noting how "misfortunes had overcome my reason," again situated failure squarely in the feminine sphere—characterized by emotion and impulsiveness—by chastising the writer for his unmanly behavior and by contrasting this behavior with a more proper course of masculine action defined by reasoned calculation, decisiveness, and assertive behavior. As these references suggest, despite his predicament, Joy, now fully cognizant of his being unsexed, of behaving in an unmanly manner, was making a determination to reassert his manhood through strength of character and reasoned action. Indeed, a consistent theme in Joy's introspective journal is his constant fear of losing his reason and his struggle to affirm and maintain his rationality (and thus his manhood) in the face of passion and emotion—in other words, his psychological struggle to reassert the dominance of masculine traits over presumably feminine traits, traits that had, at least partially, as he understood things, led him into failure. That is not to say that his new course unfolded without a hitch. On the contrary, Joy continued to battle to reclaim his manhood throughout the remainder of his journal. Later brought to tears while thinking about his family's plight and his own role in creating their predicament, Joy quickly composed himself by reminding himself of his masculine responsibilities and by rebuking himself for his feminine behavior, writing, "I could hear [Mary] chide me for giving way to sorrow." Even at low points such as these, Joy proved unwilling or, more likely, unable to let loose of the prescribed gender norms that, in his mind and in the minds of many of his peers, further rendered him a failure.[32]

Timothy Joy's journal also hints at the depth to which newer, economic-inspired interpretations of failure, shorn of all moral judgment, had penetrated New England society by 1812. Despite his pronounced tendency to interpret his failure as an outcome of personal weakness and/or character flaw, Joy, simple crossroads merchant that he was, nonetheless periodically employed the impersonal and thoroughly modern lexicon of business ("misfortune," "profit," "losses in trade," an "unprofitable," a poor "exchange") to characterize his economic travails. In so doing, he provides evidence of the depth to which the new economy had penetrated American society and that, at least on some level, he had come to appreciate that his failure in business was not entirely of his own making and that forces beyond his direct control also played a significant role in his plight. More pointedly, this recognition, whether it be conscious or not, also showed itself in occasional passages characterizing Joy's failure as a temporary situation, as "the frowns of partial fortune." This point of view, coupled with a belief that his newfound awareness of his personal mistakes would enable him to avoid similar pitfalls moving forward, permitted Joy, in his less doubtful moments, to speak hopefully of the time when he would be free to try his hand at earning a living again. As he wrote in mid-May, it was true that he was "strip'd of earthly property" at the moment, but he might "perhaps earn even more" after his release.[33]

Yet when all was said and done, Joy fervently believed, his ultimate fate, the final determination as to whether he would succeed or fail, lay with himself and his maker. Contemplating the trajectory of his difficulties as he awaited his June 3 release from jail, Timothy Joy confided in his journal his "wish for my family's sake to be possess'd of a competency," noting further that "he who has seen fit to take it from me once has the same power to bless my exertions with success in re-covering it again." "Religion and resignation props my falling hopes," he added the second day following, claiming, "[L]et me rest assured that if I lose all here, and secure my happiness in another & better world, the exchange will be advantageous." Joy's choice of metaphors is telling and reveals the frequency with which religious beliefs and the new realities of the marketplace jostled with each other in the minds of contemporary Americans. The nature of the spiritual "exchange" noted by the young debtor, how to interpret from a spiritual perspective the losses and gains that accompanied a life embedded within the cash nexus, and the terms and conditions on which this instrument of faith would be executed were a constant source of internal negotiation and consternation for him, would come to occupy the bulk of his waking hours while in prison, and stood as one of the central themes in the lengthy and introspective journal he penned during his incarceration.[34]

Chapter 3

"IF I SPEND MY DAYS IN PRISON
I STILL WILL BE A DEMOCRAT"

As March gave way to April, Timothy Joy's journal began to document a steady stream of new inmates arriving in Ipswich Prison. Like Joy, these men were debtors. Their particular fault, though, as Joy viewed the situation, was that they owed money to Federalist creditors. With the Massachusetts gubernatorial election between incumbent Elbridge Gerry (a Democratic-Republican) and Caleb Strong (the Federalist challenger) looming (April 6), Joy, undoubtedly influenced in part by his own belief that he was the victim of Federalist persecution, quickly concluded that the sudden incarceration of these men was politically motivated. "This day," he noted on March 31, "two new prisoners were brought in for debt by the Gentle Feds who now begin to hunt out all they can of the oposite party & if they owe them they must pay, vote for them, run away or go to Jail." "After what I have seen," he concluded, "I shall not wonder if Massachusetts gets shackled with a Fed Governor the ensuing year." Four days later, Joy received a visit from David Cummings, the Essex County solicitor. A local Democratic-Republican leader, Cummings assured Joy that "he did not think the Grand Jury would find a bill against [him], that [he] was committed out of spite & that after election it would be forgotten." Joy closed his journal for the day by noting, "Another prisoner just brot in—another Republican put in by a Fed for debt just before election." Joy's suspicion about systematic Federalist voter suppression, it turns out, was widely shared among local Democratic-Republicans and would soon, though unbeknownst to the young man, trigger a chaotic election-day riot in nearby Salem.[1]

At nine o'clock in the morning on Monday, April 6, 1812—election day—Timothy Joy sat ill and despairing in his cell after a restless night of little sleep. Suddenly, the quietude of the morning was broken by the arrival of "a disagreeable visitor." "Mr. Sheriff [Daniel] Dutch of Salem came just now," he coldly recorded, "& served a writ on me in behalf of Leigh & Ferguson, of Berwick, Maine, the debt 31.45 cts." "I wonder when the Gentlemen Feds," he continued, "will leave off persecuting me. How can I pay money confined as I am in jail? I now must lay here the lord knows how long to gratify these fellows malice." Fifteen miles away, Salem's Federalist selectmen—Samuel Ropes, Abel Lawrence, Michael Webb, William Mansfield, and Phillip Chase—opened the city's poll at Salem Town Hall—the same court building where Joy had been remanded to jail just seventeen days prior. Anticipating a large turnout for the closely fought and intensely partisan gubernatorial and state races and painfully aware of "the inconveniences which had heretofore been experienced from the smallness of the court house hall" where past balloting had occurred, the selectmen had chosen to relocate the polling stations to the building's ground floor, where they configured the new layout to allow voters to enter at one door in the building, to proceed down a narrow passageway past the ballot box to cast their votes, and to exit the building through a door at the opposite end of the structure. Despite their careful planning, however, the ensuing voting would be anything but orderly, though the precise details of what transpired and why it happened were a point of much contention and partisan interpretation.[2]

According to the city's Federalist newspaper, the *Salem Gazette*, the moment the polls opened, "a strong body of the democratic party, by previous concert, filled the avenue to the boxes and crowded the area of the house, and in this manner the passage to the ballot box was completely blocked up, and all approach to it utterly impossible." Chaos reigned in the tightly confined and rapidly warming space: determined men, both Democrats and Federalists, jostled for room and struggled with each other for control over the voting space, tempers flared, and the shouting and cursing of both the protestors and Salem town officials echoed through the building and spilled out into the nearby street, drawing even more people to the scene. Despite their best efforts, the Federalist voting officials and town constables could not remove the protestors, and the ballot box was rendered inaccessible. "In this manner," the paper continued, "the whole body of citizens were actually kept at bay for two hours, and the authority of the peace officers set at defiance."[3]

The Democratic protest, it turns out, was prompted by the select-men's decision, in the days following their election to office in mid-March, to drop "nearly four hundred" names from the town's voter list. The Democratic-Republican *Essex Register* alleged that with the exception of a dozen Federalists added "to save appearances," most of the voter's dropped were members of the opposition party, "some of whom had been voters for 42 years, had fought the battles of the revolution, and bore its scars in their countenances." The purpose of this paring, the outraged paper's editor argued, was "to leave off enough to secure a majority for the federal Senators in the district." Defending their actions, the selectman maintained that the names expunged from the town's voter list were the names of dead voters, those who had removed from Salem, and those names that appeared multiple times on the various lists available. Moreover, the selectmen pointed out, those who were dropped from the list were allowed, for two hours each day (Monday through Saturday) for the week prior to the election, to provide evidence of their eligibility to vote—that is, proof that they met the state's requirement of property ownership. Not surprisingly, the *Essex Register* alleged that "every person who would give a federal vote" was "put upon the list privately, without any vouchers being required. Whilst republicans, with the fullest proof of property, were rejected." The selectmen contended that few of the recently disenfranchised voters bothered to appeal their cases and that "only a very small number" of those who did were rejected. With tensions escalating because of the action, the Reverend William Bentley of Salem's East Church presciently confided in a March entry in his diary that "persons long in the habits of voting do not bare refusal with patience, and nothing but a more yielding temper promises tranquility."[4]

In the hour before the polls opened on April 6, Salem's Democratic-Republican leaders determined to try one last time to have the names restored to the list. Leading the effort were Captain Joseph Winn and David Cummings (the recent unsuccessful opponent of Justice John Prince, Jr., in the contest for the position of Salem town clerk). They, along with "a large number of persons whose names were omitted," confronted city selectmen and demanded that the names be immediately returned to the list, supplying evidence to prove the validity of their claims about the eligibility of those present. The selectmen, however, were unmoved and declared that no names would be added at such a late date. Their denial, they subsequently reported, prompted "Messrs. Winn and Cummings in a menacing manner and attitude" to declare "that if we opened the poll without complying with their requisition, it should be at our peril." Frustrated and angry, the recently disenfranchised men, led by Crispin Brewer, John Bacon, Andrew Evans, and the ironically named Alexander Hamilton, among others, stormed the polls when they opened, refusing to give way until they were allowed to vote.[5]

Unable to clear the path to the ballot box, the Salem selectmen were forced to suspend voting and to hasten a messenger to Ipswich to recall Daniel Dutch, who was there serving Timothy Joy with Leigh and Ferguson's writ of attachment, and to request Sheriff Robert Farley's immediate presence in Salem to restore order at the polls. As tensions mounted, parties on both sides attempted to reach a negotiated settlement. Finally, after two hours, the disgruntled protesters surrendered their posts, and voting resumed. The precise reason for the change of heart is uncertain. The *Essex Register* reported that the standoff ended after the selectmen promised the disenfranchised men that they would be permitted to vote in the afternoon or be provided "with a legal reason for refusing" if they agreed to withdraw from the polling place. The *Gazette*, in contrast, stands silent as to what may have happened. In any event, the peace achieved was short lived. At roughly "half past three," the Democratic-Republican protestors returned to the courthouse, intent on casting their ballots before the polls closed at four. Fearful that the ballots already cast were in danger of being destroyed, the Salem selectmen, now protected by a phalanx of Federalist voters, responded by declaring the polls closed immediately. In the tumult that ensued, Democratic-Republicans alleged that the ballot boxes "were smuggled up in one corner," that "several federalists were admitted into the window to screen from the sight of the republicans the management in sorting and counting the votes," and that "one that was admitted was seen to bring in a handful of votes." Sheriff Farley, Daniel Dutch, and other law officials scrambled to restore order, finally resorting to reading the Riot Act to dispel the thoroughly enraged crowd. Salem's election-day riot was over. The political fallout from the event, however, was merely beginning.[6]

Still incensed over the previous day's events and the Federalists' narrow electoral victory in Salem and in the commonwealth at large, the *Essex Register* bitterly wrote that "the annals of despotism and corruption cannot produce a parallel to the Salem election and the conduct of the Selectmen," who the paper decried as "petty tyrants." For its part, the Federalist *Gazette*, falling back on a tried-and-true line of attack and now bolstered by the arrival of the news of the Madison administration's imposition of an embargo on all American trade in anticipation of war with Britain, denounced the Democratic-Republican mob and the "evil works of democracy," railing that "these riotous disorganizers are enemies of our republic: they are '*tyrants* when in power, and REBELS when out of power.' They have ever been opposers of the Constitution, and will finally be its destroyers."[7]

Timothy Joy, locked away as he was in his Ipswich cell, did not, of course, have a direct role or even any immediate awareness of the events that transpired in Salem on that April election day, as evidenced by the lack of any mention of the unrest in his journal (he does discuss the subsequent trial of the rioters in early May). The events and the intense partisan climate that gave rise to them, however, are of vital importance to our understanding of Joy's actions in Haverhill and of the journal that he penned while in prison from March to June of 1812. Shorn of its political context, Joy's behavior seems rather incomprehensible. What, after all, would motivate someone to pretend to be someone else and to concoct a completely fictional story designed to question the loyalties of a leading national politician whom he does not know personally? Was it a character flaw in Joy? Or was it something else? The answer to these questions can be found in a consideration of the context and nature of early American politics. The intensity of his political partisan feeling—and his conviction that Timothy Pickering was a traitor in spirit if not in actual deed—led Joy to believe (with the help of the alcohol he consumed) that his story was true in the larger sense, even if it was not true in its basic facts. At some level—in the heat of the ongoing electoral campaign—Joy came to believe that Pickering did not love America the way that he did and that the Federalists were intent on betraying the nation and destroying the republic. Believing this, in turn, allowed Joy and a multitude of like-minded decent and honest people to rationalize and accept as true a whole host of distortions and outright lies. Living as he did in one of the most highly charged and divisive political environments in American history, Joy could not help but be influenced by and give voice to the contours of the era's turbulent politics. Indeed, Joy's intense Democratic-Republican identity is manifest throughout his journal and stands at the center, along with his religion, of what we know about the young man's life and character: it fueled his drunken tirade against Timothy Pickering; it came to shape, in part, his interpretation of his debt and how he viewed the arrest and incarceration of other debtors; it influenced his responses to people that he met; it set the course for his discussion and interpretation of the meaning of his trial and the actions of the Massachusetts Supreme Judicial Court's April–May session; and it stood as a point of intense pride and principle for him.

An appreciation of the contemporary political atmosphere is also critical in furthering our ability to grasp the intensity of the reaction to Joy's allegations at Haverhill and to the widespread news of his arrest. It would be tempting for one to assume that, as one Salem newspaper claimed,

> much is said of the Joy affair; but of all trifling this must be the greatest. Why should any man be earnest to defend or contradict upon one of the most ridiculous and most trifling of events. It appeared at once that the fellow had been trifling; his ears then should have been boxed, or he should have been taught better manners, if capable of having been taught. But to fill newspapers with such trifling, is to trifle with all their readers. A less thing could not draw the public attention, and less evil could not be done by any boyish trick whatever.

The explosive political environment in the early republic, however, ensured that such would not be the case—that a boxing of the ears or some similar form of mild reprimand would not be enough and that the claims that Joy made in Kendall's Tavern would not pass as a mere trifle.[8]

The partisan roots that supported and nourished the American political party system as it stood in 1812, though extensive and readily discernible, did not stretch very deeply into the nation's historical past. In fact, just the opposite was the case, with the Federalist and Democratic-Republican organizations, like the young prisoner Timothy Joy, tracing their birth back to the postconstitutional era of the late 1780s. It was there—in the chaos and confusion attendant in the nation's failed first attempt to forge a republic under the Articles of Confederation and surrounding the intense debates over the nation's new constitutional framework, in the murkiness of a rising democratic social and political tide and conservative efforts to suppress or reverse it, and in the debate over what actions would best promote the nation's common good—that the seeds of oppositional party strife were sown. Commenting on the politics of the era, historian Gordon Wood contends that "politics became democratized as more Americans gained the right to vote. The essentially aristocratic world of the Founding Fathers in which gentry leaders stood for election was replaced by a very different democratic world, a recognizably modern world of competing professional politicians who ran for office under the banners of modern political parties. Indeed, Americans became so thoroughly democratic that much of the period's political activity, beginning with the Constitution, was devoted to finding means and devices to tame that democracy." This democratic thrust, however, was not merely limited to the traditional realm of electioneering and voting. On the contrary, political action and thought, loosed from their moorings in the street politics and mob actions of the Revolutionary era, assumed myriad forms in the early republic—parades, festivals, public rituals and celebrations—as the people questioned their "betters'" claims to leadership and as they worked to carve out more direct control for themselves within the political process. The combination of an inverted political order and an atmosphere of general partisan rowdiness actively loosened and challenged established social structures and norms.[9]

Much of this partisan tension stemmed from the actions and policies of President George Washington's brash young secretary of the Treasury, Alexander Hamilton. Extremely distrustful of the era's democratic surge and imbued with a vision of an American nation enriched through commerce and manufacturing and run by economically and socially successful elites such as himself, the ever-active Hamilton promoted policies—funding the national debt and the assumption by the federal government of remaining state debts, the establishment of a Bank of the United States, the implementation of protective tariffs, federally funded internal improvements, the imposition of the notorious excise tax on whiskey, and the creation of the Patent Office—designed to utilize the powers of the new national government to foster capital creation, to overcome parochial affinities and thus build allegiance to the nation, to maintain elite rule, and to promote opportunity for these elites and their middling allies. By so doing, by pursuing policies that assisted and enriched those who already possessed monetary and social capital, Hamilton believed (presaging contemporary theorists of trickle-down economics) that the nation's long-term best interest would be served. Opponents of Hamilton, such as Thomas Jefferson and James Madison, worked diligently to maintain the nation's agrarian foundation, with trade as a necessary handmaiden. Committed to the ideal that property ownership and the autonomous lifestyle that it supported served as a basis for independent thought and action—key components, it was widely held, in a republican form of government—they feared the heavy and potentially abusive hand of a vastly more powerful federal government, especially one that potentially threatened this lifestyle by emphasizing commercial and manufacturing growth.[10]

The foreign policy crisis triggered by the upheaval of the French Revolution, which began in Joy's birth year of 1789, further served to distance the two groups. Jefferson and his allies threw their support behind America's Revolutionary ally and the fledgling French republic, despite the excesses of the reign of terror and French interference with American oceanic trade. Hamilton, along with his peers, supported Great Britain—who meddled even more stridently in American commerce—the economic and social model for what he hoped the United States might someday become. The combination of marked domestic and foreign policy differences between the two groups and the agonizing uncertainty about the new nation's ability to find its way in a very hostile world spawned, in turn, a deep distrust of the opposition and of their motives. More important still, this intense mutual suspicion proved powerful enough to overcome a deeply ingrained hostility to political organization—an act that was viewed by contemporary Americans as a perilous manifestation of self-interested factionalism—and led to the establishment of two loosely organized political structures: the pro-British "Federalist" followers of Alexander Hamilton and the "Democratic-Republican" supporters of Thomas Jefferson and the French cause, who justified their existence by portraying themselves as defenders of the republic against the machinations of their dangerously antirepublican opponents. Simply put, historian David Waldstreicher argues, Americans came to identify "one's own party, not as a party, but as the real nation." "In an era where Union was still seen as an experiment," Kevin Gannon thus reminds us, "national politics were played at extremely high stakes."[11]

Over the course of the next decade, the two groups jostled for political supremacy and, often uneasily, for the hearts and minds of the American citizenry, with Federalism and then (after the so-called Revolution of 1800) Republicanism taking turns in leading the republic through its difficult infancy. All the while, the two groups remained intensely distrustful of one another and often of the people whose votes they courted, refusing to acknowledge their opponents as legitimate and fearing that the newly founded nation, especially while under the control of their opponents, teetered on the precipice of complete failure and democratic anarchy.

For much of the period between 1795 and 1812, though domestic concerns remained a primary focus for the two fledgling parties, war in Europe, a war sparked by the upheaval of the French Revolution, dictated that they each devote substantial amounts of time and energy to foreign affairs. With much of Europe and, by dint of their expansive global empires, much of the world embroiled in war, the United States assumed a neutral position in the conflict. Recognizing a tremendous opportunity to expand American trade on a global scale, Federalist and Republican administrations alike sought—in the face of egregious actions on the part of both sides in the conflict and under increasingly difficult circumstances as the intensity of the conflict heightened—to maintain the nation's neutrality and to protect American interests on the high seas. While mainly a diplomatic effort, military options always remained on the table. Under Federalist rule, for instance, the determination to protect American interests led to the negotiation of the Jay Treaty with Great Britain in 1794 and also drew the United States into a brief quasi war with the French navy between 1798 and 1800—a measure that met with the full support of John Adams's secretary of state at the time, Timothy Pickering. For their part, the Democratic-Republican administrations of Thomas Jefferson and James Madison found themselves confronted with a new geopolitical reality—British domination of the seas after the renewal of warfare on the European continent in 1803 and the destruction of the French and Spanish fleets at the Battle of Trafalgar in 1805. Determined to prevent war with Great Britain while simultaneously defending American trade, protecting American seamen from impressments, and ending ongoing British encouragement of Indian attacks on the nation's western border, Democratic-Republican administrations made repeated peaceful attempts—the Non-Importation Act, the Embargo Act of 1807, the policy of nonintercourse with France and Britain, and the Macon Act of 1810—to induce a peaceful change in British policy, with little effect. Confronted with British intransigence, "War Hawks" within the party's ranks increasingly demanded military action. In the meantime, Federalists worked tirelessly to keep the peace with Britain and to reestablish their presence at the state and local levels, particularly in their New England base, in the hope that, by so doing, they would be able to reclaim control over the federal government and head off the conflict—or perhaps (if national reascendancy proved elusive, as Timothy Pickering and a handful of others had suggested in 1803 and 1804) so that they might lead a separation of the region from the United States and the creation of a new commercial republic with close ties to Great Britain. As the year 1812 began, it was clear to all that the nation and the conflict between Federalism and Democratic-Republicanism had reached a critical juncture. Nowhere was this conflict harder fought than in Massachusetts and its neighbor to the north, New Hampshire.[12]

Like the waters in Durham's Great Bay, the political tides in the New Hampshire of Timothy Joy's youth ebbed and flowed constantly, with both Federalism and Democratic-Republicanism vying for political supremacy and with neither party, after 1805, able to exercise dominance for long periods of time. During his early years, between the ages of five and fifteen, Timothy lived in a state controlled by John Taylor Gilman and the Federalist establishment of nearby Exeter (then the state capital). Closely tied (through family, political, and economic ties, as well as via the region's roads and sea-lanes) to the commercial centers of Massachusetts—particularly Salem and Boston—and well entrenched as traditional leaders, the Exeter elite used their power and prestige to dominate New Hampshire politics throughout the 1790s. In 1800, however, New Hampshire Democratic-Republicans mounted their first serious challenge to Federalist hegemony in their state.[13]

Ironically, the challenge began first in the state's financial markets. Frustrated by a lack of capital and the Federalists' stranglehold on credit via the Gilman-run New Hampshire State Bank (the only bank in the state at the time), Portsmouth Republicans, led by merchantman and U.S. senator John Langdon, organized a rival bank that quickly began making small loans to local merchants and farmers on easy terms. The Federalist response was quick and decisive, with the party-dominated state legislature taking action to force the closure of the new bank. Denouncing the New Hampshire State Bank as an undemocratic monopoly and uniting with the state's interior farmers who likewise resented rule by the so-called Exeter Junto and who were demanding that the state capital be relocated to the interior town of Concord, Democratic-Republicans mounted an aggressive campaign for the governorship behind the candidacy of Judge Timothy Walker. Although they failed in their attempt, the party did significantly lower the percentage of votes cast for Gilman, and the election revealed a deep political rift in the state, with, as historian Donald Cole contends, "[o]ld, traditional Congregational towns [in the Merrimack and

Connecticut River valleys] remain[ing] loyal to Federalism, while the more enterprising, faster growing communities [Portsmouth, the seacoast towns like Durham, and the interior of the state] were most likely to vote Republican." With this division in mind, state Democratic-Republicans devised an electoral formula that they would employ to great effect moving forward—nominating candidates for the governorship from interior towns, appealing to farmers and commercial towns by promising to end the banking monopoly and thus opening credit, and labeling their opponents as aristocrats and Congregationalists (i.e., defenders of the establishment).[14]

That this strategy paid dividends cannot be denied. In the 1802 gubernatorial race, for instance, Democratic-Republicans cut Gilman's margin of victory to fewer than 2,000 votes statewide (he actually lost in Durham), and in 1804, they reduced it further, to a mere 235 votes (once again, Durham went for his opponent Langdon), while simultaneously carrying the state for their party's presidential candidate, Thomas Jefferson, and capturing control of the New Hampshire state house (where Langdon served as Speaker of the House). The following year, Democratic-Republicans, undoubtedly aided by the intensification of British privations on American shipping and the separatist activities of Federalist senator William Plumer, who supported Pickering's idea of the creation of an independent New England confederation, succeeded in wresting control of the state from the Federalists and elected Langdon governor with a majority of nearly 3,900 votes. Among the new Democratic-Republican administration's first actions was to charter a new bank, the Concord Bank, in 1806 and to relocate the state capital to Concord in 1807.[15]

Jefferson's Embargo Act of 1807, however, dramatically hurt the Republican cause. Closely aligned with New England's commercial interests and the region's economic elite, Federalists in New Hampshire and elsewhere mounted an immediate and stiff resistance to the unpopular measure. In March of 1808, for instance, the noted Massachusetts Federalist and U.S. senator (and former secretary of state) Timothy Pickering penned a widely published letter in which he denounced the measure as one brought about by French influence on the Jefferson administration. Shortly thereafter, Federalist towns in Massachusetts, led by Boston, passed resolutions demanding the embargo's repeal and going as far as to threaten disunion—as demonstrated by the resolutions adopted by the Topsfield Caucus in nearby Essex County, which threatened to "rely for relief on the wisdom and patriotism of our state government" if the embargo was not lifted. New Hampshire Federalists were able to parlay the measure's unpopularity into electoral victory in 1809, sending Jeremiah Smith, the chief justice of the New Hampshire Superior Court and a former member of Congress, to the governor's office. The Federalist resurgence, however, proved short lived. On March 15, 1809, in one of his final acts as president, Thomas Jefferson signed a bill repealing the Embargo Act. New Hampshire's Democratic-Republicans were bolstered by the reopening of American ports and by the Federalists' recent and vociferous opposition to the federal Enforcement Act, passed to halt the rampant smuggling activities circumventing the embargo in the winter of 1809, an opposition that many deemed treasonous—the *New Hampshire Patriot*, for one, claimed that "theirs [the Federalists] is the cause of Great Britain, insomuch as they coincide with and justify her aggressions on the principles of right and justice, on the laws of nature and of nations; theirs is the cause of our enemy, because they stigmatize our government in every act, whatever its tendency, and because no subterfuge, however mean, is left unessayed to insight to distrust and opposition"). The Democratic-Republicans stormed back to recapture the New Hampshire governor's office and control of the state assembly in 1810–11.[16]

Beyond the pale of formal electoral politics, there also existed an equally important, but less well understood, world of popular political culture. Forged in, according to Simon Newman, the "social and political upheavals that had accompanied the preceding quarter century of resistance, revolution, and nation-building, all of which had complicated the relationship between rulers and the ruled," this popular political activity assumed new importance in the years immediately following the ratification of the Constitution. "The rites and festivals that comprised the out-of-doors political activity of ordinary Americans became an essential part of the political process," Newman contends, furnishing "many different Americans with the means to exercise some measure of political power—calling their leaders to account, demanding action, pressuring for change, championing ideals and sacred values, and preventing the enactment of certain policies."[17]

That this political culture was in full bloom in New Hampshire's seacoast region, home to Timothy Joy, is certain, as festivals, parades, fetes, and even riots were hallmarks of area politics. In November of 1789, for instance, George Washington visited Portsmouth, New Hampshire, as part of a national tour celebrating his election as the nation's first president. Greeted at the New Hampshire–Massachusetts border by John Sullivan, a Revolutionary War hero and "president" of the state, Washington was escorted to Portsmouth by a cavalcade of seven hundred cavalry. Entering the city at three o'clock in the afternoon on November 1, the new president received an enthusiastic welcome from a huge crowd assembled along his route into the city. Amid houses festooned with banners and flags and admirers perched in windows and on rooftops, Washington's progress was noted by the tolling of bells and the firing of a salute from thirteen cannons—one for each of the thirteen states. On his arrival at the city's Market Square, Washington was serenaded by residents (including the city's schoolchildren, wearing hats with colored quills to designate their schools) singing an original ode to the tune of "God Save the King," before his formal reception at the state house. The obvious symbolism apparent in such events—the linking of the local and national, the homage to a patriot leader of the Revolutionary struggle, the glorification of the embodiment of republican sacrifice, and the connection between the nation's past and future—was, of course, intentional and reflected the Federalists' hope of "building a secular cult of Washington with rites and symbols that would strengthen their party and its plans for the new nation." Others, however, bristled at the pomp and circumstance—"elite spectacle," as defined by Susan Davis—and the trappings of social hierarchy evident in the festivities. Often resorting to spontaneous, erratic, and disorderly public displays or "festivity," these individuals sought out alternative ways to make their point. This determination, for instance, spawned a loud and boisterous crowd to gather in Portsmouth in late July of 1795 to express displeasure with Jay's Treaty—recently lauded by local Federalists—which they viewed as a submission to British will. Protest speeches, the burning of effigies, and the smashing of windows and destruction of property all became expressions of the political discontent of local Democratic-Republicans and their fear of incipient aristocracy. In brief, partisans of all stripes mobilized to use the politics of the street to gain "control over the content and meaning of celebrations" such as those staged in honor of Washington or those in Portsmouth opposed to Jay's Treaty. The battle for the hearts and minds of the electorate was every bit as important as electoral victory.[18]

Timothy Joy shaped his partisan identity within this highly charged partisan environment, with its closely contested and fierce electoral and popular politics. The contours of political life in Timothy

Joy's Durham remain an open book. The few election tallies that do exist suggest, consistent with the pattern described by Donald Cole, that the town was predominantly Republican, giving gubernatorial candidate John Langdon an electoral majority of 95 in 1802, 61 in 1803, 95 in 1804, 106 in 1805, and 33 in 1810. Though Langdon narrowly lost Durham to his Federalist opponent in 1811, his party, now led by William Plumer, overwhelmingly recaptured the town in March of 1812. More evenly divided than its progenitor, New Durham—the town where Timothy Joy resided after his marriage in 1807 until some point in time in 1811—followed its namesake's lead and leaned toward the Democratic-Republican axis. Middleton, the town Joy chose as the place to establish his family in 1811, however, appears to have been a Federalist enclave in the years preceding the War of 1812. We can be certain, however, that this fact did not deter the indomitable Joy from casting his ballot (1 of the 26 cast as opposed to 45 votes for the Federalist candidate) for William Plumer on March 10, 1812, just one week before his hasty flight from his creditors.[19]

That voters in Durham and the rest of New Hampshire believed the act of voting to be important is borne out by the incredibly high rates of voter participation during this era. For instance, between 1808 and 1814—the years that Joy would have come of age—upwards of 70 percent of all adult males in New Hampshire were voting. Accounts of festive political life in Durham at that time are missing, though it can be safely assumed that Joy and his fellow Durhamites shared in Independence Day celebrations and other political commemoration. It is also probable, given the strong correlation between parental political affiliation and that of one's children, that Deacon Samuel, model of self-sufficient yeoman agriculture that he was, cast his ballot, like his son Timothy, for the party of Jefferson, though his defense in 1806 of the beleaguered minister Curtis Coe, who found himself under attack from antiestablishment forces as well as from religious dissenters, would likely have put him into a close working alliance with Durham Federalists. If this tempered, in any manner, the politics of the father—and that is very much an open question—the relationship certainly did not have the same effect on the son. On the contrary, it is clear from his writings that Timothy Joy wholeheartedly embraced the Republican ideology that painted his Federalist opponents as haughty aristocrats—he derisively refers to them as "Gentleman Feds" and "dear gentlefolks," for example. As a young man embarking on his life's mission to make something of himself and to provide for his family, he also undoubtedly found comfort in the Republicans' more democratic message and willingness to challenge established social hierarchies and would have readily identified with those seeking a leg up in a commercial environment dominated by old money, banking monopoly, and well-entrenched elites. It is likely as well that Timothy, raised in a time and place that revered the memory and achievements of the Revolutionary generation (in fact, being named for one such family hero) and being a proud member of the first generation of "Americans," bristled at what many perceived to be Federalism's clear willingness to kowtow to British bullying and accepted as a very real danger the myriad charges of treasonable Federalist behavior floated by the Democratic-Republican opposition. It was for these reasons and undoubtedly others as well that Timothy Joy cast his lot with the Democratic-Republican cause.[20]

It is imperative to reiterate that this party system, whether it be operating at the local, state, or national levels, perched on an ill-defined but increasingly democratic political culture—an unexpected and, from the perspective of many well-heeled elites who were accustomed to unchallenged governance by social superiors, an unwanted turn of events. Without a doubt, the need to build electoral coalitions, the need to win popular approval from the likes of Deacon Samuel and Timothy Joy, and (as the selectmen of Salem learned firsthand on that April election day in 1812) the unpredictability and assertiveness of the American electorate challenged older notions of deferential political power and necessitated the creation of a new, intensely personal political style more in keeping with the times. In the volatility that accompanied this transition, "the culture of honor," as historian Joanne Freeman has convincingly demonstrated in her work *Affairs of Honor,* stood as "a source of stability in this contested political landscape." Above all else, Freeman reminds us, "reputation was at the heart of this personal form of politics—much like, as we have seen, it was in regard to credit and business success. Men gained office on the basis of it, formed alliances when they trusted it, and assumed they would earn it by accepting high office." "Political power and victory thus," she concludes,

> required close protection of one's reputation, as well as the savvy to assess the reputations of one's peers. It also required a talent for jabbing at the reputations of one's enemies, for a man dishonored or discredited lost his influence, lost the field. Forging, defending, and attacking reputations—this was the national political game.

71

It was onto this playing field, with its well-defined rules and no-holds-barred play, that Timothy Meader Joy would blithely stray in late March of 1812.[21]

The Massachusetts political arena that Joy inadvertently stumbled into on that cold March day in Haverhill was arguably the most volatile in the entire country, for it was in that state that Federalism was making its desperate last stand against national irrelevancy. Unfortunately for the beleaguered party, things had not been going particularly well for them even here as of late. In April of 1810, state Republicans had succeeded in electing Elbridge Gerry governor and in gaining control over the state legislature—though they still were a minority in the state's congressional delegation in Washington. Gerry and his Democratic-Republican peers then used their power to oust Timothy Pickering from his Senate seat in 1811, replacing him with the Republican Speaker of the House, Joseph Bradley Varnum. State Democratic-Republicans also stepped up efforts to rally Massachusetts voters for a possible war with Great Britain and actively supported the resumption of commercial nonintercourse against that nation in March 1811. Federalist protests against the measure seemingly fell on deaf ears, and Gerry was elected to a second term in office in April of that same year.[22]

Emboldened by his reelection, Gerry embarked on an aggressive campaign against his political foes, hoping to further undercut their support before the looming war could resuscitate their political fortunes. Highlighting British interference with American shipping during the summer of 1811, Gerry sought to tap patriotic sentiment and to rally Massachusetts voters to the Democratic-Republican standard. To further ensure the success of his party in upcoming elections, Gerry, who had consented to run for a third term in office, and the Republican majority in the legislature actively redrew state senatorial district boundaries so as to weaken the Federalist opposition—this is the origin of the term *gerrymander*—and, in February of 1812, embarked on an aggressive antilibel crusade against the Federalist press. News of the Henry Affair in early March 1812, with its myriad charges of Federalist disloyalty and treasonous collusion, provided yet more grist for the Democratic-Republican mill and yet another opportunity for the party to castigate state Federalists as royalists, aristocrats, and dangerous usurpers and to thus rally further support.[23]

Cornered and under constant attack, Massachusetts Federalists fought back tenaciously, denouncing the buildup toward war and the impact that such a war would have on Massachusetts commerce and focusing intently on state issues to build support for their candidate for the governorship in 1812, Caleb Strong, a former member of the U.S. Senate and a delegate to the Philadelphia Constitutional Convention. Reproving the Democratic-Republican assault on the press, a change in the pay structure for members of the state legislature, the Republican gerrymander, and rumors of a looming renewal of embargo on all American trade, Strong and his supporters launched an aggressive campaign designed to stop their opponents in their tracks and to shore up Federalism's position in Massachusetts. Within this white hot political climate, the claims made by Timothy Joy at Kendall's Tavern, a mere three days before Haverhill opened its polls, were certain to elicit an intense political response.[24]

The precise nature of the conversation being shared by the men seated at the corner table in Kendall's Tavern when they first drew Timothy Joy's attention on that fateful March afternoon is altogether uncertain. Certainly, the discussion was a political one likely touching on the upcoming election, the threat of war with Great Britain, the recent revelations made by John Henry, and undoubtedly, given that the primary men involved in the discussion were Democratic-Republicans, the suspect loyalties of their political opponents. What is clear is that Joy, emboldened by drink and feeling safe in the presence of others who were openly sympathetic to his own political views, became an active and vocal participant in the discourse and openly concocted a tale of Federalist intrigue, a theme that had long circulated as a common subtext in New England political circles and in the broader political culture. That he chose to feature Timothy Pickering in the lead role in his fictitious conspiracy is also not surprising and would not have struck any Republican in the room as far-fetched, especially in light of Pickering's support for New England's separation from the union in 1803–4, his strident protests against the Jefferson and Madison administrations, his well-known prickliness and litigious nature, and his formal censure in January of 1811 by the U.S. Senate for reading confidential documents in an open Senate session. Above all else, Joy's impassioned allegations stemmed from his deep-seated partisanship and reflected his heartfelt conviction that the members of the opposition party were not well-intentioned contestants for public office. Because of the policies that they endorsed and the vision of society that they adhered to, as well as Joy's belief that his own party's ideals reflected true American ideals, he considered the Federalists very real dangers to the nation, to its values, and to its form of government. It was thus likely not a particularly large leap to make for him when he—under the assumed identity of the fictional British soldier Nathaniel Emery—asserted to his messmates that "there were traitors in every country—that we [those assembled at the table] had them in this"—in the process, unwittingly inserting himself onto center stage in the Massachusetts election.[25]

As discussed elsewhere, Joy's claim of knowledge of a treasonable correspondence between Timothy Pickering and British officials serving in Canada sparked an intense response from both the Democratic-Republican and Federalist camps and sent shock waves through the Massachusetts electorate. The nature of those responses and of Joy's interpretation of them are very revealing. Initially, of course, Haverhill's Democratic-Republicans, immersed as they were in local electioneering and still abuzz over the recently published revelations (these stories continued to appear in local papers well after Joy's arrest) about the Henry Affair, must have been thrilled by what they were hearing from the stranger at Kendall's, hence their rapid effort to depose Joy, alias Emery, and, as some accounts suggest, to quickly disseminate the information for publication. If the young man's claims were true—and they had no reason or inclination to believe otherwise—their party had just gained a tremendous leg up in the electoral campaign, and, perhaps even more important, their opponents' true colors, which they had been trying to reveal for years, had finally been exposed for all to see.

For their part, local Federalists, as evidenced by Bailey Bartlett's request to be included in any deposition proceeding and by the rapidity with which Haverhill partisans alerted their compatriots in Salem about what had transpired in their town, sought to defuse the situation as quickly as possible and to prove Joy's story a false one—such claims, after all, were nothing new, and they had been busy for the better part of the past two weeks dealing with the Henry Affair. They also rallied in defense of Pickering's honor and reputation, attributes once again under assault from below, an ominous trend made all the more common by the era's democratizing politics and festival politics, which increasingly empowered an electorate comprised of thousands of men like Timothy Joy and emboldened these men to speak their minds and to openly question their leaders. Rallying around their "upright and distinguished" leader, Federalists were quick to point out the "good name of an aged patriot, who has devoted his life to his country, and whose character is assailable only by the tongue of slander, and the pen of the libeler," and to contrast that to the "vagabond" and "imposter" Timothy Joy, who, along with his Republican coadjutors, perpetrated a "most base and infamous affair." Indeed, the culture of honor and the determination to defend it at all costs, as well as the pervasive fear of charlatans and confidence men in a world of increasingly impersonal interaction, was patently manifest in the official complaint sworn out against Joy, which accused him of "contriving to injure & prejudice Timothy Pickering . . . and to deprive him of his good name, fame, & reputation and to bring him into disgrace, infamy & contempt and to cause it to be suspected, that said Timothy was guilty of the crime of treason against the United States." Such a blatant assault on Pickering's integrity, especially coming as it did from an embarrassed transient, could not be allowed to pass unchallenged.[26]

Joy's subsequent arrest and his admission that he had fabricated his entire story allowed the Federalists to immediately turn the tables on their political foes—who they labeled in the local press, in reference to the bloody excess of the French revolutionaries, "Jacobin demagogues"—and to allege a conspiracy on the part of Haverhill's Democratic-Republicans to steal the forthcoming election (again, a charge easy to accept as credible by the Federalists, given the political climate of the era). To ferret out the extent of this conspiracy, Justice John Prince and the Essex County prosecutor, Samuel Putnam, grilled Joy at his arraignment hearing, continually prodding him in an effort to force him to implicate Francis Eaton, Moses Wingate, and the other Haverhill Republicans as the plot's masterminds. The effort, the Federalist press reported, was successful, and Joy admitted to entering Eaton's office above the Haverhill Bridge—"with that secrecy," one Federalist publication alleged, "that always accompanies villainy"— and to being "questioned very hard, and [being] induced to make the statement." "Thus we see," a Federalist broadside detailing the "plot" asserted,

> the wicked measures to which a party resort to answer their purposes!
>   . . . Such conduct as that at Haverhill, deserves the utter detestation of every man who has a spark of honor or honesty . . .
> They will judge rightly of a cause which seeks support by such

means, and will distrust their stories of plots, conspiracies, treasons, &c which so abound before our elections.

The contest had reached a heightened level of intensity, and the affair at Haverhill (at least for the moment) had become a political hot potato.[27]

With momentum now solidly with the Federalists, state Democratic-Republicans mounted a public relations campaign of their own, desperately trying to distance themselves from Joy and his libel and working tirelessly to rescue the reputations and honor of Eaton and his Haverhill peers. Decrying Federalist attempts to paint them as stooping "to abject and contemptible arts for electioneering purposes," Haverhill Republicans were quick to point out that Joy's statement was "made voluntarily and unhesitatingly." "Why," they continued, "are the Republicans denounced as Demagogues and Scoundrels for the exertion of rights and the performance of duties, dictated by the most pure and patriotic motives?" Most troubling of all, though, was "the peculiar mode in which [Joy] was questioned by the Council for the Government." "During his examination," the Republican *Portland Eastern Argus* claimed, Joy was made "to implicate the Republicans of Haverhill." "The course adopted," the paper continued, "was . . . most unwarrantable, unprecedented, and outrageous." The prosecutor, it went on, "manifested throughout a desire to exculpate this vile wretch, by making him accuse the republicans of Haverhill; THEY were made the party accused, and Joy the witness." The intent of this subterfuge, of the effort to create a Democratic-Republican plot where none existed, the *Essex Register* boldly concluded, was to endeavor "to throw the odium of its invention upon the republicans" so as to "screen themselves from the effect of the serious disclosures of HENRY." "[B]ut it will not do," the paper claimed, explaining, "These documents [Henry's] are too well authenticated to be done away by so shallow an artifice." Salem's famous diarist the Reverend William Bentley agreed, writing in his diary, "An attempt to keep Henry's Affair out of sight by the trifling affair of the boy at Haverhill, and party has been successful at this small game. Above one hundred have already been struck off the list of voters . . . So we go, and so we shall go."[28]

As Massachusetts Democratic-Republicans and Federalists spun the incident at Haverhill to suit their particular political purposes, Timothy Joy took pen in hand and gave voice to his own interpretation of the events that had precipitated his arrest and incarceration.

Though confessing that he had a rather incomplete memory of the events at Haverhill, Joy nonetheless assumed responsibility for what he had done. Dragged before Justice John Prince, Jr., Joy noted how he had admitted guilt (though he attributed his behavior in Haverhill to his distress and "a disordered brain"), apologized for his wrongdoing, and supplicated himself before the court and asked for mercy. The court's response, unfortunately, was not what he had hoped for. That response did, however, reinforce Joy's preconceived notions about Federalist haughtiness and high-handedness and thus rendered itself susceptible to a highly partisan interpretation by the young Republican, an interpretation no doubt reinforced by what he was learning about the fallout from the incident from those who visited him in jail. After having demonstrated the truth of his claims regarding his circumstances and thus theoretically setting the stage for the court to accept his apology as an earnest statement of fact, Joy was chagrined when

> the Fed Justice called in a cloud of Fed witnesses & among the rest the son of old namesake who decoyed me into the hands of the Fed officer, to prove what a poor unfortunate distrauted man said at Haverill against a Fed of windham, and employ'd a Fed lawyer to examine a man who hardly now knew how to arrange his ideas much less how to answer one who possessed all the art of a Fed crossquestioner, but after a long examination which continued about two hours, his Fed Honour with the advice of his Fed Council required poor me to find bail in the sum of five Hundred Dollars or else be committed to prison there to lie in dirt untill the sitting of the Supreme Fed Court at Ipswich which would commence its Fed session on the fourth Wednesday of April ensuing.

Clearly, as manifest in Joy's sarcastic and derogatory use of the modifier "Fed," he ascribed his imprisonment, at least in part, to partisan enmity. As a subsequent Republican visitor to the jail, who Joy chooses not to disclose, told him, "I owed my imprisonment to the Feds & not to them." "This," Joy sourly writes, "I knew before."[29]

This intensely partisan perspective, because it reflected Joy's own understanding of the world in which he lived, became a central theme of his prison journal. Among the more interesting applications of this partisan lens was its relevance for Joy in shaping his understanding of the issue that had led him to Haverhill in the first place, the issue of imprisonment for debt. Very early on in the journal, Joy relates the story of his first cell mate, Neil McCoy. According to Joy, McCoy was imprisoned for "being in debt to the Feds and refusing to vote for their candidates." This behavior, Joy alleges, "incurred their resentment," and McCoy "of course was deprived of his employ & thrown into prison . . . while his wife & three small children were left to beg their bread." "Oh—the humanity of the Feds," he derisively wrote, adding, "Who after reading this would not be a Fed."[30]

McCoy, it seems, at least as Joy came to view things, was not the only Republican debtor locked up for political purposes. Just prior to his transfer to Ipswich, Joy notes the incarceration of an unnamed partisan who "informed me that a malicious Fed had purchased a note against for about twenty dollars & not withstanding two responsible men offered to be his bail had dragged him from his home & family consisting of his wife & seven children to Prison for the express purpose of keeping him from voting at the ensuing election." As the April Massachusetts election drew near, Joy noted, as previously mentioned, a steady stream of newly jailed Republican debtors. Joy also offers at least one tantalizing suggestion that he saw or had come to see the pressure being applied to him by his own creditors as at least partially politically motivated. When served with the writ of attachment on behalf of the firm of Leigh and Ferguson on April 6, Joy scrawled, "I wonder when the Gentlemen Feds will leave off persecuting me." While certainly not conclusive evidence that he saw his own failure as directly connected to his partisan affiliation, the comment does nonetheless suggest that Joy had come to understand the current credit crunch and the contemporary political climate as having a clear partisan and class dynamic, with wealthy creditors affiliating with Federalism and those in the debtor class identifying with the Democratic-Republican Party, and that he saw this class dichotomy—perhaps exacerbated by the intensity of the era's politics, the rise of a restive democratic spirit, and the waning of Federalist power—as at least partially to blame for the myriad economic failures then plaguing the American people. Joy's journal thus offers a tantalizing and previously ignored perspective—the role of partisan conflict—on the issues of debt and incarceration for debt in the early republic.[31]

Joy's latent egalitarianism and his growing awareness of the class dimensions of the dynamics of political power stand as one of his journal's most consistent themes. While being conveyed along the post road from the Salem Jail to Ipswich Prison on March 24, for instance,

Deputy Sheriff Amma Brown pointed out Timothy Pickering's residence in Wenham to the shackled Joy. One can easily imagine the tangle of emotions coursing through Joy at that moment—the sinking feeling in the pit of his stomach as Brown motioned toward Pickering's home, anger for what had happened to him, hostility for the ideals that Pickering represented, resentment stemming from his failure and Pickering's obvious (and perhaps, in Joy's mind, undeserved) success, embarrassment for what he had done and said. Writing later that day, he recalled,

> He shewed me the residence of Old namesake. It is situated in Windham about a quarter of a mile from the post road. The house is a large two story building, wears an ancient aspect. I suppose he wishes in everything to represent his brethren the ole Brittish Lords in his buildings as well as in his writings. It puts one in mind of the old feudal times. But enough of this old castle and its owner.

The meaning of Joy's overt connection between all things British, on the one hand, and Pickering and all that he and his party represented, on the other, is, of course, blatantly obvious: he considered Federalism nothing more than Britain's aristocracy cast anew in America. The Revolution had led to a physical break with Great Britain, but there was still much to do to root out what remained of British-style aristocracy, arrogance, tyranny, and privilege.[32]

As Joy's day in court arrived in early May (on the brink of yet another state election—this time for seats in the state house), he returned to this theme often. When asked by Justice Samuel Sewall—a Federalist—to enter a plea in his libel case, Joy wrote, "I answered that I was guilty of writing the paper mentioned in the Indictment but not with malicious design & that I should not contend with the Commonwealth." "This answer," Joy snidely remarked, "did not satisfy my lord Judge [Joy later refers to Sewall as "Mr. Powerful"]. He must have his own way so poor I was obliged to plead guilty." After testimony from witnesses and statements about Joy's character were made by his brother Eben and by Valentine Smith, "my Lord Judge was but a few minutes . . . in making up his blessed Judgement." Fined fifty dollars and sentenced to an additional thirty days in jail, Joy crowed, "Bravo! Fine doings, what a charming sentence this." "Who would have thought," he continued, employing a very interesting choice of terms, "that a *democrat* [emphasis added] would come off so cheaply." With a full view of his situation now in hand, Joy launched into a screed.

> I had been imprisoned only forty four days and nights, but law suz, the Judge was a Fed thats all how it com'd to pass. Every one cried injustice & asserted that had I belonged to the black fraternity fiends, yclep'd Federalists, I should have been discharg'd, but thank fortune its no worse, that is to say thank the laws which brail up the power of these fat faced gentry, for if they were allowed their full scope there would be many an honest democrat made headless by the guilotine, but the old adversary knows his bounds & so do they . . . I glory in my sufferings knowing as I do that everybody knows the cause of my detention, that it is now merely for my political principles.

Joy had fully internalized the partisan conflict that characterized the era and had come to see himself as a political prisoner, a martyr for the cause of values and ideals that were democratic—in regard to both the political party and the political philosophy.[33]

In stark contrast to the aristocratic haughtiness and tyrannical proclivities of his Federalist foes, Joy also highlights, in very lengthy journal entries, the character of two men (Sheriff Robert Farley and a man he simply refers to as Leach) who embodied the republican values that he associated with his own Democratic-Republican Party (the party to which they both belonged) and with the ideals of the Revolution (a conflict in which they had both participated). Born sometime between 1757 and 1760, Sheriff Robert Farley was the son of one of Ipswich's most respected men, Major Michael Farley and his wife, Elizabeth. As a youth, Farley went to sea, finding employment in the West Indies trade. When the Revolutionary War began, the young man volunteered for service aboard a privateer. "His courage and good conduct," Joy writes, "procured him the good will of the ships crew & he was soon made an officer." Unfortunately, Farley and the ship's crew were captured by a British man-of-war in 1780 and were "put in irons & confined on board the Jersey Prison ship." There, Joy relates, he "suffered all the horrors of close confinement for five months during which time eleven hundred of the Americans died aboard that ship among whom were all his ships crew except himself & the first mate." After gaining his liberty, Farley reenlisted for the duration of the war.

At war's end, Farley returned to Ipswich, where he engaged in the fish trade, primarily with the West Indian islands. "He then for a number of years," Joy writes, "shone conspicuous as an honest merchant, but the loss of two of his vessels . . . , captured & condemned by his sworn foes, the Brittish, reduced this worthy citizen to a state of dependence hitherto unknown to him." In consideration of his past service and for his partisan support, Governor Elbridge Gerry appointed Farley high sheriff of Essex County in 1811, a post that brought him into contact with Timothy Joy. A constant source of comfort to the young man, Joy effusively praised Farley—who he called a "true Republican"—for his selfless nature, fatherly advice, and evenhandedness. "Having suffered himself," the young prisoner scribbled, "he knows how to sympathize with others." Joy wrote, "I can never say too much in his praise."[34]

Joy's decision to also include Leach's story tells us a great deal about the importance that Joy attached to his partisan identity and about how closely he connected the ideals of his party with those of the Revolutionaries. Joy became familiar with Leach's story during the May session of the Supreme Judicial Court. Beyond his own trial, that session featured the trials of the men involved in Salem's election-day riot of April 6 and the trial of Warwick Palfray, Jr., the embattled editor of Salem's Democratic-Republican newspaper, the *Essex Register*, who faced slander charges for his paper's coverage of the actions of the Salem selectmen related to the chaos at the polls on that day. While Palfray's case ended in a hung jury, the Salem rioters were not as fortunate. "The rioters are condemned," Joy recorded, "eight of nine were found guilty . . . They were oblig'd to procure bonds for their appearance at the next term of the Supreme Court holden in Salem where they must appear to receive their sentence." "O depart ye Republicans into the dungeons prepared for you by we Feds," he concluded, "Because you dared to assert your right to suffrage." This same issue—the loss of voting rights—led Joy to relate Leach's story, as told to him by Sheriff Farley.[35]

Like the others involved in the melee at the Salem courthouse on election day, Leach, who Joy describes as "an old revolutionary officer who was several times wounded when defending the liberty of his dear Country" and as a man "worth a handsome property in Salem," discovered, when he attempted to cast his ballot, that his name had been removed from the polling list by the town's Federalist selectmen. Hoping to rectify what he knew to be a mistake, Leach approached the selectmen, but, as Joy phrases it, "in vain did he remonstrate, in vain did he call in evidence numerous citizens, to prove his right. The answer was, it is too late now, the polls are opened, to put on any new names." "[W]hy," Joy reports the selectmen asking, "had you not apply'd before?" Responding to the question, the old veteran straightened himself and boldly replied that he "had not an idea, that he who had been a voter for twenty five years and still a citizen worth five thousand dollars would be struck off the list merely because he was a Republican." At this, Joy reports, "[o]ne of the selectmen had the impudence to insult him saying, 'we shall never have any peace or good order so long as one of these seventy five's are suffered to live.'" That such a comment might have been made does not strain credulity. Certainly, from a Federalist point of view, the democratic tide unleashed by the Revolution and the social upheaval that resulted from the elevated sense of worth emanating from the ranks of commoners who lent their hand in winning American independence—trends staring them in the face on that chilly April morning—were problematic by-products of the spirit of the "seventy-fivers."[36]

Angered to the point of outrage by this comment, Leach confronted the selectman who uttered them (a "Mr. C"—undoubtedly Philip Chase) and said, "[R]epeat those words again & I will close your jaw forever." Wishing to avoid fisticuffs, Chase remained silent. Leach then initiated an action for damages in the amount of fifty thousand dollars against the selectmen for depriving him of his suffrage. Asked to present his case to the court, Leach gave an impassioned speech.

> Sire . . . you behold in me an injured citizen, who has been deprived of his right by those very men who when babes I fought to defend, when Brittain dared to invade our rights I Sir, volunteered my services with many other heroes who in the arduous struggle for liberty exposed their persons to the shot of the enemy & their with their lives in their hands met the haughty foe at the point of the bayonet. I sir, have bled in my countries cause thrice was I wounded while fighting to secure that right which now in my old age I am deprived of by those who were then 'mewling & pewking in their nurses arms.' When I hear these men saying that they expect no peace or order so long as one of those men exist who fought & bled in the cause of freedom, I look on my scars and sigh, Oh my ungrateful Country! But sire I will not give up my right without a struggle. It is the

first time I ever was a party in a lawsuit & nothing but the being deprived of my right of voting, wrongfully by a faction who
wish to sway the scepter of tyranny & oppression oer the sons
of freedom should have driven me to it, so long as God spares
my life Sir, shall that life every moment of it be devoted to the
cause of liberty.

Despite Leach's moving address, however, as Joy notes in closing the
entry, Justice Sewall "would not consent for the case to be tryed this
term as his clients [Salem's Federalist selectmen] had not time to procure false witnesses sufficient to prove themselves innocent."[37]
Joy's decision to include the account of Leach's court appearance is
well worth considering. Beyond the compelling nature of the story itself, it is clear that Joy was moved to record it in his journal because it
resonated with him. It reinforced his deeply held beliefs that those who
shared his political perspective were in the right and that they, in
marked contrast to the Federalist opposition, understood and appreciated the true meaning of the nation's Revolutionary experience and thus
were the only ones to be entrusted with the nation's safekeeping. "[I]t is
useless to attempt to recount the many instances of Federal injustice
and oppression," Joy regretfully wrote elsewhere in his journal, ex-
pounding, "It would require the age of Methuselah to complete the history of one year." Reflecting back, through his now well-polished partisan lens, on all that had happened to him since his March flight from
Middleton and his subsequent arrest and imprisonment, Joy penned the
following paean to the movement that he so readily identified with,
"Huzza for democracy, if I spend my days in Prison I still will be a
democrat." If there had ever been any doubt about his commitment to
the Democratic-Republican cause, none remained now.[38]

Chapter 4

"HAVING GOD FOR MY FRIEND
WHAT MORE DO I WANT?"

May 10, 1812, was the Sabbath. Timothy Joy, however, still lingered in his Ipswich Prison cell after fifty-two days of confinement. Just six days prior, he had pled guilty in the Supreme Judicial Court of the Commonwealth of Massachusetts to his libel against Timothy Picker-ing and had been fined for his transgression, as well as being sentenced to an additional thirty days in prison. Sick, lonely, humiliated, and de-jected, Joy, as he had on a number of prior Sabbaths, sat down to wor-ship and sought solace in prayer. Though frequently providing comfort to him during his time in prison, Joy found that his entreaties to God brought, on this occasion, no relief from his anguish. Dejected and forlorn, the desperate Joy confided in his diary, "I have besought the Lord to look in pity upon my sufferings, but my mind still labours in darkness, and sometimes I almost despair of ever again enjoying any comfort." The next day, Joy's distress mounted. "My head," he wrote, "grows dizy. I wish I could drink the waters of lithe & consign to oblivion past events, the rememberance of which drives me to distrac-tion." Fearing himself to be on the brink of insanity, Joy once again be-seeched the Lord for guidance and opened his Bible. This time, how-ever, his prayer was answered, and his gaze (directed by God, as Joy tells it), fell on "1 Luke 6th 21st." The words "Blessed are ye that hunger now for you shall be filled" immediately resonated with Joy, and he felt calm, giddiness, and awareness rush suddenly through his body. "I feel satisfied," he testified shortly thereafter, "that I have at last got into the true channel."[1]

Jail-cell awakenings of this type, of course, are standard fare—to the point of being a virtual staple—in both popular and historical accounts of life behind bars. The stress of separation from one's family, fear of the unknown, regret, guilt, doubt, anger, and solitude can easily prompt those who have been incarcerated to seek out spiritual comfort, guidance, hope, and redemption in the midst of an abundance of misery, confusion, and despair. Likewise, deeply personal spiritual autobiography and highly allegorical redemptive fiction, such as *Pilgrim's Progress* and *Robinson Crusoe,* were very familiar genres for those, such as Joy, steeped in the New England Puritan tradition. The commonality of the conversion theme and the emblematic manner in which it manifests itself in Joy's particular case, however, does not negate or trivialize its importance. On the contrary, Joy's struggle for spiritual clarity and his battle to reconnect with his faith—a struggle both exacerbated and prompted by his economic failure, his numerous falsehoods, his guilt, his knowledge that he could not offer direct assistance to his wife and children, and his lengthy incarceration—is very much worth examining, as lived religion on an individual level, for what it reveals to us about his personality, his frame of reference, his feelings, his spiritual confusion stemming from his exposure to Arminianism (a doctrine preaching, among other things, free will), and his personal understanding of the rapidly changing world in which he lived. Without a doubt, for Timothy Joy and for the majority of his contemporaries, religion served as one of the primary lenses through which to interpret things experienced and life in its many permeations, as it was lived.[2]

Historians have long recognized the vital place of religion in the lives of Americans in the early decades of the nineteenth century. As the United States struggled to gain its legs, the American people found themselves confronted with change on a scale never before imagined. The rapid physical expansion of their nation, the wide dispersion of its population, the strain inherent in the nation's efforts to define the meaning of democracy, and the explosive growth and expansion of a commercial economy, along with its attendant social and cultural transformations, left many feeling out of kilter and adrift in a sea of chaos, tumult, and disorder. In response, many Americans sought a spiritual anchor to tether themselves to during this time of change, initiating a period of intense and enthusiastic evangelical fervor known as the Second Great Awakening. Though Timothy Joy's life paralleled what are generally considered to be the Awakening's earliest manifestations, and although he did not embrace the movement's more familiar evangelicalism, it is nevertheless useful to consider his experience and his quest for spiritual answers in the face of unyielding and frightening temporal change, as representative of the experiences and personal responses of myriad Americans of this era and of the broader movement as it unfolded across the nation, especially in the years after the War of 1812.[3]

Although religion had always played a central role in Timothy Joy's personal life, his individual battle to rediscover and clarify his faith, to set his life right, and to gain spiritual assurance while in prison was a long, drawn-out, contested affair, captured, in all of its dramatic complexity, in his prison journal. At the same time, as historian Daniel Shea reminds us, despite the journal's intimate description of his personal spiritual travails and his quest for personal assurance of salvation, a Calvinist like Joy, "as a member of a family, a church, and a body politic, . . . could never speak simply to hear his own echo, nor was he free to consider his autobiographical reflection of himself totally apart from the faces [and forces] that surrounded it." Rather, Joy's detailed recounting of his private sacred journey and his effort to fathom the vital questions of whether personal salvation could be lost once obtained or whether he was saved at all also represented a communal enterprise, a social commentary and cautionary tale, and a moral imperative and thus must be considered within this broader context.[4]

That Timothy Joy commenced the writing of his journal after his arrest and subsequent confinement begs the question of his intent in creating the document. Although Joy indicates that his reason for initiating the journal was "to commit to paper while in my rational moments the most extraordinary circumstances which have happened to my Imprisonment, as correctly as I can remember them wishing, should I lose my reason that this paper may be carefully preserved & sent to my family," his more immediate purpose for penning his entries seems to have been to employ the journal as a reflective tool to examine what he clearly viewed as his fall from respectability and his descent into sin, a descent that reinforced his belief in the truth of human depravity and that provided overwhelming evidence, at a minimum, that he had lost his way or, more ominously, that his eternal soul was in great peril. Whatever the intended lesson and whatever the ramifications for his eternal soul—it would take Joy many weeks to puzzle through this—what was clear in his mind was that his current situation was a direct by-product of his neglecting of his faith. Obviously agitated by all that had just happened to him and in a deeply confused state of mind, Joy nonetheless assiduously strove, in the journal's opening pages, to identify the precise moment when he had let his guard down and when he allowed himself to stray from God. In retelling the story of his flight from Middleton and his frenetic travels to Haverhill, Joy injected a telling commentary. Upon reaching the Gilmanton Iron Works, eighteen miles to the west of Middleton, the desperate young man stopped to exchange his horse for "one young and sprightly." "[H]ere," Joy lamented, "was the beginning of my troubles, if I may use the expression." Asked his name by a local, Joy, "being off my watch," "deny'd" his name and offered up an alias. This moment (not the moment when he decided to flee his creditors), Joy believed (though he was writing with the knowledge of how his situation would all play out), marked his spiritual fall. Recalling the incident, he wrote,

> Oh what horror did now seize upon my soul. I had told a falsehood. Where now was my religion. All vanished all gone. I then began to despond. The adversury persuaded me that I never knew what it was to be regenerated and born again, that I had been deceiv'd, else I should have been kept from sining. I accordingly settled down in this dangerous opinion & concluded myself lost & undone both soul and body.

Timothy Joy's insistence on scrutinizing everyday occurrences for visible signs of God's favor or displeasure—what historian Charles Cohen identifies as looking for God's presence through "sighs and smiles"—though not in agreement with formal Puritan orthodoxy, was nonetheless a commonplace and, one might argue, an instinctual response to the basic human desire to decipher one's fate. It forced the failed businessman to confront the profound question of whether one's salvation could be lost—a question entirely inconsistent with the Calvinist principle of the perseverance of the saints (i.e., once an individual was saved, they were always saved) but doctrinally central to Arminian-based faiths, such as Freewill Baptism, to which Joy had been exposed at various points in his life. This deep confusion over the fate of his soul and how to attribute meaning to his fall was still very much an open question in Joy's mind, a realization that threw him into a state of spiritual vertigo.[5]

Subsequent events—especially those that unfolded in Haverhill—along with the social stigma attached to his personal economic failure, only served to reinforce this dreary confusion in Joy's anguished mind as he continued his intense reflection and self-examination. The fabrication told in Kendall's Tavern, Joy determined in hindsight, was the direct result of his spiritual distress. "[D]espairing of ever enheriting eternal life," he confessed, "I was so desperate I cared not what I said or did." That indifference, he now believed, led directly to his slander of Timothy Pickering. Cognizant that no mercy would be shown to the reprobate, Joy noted in his writing that he developed, by the time he reached Salem, a deep sense of foreboding, "as tho some heavy judgment awaited me as a correction for my past follies." Judgment, in the form of his arrest, of course, was not long in coming. In an intriguing passage, Joy recalls an exchange that took place while he was being searched in the shop on Derby's Wharf. He recalled that while local law officials "were searching me it seemed as though one spoke to me & told me that it was a mercy of God that I was so soon overtaken by Gods judgments, so that I might be brought to repentance, ere it was too late." "I saw God was just & merciful," he continued.

> Just in bringing me to punishment for my transgression, merciful in not suffering me to go on till by my disobedience I should have sealed my own damnation. I could truly say with David Psalms 40th Chap 12 & 13th verses innumerable evils have compassed me about: mine iniquities have taken hold upon me, so that I am not able to look up: they are more than the hairs of mine head: therefore mine heart faileth me. Be pleased O Lord to deliver me: O Lord, make haste to help me.

Curtis Coe, Joy's childhood minister, would have been proud, for as he had reminded the young man, along with the rest of his congregation, in his 1806 valedictory sermon, "a view that the heart is so exceedingly evil, yea desperately wicked, may well serve to abase the pride of man, and lead us to plead guilty in the presence of Jehovah." Recognition and acknowledgment of his depravity and of the fact that damnation was the deserved fate of the unregenerate sinner was a vitally important first step for Timothy Joy on his path toward clarity. Still, much spiritual heavy lifting lay ahead of him before he would receive the blessed assurance that he so fervently sought. That lifting and Joy's awareness of it began almost at once for the young man.[6]

On the day after his arrest, Sunday, March 22, Joy found his first tentative step toward self-realization and spiritual comfort sorely tested. Now painfully confused about his uncertain spiritual state and fully aware of his own culpability in his sins, Timothy Joy hoped to immediately commence his penitence and to embark on his journey toward what he hoped would be his reconciliation with God. His incarceration, of course, loomed large as an impediment to that goal. Deeply saddened at the prospect of being unable to attend worship (from his second-story cell window, he could see the congregants of neighboring St. Peter's Episcopal Church gathering together for service) and desperately hoping to find guidance in the scriptures, Joy requested that he be brought a Bible so that he "might read & contemplate by myself." His heart sank when, to his great dismay, the jailer (Joy identifies him as Thomas Hudson) informed him that prisoners were not allowed books. "My tears flowed afresh & my head grew dizzy," he continued, adding, "For a considerable time I hardly knew where I was." Composing himself, Joy determined, despite the lack of a Bible, to hold a meeting of his own. "I prayed sung shouted & felt happy," he joyfully noted, explaining, "I saw that the Lord had not quite forsaken me, for I felt the same good spirit working in me that I was wont to feel when encompassed by the children of God at Middleton . . . I felt the promise of God verified where he says in Psalms 40th 15, Call upon me in the day of trouble I will deliver thee & thou shalt glorify me."[7]

Later that same day, a form of figurative deliverance arrived in the person of the wife of his cell mate, a man by the name of Neil McCoy, an incarcerated debtor and father of three, from nearby Danvers. McCoy's wife, who Joy describes as "a good looking woman of about twenty eight years of age" but who he unfortunately never names, undoubtedly empathized with Joy (or perhaps, more likely, with Joy's now unaided wife, Mary) and took a deep interest in the young father's plight, immediately setting to work to alleviate his anxiety, by walking two miles to seek out "a young man by the name of Pierce a native of N H who Mr. McCoy recommended to me to carry a letter to my parents." Perhaps even more important, on the following day, McCoy's wife, "after consulting her husband, sent [Joy] down from Danvers . . . her own Bible & a book entitled the beauties of the Bible, likewise a table & chair, a plate knife & fork, two mugs & some small articles to make me comfortable." "Thus," Joy continued, "the Lord raised me up friends when I little expected it." McCoy's fortuitous release later that same day led Joy to conclude, not surprisingly, that God had "recompenced them for their kindness." Now properly equipped for sincere self-reflection, Joy commenced a running, real-time account of his daily life in prison and of his journey toward spiritual truth.[8]

For the duration of his time in prison, Joy's daily routine included silent prayer and much introspection. As he described it, his typical day looked something like this: "After eating breakfast I usually walk around my cell for the space of half an hour, sometimes longer, then sit down & read two or three chapters in the Bible & draw from them all the comfort possible, which supports me until after dinner. I usually set down the occurrences of the day just before night. & I write on other subjects about two hours in the day, when I am dull & melancholy I go to writing or reading, but sometimes these fail to amuse & my tears mark the pages as they turn." As indicated, Joy's continual self-examination led the young man, on a daily basis, to the scriptures and to lengthy reflections on their intent, their meaning, and the lessons that could be drawn from them. While he found many passages inspiring and calming, these exercises in humility and understanding just as frequently spawned a painful awareness of how far he had strayed from his faith. They also revealed to him that, try as he might, he could not merely will himself into salvation. Was he fit for grace? The anguish was excruciating for Joy. Now that Joy was painfully aware of his sinfulness, that God's grace held the promise of salvation and eternal life, and of his own inability to influence, in any way, the manifestation of that grace as blessed assurance, his mood oscillated between, as historian Charles Cohen phrases the experience, "refreshment and depression." On Thursday, March 26, for instance, Joy closed his daily rumination by noting, "after reading a chapter & committing myself to God in prayr went to bed as happy in my mind as ever I was in my life." Just three days later, however, Joy confided, "This day I felt uncomonly dark in my mind. I was in a wilderness of doubts & fear respecting my future state almost all day." As March gave way to April and Joy's health began to deteriorate, his melancholy intensified, especially in the days immediately preceding his awakening, as did his "meditating on the scriptures." Again, Joy's writing is instructive and reinforces a critical point, expounded by John Owen King, that this despair was "the occasion rather than the cause" of his awakening. Joy's pervasive doubt thus spawned what King identifies as "a compulsive quest for certainty."[9]

One wonders as well whether John Bunyan's *The Pilgrim's Progress from This World to That Which Is to Come* (1678) was also influencing Joy's interpretation of his present situation. Like Joy, Bunyan penned his spiritual coda, a defense of Calvinist theology and a metaphorical spiritual journal, while imprisoned. The book was very widely read in early New England and would have been precisely the type of thing that Timothy Joy might have had access to either in the Durham home of his father the deacon or in prison. Though he never formally acknowledges the work in his journal, the parallels between the path pursued by Joy toward redemption and those followed by the book's protagonist, Christian, are certainly intriguing. Bunyan's allegorical tale traces the spiritual pilgrimage of one Christian, prompted by his reading of the Bible and his recognition that he is dead in sin, as he journeys from his earthly home, the degenerate City of Destruction, to the afterlife in the Celestial City. Along the way, Christian, later accompanied by other pilgrims such as Faithful and Hopeful, is enticed from the straight and narrow (the [spiritual] King's Highway) and/or tested by characters bearing telling names, such as Mr. Worldly Wiseman, a young man named Ignorance, a ferryman named Vain Hope, a scoffer named Atheist, and a giant named Despair. To reach the Celestial City, Christian must also pass through the Slough of Despond, a murky swamp where he nearly sinks under the weight of his sin; Hill Difficulty (one of three paths available to Christian—the others being Danger and Destruction); the materialistic and commercial city of Vanity and the worldly enticements of the never-ending Vanity Fair; the Valley of Humiliation and the neighboring Valley of the Shadow of Death; the Doubting Castle; the Enchanted Ground; and the River of Death. Certainly, Timothy Joy could have identified with Christian's plight and his journey, having been tempted into the worldly pursuit of wealth by the "Vanity Fair" that characterized the early national New Hampshire coastal region, encountering his own "Slough of Despond" in Haverhill, recoiling at his actions in his "Valley of Humiliation" at Salem, catching a glimpse of the "Valley of the Shadow of Death" as he battled illness in his Ipswich cell, and grappling with his spiritual doubts and his own personal battle with "Despair."[10]

In this manic state of mind, Joy found himself drawn to "the lamentations of Jeremiah & the Psalms." "There," he confided, "I find comfort & consolation." In an early April entry, after a particularly uncomfortable and sleepless night due to a bout of painful inflammation of his face, Joy noted the particular resonance of "the 18th, 19th, 20th & 21st verses of the 31 Chap. Of Jeremiah." That the Old Testament book of Jeremiah would resonate with Joy at that moment in his life should not come as any great surprise to anyone with any familiarity of Jeremiah's story. Undoubtedly, Joy saw something of himself in the persecuted and much-maligned prophet. An intensely introspective man who experienced imprisonment at various points in his life, Jeremiah, like the recently married Joy, also found himself battling to fulfill social expectations of manhood in a volatile commercial environment that increasingly rendered these expectations fleeting and/or illusory, as well as with a role—in Jeremiah's case, divinely ordained—that was thrust upon him. Joy most certainly embraced Jeremiah's lamentations—offered in a manner strikingly similar to that employed by the Reverend Curtis Coe when he bade his Durham congregation, Timothy among them, farewell in 1806—about the predominance of worldly pursuits and false prophets in the contemporary world and his plea to renounce evil and sin and to turn to God. Indeed, it was from Jeremiah's name and his incessant lamentations that the Puritans' sermon archetype the jeremiad (which Coe's valedictory was)—with its stock denunciation of the materialism and immorality of the secular world, along with the hope of redemption—took both its title and its form. Believing himself entirely lost, Joy—perhaps recalling Coe's stern warning about "that place of punishment where the worm dieth not and the fire is not quenched" and his admonition that "if sinners persevere in rebellion, fiery indignation and endless curses must fall on their guilty heads"—took to heart the prophet Jeremiah's message of repentance and his dire warnings of impending judgment:

I have surely heard Ephraim bemoaning himself thus; Thou hast chastised me, and I was chastised, as a bullock unaccustomed to the yoke: turn thou me, and I shall be turned; for thou art the Lord my God. Surely after that I was turned, I repented; and after that I was instructed, I smote upon my thigh: I was ashamed, yea, even confounded, because I did bear the reproach of my youth. Is Ephraim my dear son? Is he a pleasant child? For since I spake against him, I do earnestly remember him still: therefore my bowels are troubled for him; I will surely have mercy upon him, saith the Lord.

Accepting this article of faith with his whole heart, Joy imploringly wrote, employing scripture from Psalms 130:7, "I will hope in the Lord, for with the Lord there is mercy & with him there is plenteous redempsion."[11]

Despite the feeling of comfort that Joy experienced after contemplating Jeremiah that evening, and perhaps because he had now been exposed to what was possible for the repentant and redeemed pilgrim,

Joy continued to wallow in fear about his lost soul and desperately struggled to gain blessed assurance that he was indeed saved. His efforts were in vain, however, and despite his many repeated attempts to find solace and direction in the scriptures, the Bible, he lamented, "seemed like a sealed book." "I mourn & cry to God but find no comfort," he agonizingly wrote on April 5, asking, "When O lord will thou apear for my soul."[12]

The following day, Joy's spirits sank even lower. Thoughts of Mary and his children flooded his consciousness, and undoubtedly prompted by his lingering illness—he was still complaining about swelling of the hands and much pain—he began to doubt that he would ever see them again. If this were not enough for the disconsolate Joy, his emotions were further strained by the arrival of Sheriff Daniel Dutch, who served Joy with a writ on behalf of Leigh and Ferguson. Desperate to exorcise himself of his unbearable hopelessness, Joy took his pen in hand and wrote a long letter to his brother Eben and, as he confessed to his journal, "wept all the time like a child." Still unable to compose himself, he ended his day's entry with "Now I will leave off for I am quite overcome . . . Oh that I could banish my thoughts with my pen but I cannot. God be merciful to me for thou art alone able to help me." Although not knowing it at the time, Joy— soon to lose yet another human source of personal comfort, his cell mate, Elisha Gurney—was bottoming out. Human assistance would and could no longer avail him. Only God could sustain him. As difficult as this recognition was for Joy, however, it also marked a critical final step toward grace; Timothy Joy was soon to give himself up to God, to abandon what Curtis Coe had called "stubbornness of the will," and to finally accept Christ's free offer of mercy.[13]

Timothy Joy arose later than usual on the morning of Thursday, April 9. Despite his fragile health, Joy had, nonetheless, stayed up longer than normal the night before (until the town bell struck nine), reading the Bible by candlelight. Now fully awake, he and Elisha Gurney engaged in conversation in their frigid quarters, and Joy commenced a new entry in his journal. Gurney, now beginning his tenth month of confinement, had been imprisoned for "secreting some articles in his house in the time of the great fire in N[ewbury] Port [on May 31, 1811]." A man of approximately sixty years, by Joy's estimation, Gurney, much to his relief, proved to be "a very sensible man, serious and sober, used no profane language, read considerable in the bible & was very fond of prayers evening & morning." Perhaps even more endearing to Joy was the fact that his cell mate "would do anything I asked him to do cherfully & endeavored to cheer up my drooping spirits all in his power." The two men had been sharing quarters since Joy's transfer from the Salem Jail to Ipswich Prison on March 24. Joy noted in his March 24 diary entry that the cell (he refers to it as a "room") "was clean & wholesom," not at all like the dingy cell he had occupied in the Salem Jail, which he had referred to in his diary's opening entry as "open & cold." In a later, May entry, Joy described the Ipswich cell in detail. The room, he wrote,

> is sixteen feet long & ten wide. The door opens into the entry way. It is made of huge iron bars riveted together lengthwise on the inside & crosswise on the outside. The bolts are secured to the door on the outside by clasps made of thick iron bars and riveted through the door. The both are as large as a mans arm & are shoved into the stone wall about a foot & fastened with two huge padlocks. In the upper part of the door is cut a hole four inches wide & three feet deep through which I receive my provision. There is an iron shutter staple & lock to this, & when the prisoners behave bad it is fastened up . . . These doors weigh upwards of one thousand pounds. My windows [he indicated that there were two in the March 24 entry, where he recorded that each contained nine squares of glass] are darkened by a double grating made of bars two inches square. The bars which compose the inner grating are all plated with steel so that it is impossible to saw them off.

Joy also conveyed that the four-year-old prison building, situated on Ipswich's Jail Lane (modern-day Green Street), "was three years in building & cost thirty thousand dollars. It is three stories high, it is founded on a smooth solid ledge so there is no danger of its ever setting. The walls are three feet thick & the stones some of which are twelve feet in length are all dog'd together with large square iron bars."[14]

As the two men casually conversed with one another, they probably did not pay much heed to the familiar sound of footsteps echoing in the corridor outside of their cell; visitors, after all, as Joy's journal makes very clear, were nothing new to them. Nor would they have started when keys were thrust inside the padlocks used to secure the two iron bolts that shut them in. On this day, however, a surprise was indeed in store for them; Elisha Gurney was being released.[15]

Timothy Joy's emotions certainly ran very high at that moment. While thrilled at his friend's good fortune and elated spirits, he was also thrown into an anxious panic at the prospect of finding himself, for the first time since he was incarcerated nearly three weeks before, entirely alone. Returning to his journal later that same evening, he dolefully wrote, "he [Gurney] was so overjoy'd he could hardly bid me farewell as he hurried out of the room. But it was otherwise with me. The thoughts of being left alone in this gloomy place overcame me to such a degree that it was sometime before I could speak & after I recovered who had I to speak to, alas none." Now completely alone, with only his guilt and personal thoughts for company, Joy began "brooding over my misfortunes till I wept." Floundering in despair, he turned, as he had done on many previous occasions, to God for solace, falling to his knees and beseeching "him to support & comfort me," almost simultaneously feeling, Joy excitedly scribbled, "my petition granted before I rose from the floor. The heavenly crum I then receiv'd from my fathers table sustained my drooping spirit in a remarkable manner." "Being thus comforted," Joy ended his daily entry, "I do not feel so lonesome as I expected I should, having God for my friend what more do I want."[16]

Recalling the previous night's emotional journey, the still euphoric Joy excitedly detailed the particulars of his spiritual replenishment in his journal the next day. Retiring for the evening on April 9 in his now solitary cell, Joy attempted to pray. But, as he later related, "it seemed as though my mouth was sealed up." Breaking down into tears once again, the traumatized Joy "cryed unto the Lord" and immediately felt a sudden rush of happiness coursing through his body. "I felt so happy," he recalled, "I hardly knew what to do with myself." Thus filled with the Spirit of God, Joy "prayed, sang, shouted, laughed, wept, prayed again," and then lit his candle and read in his Bible until the Ipswich town clock tolled nine. "I have never since I have been in Prison," Joy assuredly noted, "felt the presence of the Lord in such a degree as I did last night." Buoyed by this blessed presence, Joy then recommitted himself to God and to living a proper Christian life.

Oh the comfort & satisfaction there is in serving God, the God of love—the God who condescends to visit the poor backsliden prisoner. O may I never more swerve from the path of the riteous which leadeth to true hapiness and felicity. . . . I am determined by the help of God to serve him the rest of my days hav-

ing a hope of blessed Immortality after I shall quit this troublesome world.

"It is not from this world that any ray of comfort can proceed to cheer
the gloom of the last hour," Joy confidently wrote, "but futurity still has
its prospects; there is yet happiness in reserve sufficient to support us
under every affliction." "Hope," he enthusiastically continued, "is the
chief blessing of man . . . O may I never give up this hope during life
and I am sure it will stand by me in death." Recognition of his own incapacity and the direness of his circumstances had led Joy to an appreciation of the majesty of God and had opened the door for a true
awakening of the young man's spirit.[17]

Joy does not divulge in his journal the exact scriptural verses that
precipitated his spiritual ascent culminating in his epiphany on April
10. Perhaps he revisited Jeremiah. Or maybe he was inspired by the
New Testament and Paul's second epistle to the Corinthians (a book
he later quotes at length when grappling with another bout of uncertainty), wherein Paul wrote, after three times requesting that the Lord
"remove a thorn in my flesh,"

And he stated unto me. My grace is sufficient for thee: for my
strength is made perfect in weakness. Most gladly therefore will
I rather glory in my infirmities, that the power of Christ may
rest upon me. Therefore I take pleasure in my affirmities, in re-
proaches, in persecutions, in distresses for Christ's sake: for
when I am weak, then I am strong.

We do know, however, that scripture served as an accelerant for the
spiritual flame that now engulfed Joy. "I found great comfort in reading the scripture," Joy happily noted, adding, "Sometimes when I
found a blessed promise to the afflicted I should shed tears of joy over
& over would I read it until I could retain it in my memory." Awakening "greatly refreshed" on the morning of April 11, Joy poured out his
heartfelt thanks to God. "How good is our God to condescent to notice such a wretch as me who has once deny'd him after being made acquainted with his excellencies," Joy tellingly wrote, "I shudder to think
what an abys I have escaped through the interference of divine providence." Just a few days later, he added, "Religion is my only support &
I have many happy seasons in prayr more especially since I have been
left alone. I feel myself more confirmed in the blessed doctrine of per-

severance of the saints than ever. Oh that I had always believed as I do now. If I had I should not have been here." Still, the test he was presently enduring had yielded dividends, as the young man came to acknowledge the truth in Reverend Curtis Coe's 1806 pronouncement that "though a variety of means are necessary to conduct souls to endless rest, yet God by his grace preserves them from finally forsaking his good cause." For the now assured young man, everything suddenly made sense.[18]

It is important to point out, however, that religion served myriad purposes for Timothy Joy. Beyond the spiritual service rendered by Joy's renewed faith, his religion also served as a balm to soothe his more temporal concerns. His debt, his flight, his lies, his arrest and subsequent incarceration, the distance between himself and his loved ones, his illness, his solitude, and, as I discussed in chapter 3, his political outlook—all this fell into place as a function of human depravity and/or as part of a divine plan to set him back on the straight and narrow and to save him from falling into the "abys." More to the point though, Joy's Congregational faith also provided him with a ready means of explaining/interpreting what had happened to him. Viewed through the lens of the Puritan tenet of predestination, his failure, though grounded in the era's market discomfitures, stood as a tangible sign of divine disapproval of Joy's neglect of his spiritual duties/obligations (a point undoubtedly further driven home by the consistent respectability of his father, Deacon Samuel, even in the face of the same forces that had brought Timothy to his knees). "Oh that I'de kept Gods law," Joy wrote on April 15 in recognition of this new epiphany. Furthering the point, he included the following verse in the same entry, "Unto the will of a just God, Who justly punishes / Those who have cleans'd by his blood, And then believed lies." This interpretation of events (that he was saved but had drifted) certainly helped to ease Joy's anxiety. It also, however, dispelled a portion of the tremendous guilt borne by Joy and positioned him to deflect those (including himself) who might choose to interpret his failure as a sign of incompetence and/or inability. It is far easier and certainly more socially agreeable to accept a personal collapse grounded in a moral lapse—the fate of all depraved humanity—or to argue that misfortune is a wake-up call from God than it is to accept that failure is entirely the result of sheer incapacity and ineptitude.[19]

Furthermore, if one could attribute the root cause of their failure to the spiritual realm, then it became a relatively simple matter for the individual to pick oneself up and start over again. The teachings of a new generation of theologians, such as the Freewill Baptist minister William Buzzell of Middleton—whose church Timothy had apparently been attending before his arrest—and liberal Calvinist theologians Timothy Dwight and his student Nathaniel William Taylor, emphasized human moral agency (in the words of historian E. Brooks Holifield, this led to the belief that sin was "not necessary, but it was certain" until subdued by divine grace) and the idea that, in the spiritual realm at least, an individual had a measure of influence, as contrasted to lack of influence in the impersonal world of the marketplace. Even for more orthodox Calvinists like Joy, Puritanism's sometime tacit, albeit inadvertent, equating of God's spiritual favor with tangible signs such as economic success served as a sort of self-fulfilling prophecy, urging the unsuccessful back into the field, time and again, to try their hand and to hopefully, by dint of succeeding, prove their spiritual (not to mention their social and economic) worthiness. Hope sprung eternal in a system that hinged on a belief that commitment to one's faith, a fleeting but inexhaustibly renewable asset, would lead to God's grace and material comfort. Even in those cases where such a positive outcome proved elusive, however, religion held out the promise of something better, of eternal rewards far richer than anything attainable on earth. "Were you to gain the world and command the stars," Curtis Coe reminded his Durham congregation in his parting sermon, "it could not profit, under the loss of the soul." As Joy himself phrased it,

> The worlds false joys can please no more
> When heav'nly are in view
>
> The frowns of partial fortune here
> The virtuous may despise,
> They're only happy who can fear
> Not poverty, but vice.

Minimally, it is likely that the world viewed through the lens of religion enabled Joy to redefine the meaning of success—salvation and grace—in a world where material success and security were increasingly illusory and fleeting entities for many young men like himself. Rather than feeling adrift in a world dominated by the impersonal forces of the market, Joy now felt assured and safe in the embrace of God. In the spiritual realm, he had gained the success he so desperately sought even if success had evaded him this far in the world of men. In short, for Timothy Meader Joy and a great many of his peers, religion served as a constant and ready source of comfort and stability in an America very much characterized by chaos, change, and upheaval.[20]

That the spiritual did not completely eclipse the temporal for Joy, even in the aftermath of his renewed awareness of God's majesty, is further borne out by his journal entries over the course of the next few weeks. Commentary on fellow prisoners and their activities, the anguish of separation from his family, a protracted and debilitating illness (very likely scurvy), the comings and goings of visitors, politics, and his upcoming trial all occupied Joy's mind and thus worked their way into his journal, often shunting spiritual matters into the distant background. It is worth considering, of course, how much of this was a function of the fact that Joy was now at peace with himself and his God. With his spiritual house now in order, Joy may have felt freer to allow his thoughts to stray to more mundane matters.[21]

His entry for Friday, April 17, provides a case in point. Joy began his entry for the day complaining about being "consumed by pain & sickness . . . I can but just reach the scuttle to take in my medicine. The inside of my mouth is to a blister & my face swolen to an enormous size. I hardly know myself when I view my face in the glass. My teeth are every one loose & my gums swollen. I can chew nothing." Under such trying circumstances, Joy's mind wandered not to God—beyond a brief and almost reflexive "I am wonderfully supported by the hope I have of blessed immortality"—but instead to his "dear wife & Children, Parents & friends," leading him to compose the following gloomy poem:

> My Lamentation, in this stormy night,
> Black night o'er the concave is spread.
> Hoarse winds thro' the grates how they roar
> In vain do I lie in my bed,
> While the sea rolls its surf on the shore.
> Hail scene of terrific dismay!
> Thy horrors compare with my own,
> As fill'd with deep anguish I lay,
> As bursts from my bosom the grown.
> I once knew the pleasures of peace,
> And Innocence dwelt in my heart,

Fair Friendship gave rapture to ease,
And love could its transport impart.

What extacy dwelt in my soul,
When my Mary with hapiness smil'd.
What Joys thro' my bosom oft stole,
When her tear soft compassion beguil'd.

Alass! now how chang'd is the scene,
In Prison I languish & mourn.
My heart torn with anguish so keen,
Oh I would I had never been born:

The sport of Dame Fortune to be,
And the child of affliction and woe;
Given up to the passions a prey,
I down to the Grave soon shall go.

Methinks on the crags of the rock,
Swift destruction some shattered ship seeks?
How its timbers are torn with the shock,
How the agoniz'd passenger shreiks.

Compar'd with my anguish how faint,
Are the horrors that fill him with care;
His fancy destruction my paint
But he knows not the woe of despair.

What waves on the vessel are driv'n,
How the surf throws its foam on the deck!
What thunders roll dreadful thro' heav'n!
What lightnings illumine the wreck!

But soft—see the storm dies away
The beams of the morning appear,
Hope to him may a promise display
But my bosom she can never cheer!

The poem, while certainly not remarkable for its prose, stands, nonetheless, as the only piece of purely secular poetry—it is also the

longest—penned by Joy (he wrote nine such pieces) during his imprisonment. It attests to the omnipresence of the temporal world for him,
even in the aftermath of the most moving of religious experiences.[22]

By late April, Joy's journal entries became even more explicitly
worldly, as his thoughts increasingly gravitated toward his looming
trial in the Supreme Judicial Court. On Sunday, April 26, Joy excitedly
noted the arrival of his brother Eben and his brother-in-law former
New Hampshire state representative and Durham town clerk and selectman Valentine Smith (who Joy refers to as "Mr. Smith"). Their arrival on the Sabbath, a day that normally led to much spiritual reflection by Joy, along with the weight of the impending trial, clearly
directed his thoughts in another direction, and as a result, he made no
mention of any form of worship, an uncharacteristic omission for the
devout Joy. The days that followed were agonizing for Joy as he waited
for events to unfold.[23]

Ebenezer and Valentine Smith busied themselves trying to arrange
an acquittal for their relation. For his part, Joy's mind must have raced
as it ran through the myriad possible outcomes. On April 28, Joy ner-
vously wrote, "The long waited for day has at length arived & the
Supreme Court has commenced its sitting. When the bell rang to call
the court it sounded to me as dismal as tho it were tolling for a funeral.
Nothing has yet been effected by my friends except that they have employed an Attorney to plead my cause, so I must be led a criminal before the Court & the Lord have mercy on me." Understandably pre-
occupied, the anxious Joy barely wrote anything for the next two days,
hoping against hope that his case would be dismissed. Then, on May
1, his mood took a dramatic turn for the worse. "My hopes are all fled
& plung'd in despair," he fearfully noted, explaining, "My persecutors
ever active sent of a Deputy Sheriff yester afternoon to Haverhill to
procure evidence against me & this morning they throng the court
house . . . My attorney Esqr Andross has been with me and gave me
no reason to hope that I should be liberated by paying a small fine."
"What the result will be," he gloomily confessed, "God only knows."[24]

The following morning, a Saturday, Joy's case went before a grand
jury, where, Joy confided, "there is no doubt but they will find a bill
against me." While awaiting news of the grand jury's findings, Joy received two visitors, Francis Eaton, the Haverhill attorney that he had
met and engaged in conversation on that fateful day in March in
Kendall's Tavern (or, as Joy phrased it, "the one who led me into this
scrape & persuaded me to write what I did at Haverhill"), and Moses

Wingate, the Haverhill town clerk who deposed Joy. Apparently shocked by Joy's haggard appearance, Eaton, Joy tells us, "just looked in then started back & looked pale as a sheet. He looked me in the face some time but never utered a word." Wingate then "spoke a few words but was soon hurried away by Eaton." Taking some degree of pleasure from Eaton's obvious discomfort and shock, Joy had seemingly come to view the attorney as his own version of Bunyan's character Mr. Worldly Wiseman, a charlatan who lured the pilgrim Christian from the straight and narrow—the path of God—by promising to take him to a place where he could relieve his burdens. "I never saw a mans countenance," Joy assuredly wrote with an obvious degree of satisfaction, "show more guilt than his in my life." He concluded his entry for the day by noting, "I have heard that the Grand Jury have found a bill against me & of course my tryal will come on monday or tuesday."[25]

At three o'clock in the afternoon on Monday, May 4, 1812, Timothy Meader Joy was led from his cell to the Ipswich courthouse. There, the indictment for libel against him was read, and he was asked to enter a plea of guilty or not guilty. "I answered," Joy wrote later that day, "that I was guilty of writing the paper mentioned in the Indictment but not with malicious design & that I should not contend with the Commonwealth." The judge presiding over the case, the former Federalist member of Congress Samuel Sewall (the great-grandson of the judge in the Salem witch trials), who Joy derisively referred to as "my lord Judge," demanded a simple "guilty" or "not guilty" plea, to which Joy responded with "guilty." Joy was then fined fifty dollars and sentenced to an additional thirty days in jail. Now able to see a definite end to his confinement, Joy, his mind temporarily eased, cheerfully wrote, "I now contemplate with pleasure the day when if it please God I shall once more embrace the dear objects of my fond affections."[26]

For the next five days, Joy's diary became a running commentary on the actions of the court and the era's hard-fought and intensely partisan politics. The regular spiritual reflection that had characterized so much of the journal's content and that had been in the forefront of Joy's consciousness just three weeks before is made all the more conspicuous by its absence. It would not be fair to conclude from this shift in emphasis, however, that he had been disingenuous about his progress toward redemption. Rather, it is very likely that the rush of events, along with the exhausting, yet calming, journey to spiritual assurance, allowed the young man's mind to wander in new directions. Joy's wandering was short lived. His lengthy and, as he perceived it, egregious and regrettable dereliction of his spiritual duties, undoubtedly exacerbated by the mental and physical toll of his long separation from his loved ones, bore down on his conscience, as previously mentioned, on Sunday, May 10, triggering yet another deep inner struggle for the young man. "I have been too negligent of late in attending to the things of the kingdom," Joy noted contritely, admitting, "My mind has been agitated with a spirit of revenge against my persecutors & I have written what I wish I had not." Now fully cognizant of his neglect, Joy steeled himself for the task at hand. "I am determined," he wrote, "to search my own heart. I know that I have been very wicked but then Christ came not to call the riteous but sinners to repentance." After further introspection, Joy, though still very much agitated, continued, with a measure of momentary confidence, "I know that I do not feel the same relish for sin & sinful pleasures I once did. I know too that I love the servants of God . . . I believe I have some ground for my hope."[27]

Full spiritual clarity still, however, remained elusive for Joy. The following day, he took his pen in hand and woefully scribbled, "I would fain get rid of my melancholy, but cannot." Turning to the scriptures, as he had in the past, Joy found no comfort. Rather, he wrote, "I have been studying the scriptures til I am left in uncertainty." "Oh that I could be but guided aright," he plead, noting, "I should then be happy." The depths of the young man's despair seemed to know no limit, and he woefully took stock of his present situation: "My peace of mind is gone, my vain hopes of happiness fled. My health ruined—my reason—Oh my God how miserable am I." Concerned that he was being tested yet again, Joy anxiously confessed, "I wish I could be more resign'd to the will of divine providence & study up into the mysteries of religion. I fear it is another plan of satan to bewilder my understanding, but I hope for the best." "I hope that God will enlighten my understanding," he closed, "that I may disern good from evil."[28]

The next morning, May 12, after "passing a restless night" and "earnestly praying God to strengthen & assist me," Joy determined to make a final push for clarity and prepared himself, should he fail, to "give up the point & let despair take its full scope." The moment of truth had come. Was the assurance that he had fought so hard to receive on that cold April evening real or merely a fleeting glimpse of an elusive calm that he could never hope to experience again? Fortunately for the young seeker, the answer to his question was not long in coming.[29]

Joy recalled later that day that when he had been thumbing through his Bible, "it pleased God to direct me to this passage of scripture which at once dispell'd the gloom which beclouded my mind." The passage, Luke 6:21, read, "Blessed are ye that hunger now for you shall be filled. Blessed are ye that weep now for ye shall laugh." Heartened by what he read, along with "many more such comforting passages," Joy submitted himself to God, introspectively writing, "It is passing strange but so it is that those very passages which in my hour of darkness read death to my soul now speak life in all its beauty." Facing the heart of his previous confusion head-on, Joy continued,

> If I were a castaway should I feel as I now do, should I find any comfort in reading the scriptures? Should I have such melting seasons in pray'r. I think not, & I think further that I have nourished false doctrine which has been the cause of all my misfortunes & darkness of mind. I mean the doctrine of falling from grace. This doctrine drove me to despair, depriv'd me of my reason, & for awhile kept my mind captive in more than Egyptian darkness, but thank God light again shines in upon my benighted Soul I see things in a different from what I formerly did. And I feel more calm & established in my belief of Gods all protecting power than I did in the belief of his partial mercy. If those who have been regenerated, born again & cleans'd by the blood of Christ, and received into the family of saints, can be wrested out of the hands of a savior who bled & died, that they might live, then the power of Satan [is] greater than the power of God & the whole plan of redemption is rendered abortive at the will of the adversary.

Returning to the scriptures, Joy concluded his entry with clarity of mind and with renewed confidence in his understanding of the mysteries of his faith, quoting from the book of John, "My sheep hear my voice & I know them and they follow me and I give unto them eternal life, and they shall never perish, neither shall any man pluck them out of my hand. My Father which gave them to me, is greater than all: and no man is able to pluck them out of my fathers hand."[30]

An understanding of Joy's deeply contested struggle is critical if one hopes to understand the intensity and significance of Joy's spiritual journey. This ideological battle, moreover, offers a glimpse into a broader struggle then underway in pulpits and schools of theology across the country, one that continues down to our present day. At the heart of this dispute stood the conflict between the Calvinist belief in the perseverance of the saints (the concept of eternal salvation, which held that those who are truly saved cannot fall away from their faith or be condemned because of their actions) and the Arminian-based notion—which Joy would have been exposed to in the Middleton Freewill Baptist church and perhaps, even earlier, through the Lee church's Reverend John Osborne—that individual salvation was conditional (that God's Grace, once given, could just as easily be lost as a result of a conscious repudiation—through word or deed—of one's faith). As Joy's reflections make abundantly clear, this tension was central to his distressing religious uncertainty and its attendant anxiety. In the end, however, as the journal entry of May 12 readily demonstrates, Joy rejected the challenge to the faith of his youth posed by his exposure to Arminian doctrine and instead fell back on his Calvinist roots and the belief that once an individual was saved, they were always saved. "The friends of God may have real or apparent decays in virtue and holiness," Joy had been reminded by Reverend Curtis Coe in his 1806 valedictory sermon, "yet they shall never finally apostatize from the faith of the gospel."[31]

A tremendous sense of inner peace and serenity quickly settled upon the now confidently assured Timothy Joy. "An heretofore unnown calmness pervades my Soul," Joy recorded the following day, "I never in my life felt more peace of mind . . . I feel satisfied that I have at last got into the true channel, at least I hope I have, & pray God to direct me through." The strenuous cycle of conversion, forged initially in intense fear and desperation, had come full circle as Joy was overwhelmed by love and inner calm. The change in his demeanor remained a source of wonder for Joy as he counted down the days until his June release. "I hope I shall always be thankfull to my Maker," Joy earnestly noted, "for his goodness to me in removing the thick darkness from my mind & bringing me once more into the light of hope." "This alteration," he continued, "is great indeed . . . When I look into my soul all is at peace." With his renewed confidence and spiritual assurance, Joy also took time, in a manner strikingly similar to that employed by Reverend Coe in his valedictory sermon, to assess the current state of the world and, perhaps more important, how he had allowed it to preoccupy his mind in the past. "I am lost in astonishment," he wrote in a Sabbath entry on May 24, "to think how careless & unconcerned many waste their precious moments in vain pursuits and idel recreation which ought to be

improv'd in making their peace with their justly offended maker." "We
have no fixed abode," he continued,

> but are swiftly passing through time into eternity, where we
> must be fixed in happiness or misery forever. Then how great
> the folly of suffering our main attention to be taken up with the
> present objects and seeking our chief happiness in this world, as
> tho' we were settled here forever, and had no concerns with an-
> other state. This is too much the case with multitudes, when we
> look around us, we see people engaged some in the business &
> others in the trifles of time: but as for the weighty concerns of
> eternity, they are by many at least put far out of mind and ne-
> glected as Idle fictions and not treated as important realities. Oh
> may I never again waste my precious time as I have heretofore,
> but improve every fleeting moment in making preparation for
> another and a better world.

Timothy Joy now fully understood the reason for his secular failure and
for the test that God had given him. To him, his new path was clear.[32]

On the evening of June 2, Joy sat down to make his final journal entry. While certainly eager to be free again and to hasten home to his
family, he took a final moment to reflect on his arduous spiritual trial
and to pen a brief covenant with his maker. "I desire to be thankfull to
almighty God for his abundant goodness in keeping me & bringing
me through so many tryals & perils in safety," he humbly wrote, requesting, "O may my future time be spent in an acceptable manner in
the service of the most high." He earnestly concluded, "Adieu ye damp
solitary walls. Ye have often witnessed my sighs & groans, you have often been wetted with my tears, bear witness of me forever, that I have
vow'd to serve that God, whose kind care of me has been indeed wonderfull, all the days of my life, & if I do not perform my vow, may you
again receive me & inclose me forever." With his physical being about
to join his spiritual being in casting aside its incarceration, Timothy
Joy's pilgrimage had reached its conclusion. His entry into the "Celestial City," he now more confidently than ever believed, was assured.[33]

Ipswich Prison, March the 20th, 1812.

Confined in a dismal awful Prison and sometimes so absent in mind as not to recollect the circumstances which have occured to me since I left my home I have thought proper to commit to paper while in my rational moments the most extraordinary circumstances which have happened to my Imprisonment, as correctly as I can remember them wishing, should I lose my reason that this paper may be carefully preserved & sent to my family my circumstances being very much embarrassed at Middleton & W I came to the resolution of quiting this place country for a season, & going to Salem there to endeavour to get into some line of business or other to earn money to pay my debts my family being dear to me I often before I started doubted my duty to remain but on the 1st of the present month, my creditors broke upon me and took every article I possed in the world, except some household goods I had previously sold to my brother this circumstances, I had but one alternative, to fly or go to Prison being naturly timid & by no means used to misfortunes I new not which to turn, but

Opening page of Timothy M. Joy's prison journal. ("Diary of Timothy M. Joy (Written in Ipswich Prison, Salem, Massachusetts, 1812)," box 7, Henry B. Joy Historical Research Record Group, Bentley Historical Library, University of Michigan, Ann Arbor.)

Reverend Curtis Coe, pastor of Durham, New Hampshire, Congregational Church, 1780–1806. (Joseph Gardner Bartlett, *Robert Coe, Puritan: His Ancestors and Descendants, 1340–1910, with Notices of Other Coe Families* [Boston: privately printed, 1911], 176.)

Ffrost store. Though taken well after Timothy Joy's death in 1813, this image captures a building type that would have been typical at Durham's Oyster River Landing in the early nineteenth century. (Series X, box 1, folder 19, Durham Town Records, Milne Special Collections, University of New Hampshire, Durham.)

Portrait of Timothy
Pickering by C. W. Beale.
(Photograph courtesy of
Peabody Essex Museum,
Salem, MA, PEM# EI224.)

Derby Wharf, where, in
March of 1812, Timothy
M. Joy was arrested for
defaming the character
of prominent Federalist
politician and local resident
Timothy Pickering.
(Photograph courtesy of
Peabody Essex Museum,
Salem, MA, PEM# 19736.)

View of the COURT HOUSE, in Salem, Massachusetts.

(above) Engraving of the courthouse in Salem, Massachusetts, 1785, by S. Hill (from *Massachusetts Magazine,* 1790). The courthouse was one of Salem's most important public buildings in 1812, and it was here, in the second-floor courtroom, that Timothy Joy was charged with defamation and then remanded over to local officials for incarcerations. (Photograph courtesy of Peabody Essex Museum, Salem, MA, PEM# 19138.)

Another Plot!

The heat of Election hatches a brood of Plots and Falsehoods.

Last Friday a stranger of good address and personal appearance, and about 28 years of age, arrived at a tavern in Haverhill, and stopped for refreshment. After conversing with some of the inhabitants, and exciting their curiosity, and knowing that the *Henry Plot* was designed as a powerful electioneering engine for the democratic party, to which this impostor belongs, he pretended that he was just from Quebec, and had in his possession evidence of most horrid treason committed by men esteemed the most upright and distinguished in the nation—and that he had actually seen the treasonable correspondence with British officers. As the election for town officers in Haverhill was to be held on Monday next, the Jacobin demagogues caught at the bait, caressed the vagrant, took him to an office above the Bridge, and after much importunity persuaded the man to copy and sign a certificate which one of these disturbers of the peace had prepared. All this was done with the secrecy that usually accompanies villainy :—for they refused to permit Bailey Bartlett, Esq. to be present and examine him. After he had left Haverhill, where he called himself *Nathaniel Emery*, the good people of that town were alarmed for the public safety, and became in an uproar ; for the DAMNING CERTIFICATE of this vagabond, was triumphantly exhibited as undoubted evidence of Federal Treason, by Mr. Francis Eaton, a democratic lawyer, and Postmaster in that town.

So great was the ferment and excitement produced by this most base and infamous affair, that reflecting men thought it expedient to investigate and sift this mountain of falsehood ; accordingly the man was pursued to Salem, where he arrived late at night, and called himself *Timothy Joy*, and at this place also said he was just from Quebec. In the morning, as soon as it was ascertained he was in town, a warrant was obtained, and he was apprehended and examined before JOHN PRINCE, jun. Esq. He denied none of the facts, admitted his guilt, and was ordered by the Magistrate to recognize in the sum of five hundred dollars for his appearance at the Supreme Judicial Court. As he was unable to obtain bail, he is now committed to prison for trial for his crime. An immense concourse of people attended the examination, and all were disgusted and alarmed at the unfolding of the shameless and abandoned arts and devices resorted to by our demagogues to excite the feelings of the public at every election, to destroy by base calumny the fairest characters, and to sustain by the most iniquitous means the tottering cause of Democracy.

Upon examination he confessed, that he had signed a paper yesterday at Haverhill, charging Col. Pickering with holding a treasonable correspondence with the British, and alledging that he had seen the letters from Col. Pickering to a Col. Hamilton—that he never was in Canada, as he pretended—that he was questioned very hard, and induced to make the statement—that he was desired to go to *an office* above the bridge, and there the gentleman [no, said he, if he *had* been a gentleman he would not have used me so] wrote the paper which he the prisoner at their request signed, and left there—that they wanted him to swear to it, but refused, because (as he now said) he thought it was bad enough to lie without swearing to it. He said, that when at Haverhill he called his name *Nathaniel Emery*, but that his real name was *Timothy Medey Joy*—that he lives at Middleton, N. H.—had been a trader, but was now embarrassed—that he bore no ill will to Col. Pickering, knew nothing evil of him, was sorry for what he had done, and should not have done it if he had not fallen into such company at Haverhill.

In corroboration of his statement, writs served upon him at Middleton, and sundry small notes and accounts dated there, were found upon him. *Isaiah Webster*, the mail-carrier between Haverhill and Salem, who was called as a witness, stated, that *Francis Eaton* at Haverhill handed to him in his office, on Saturday morning, a paper signed by N. Emery, and told him that it was concerning a treasonable correspondence between Col. Pickering and an officer in Canada.

Thus we see the wicked measures to which a party resort to answer their purposes ! They are willing to conspire to blast the good name of an aged patriot, who has devoted his life to his country, and whose character is assailable only by the tongue of slander, and the pen of the libeller. It is to be feared that this nation will not wipe away the stigma of ingratitude from the character of republics. Such conduct as that at Haverhill, deserves the utter detestation of every man who has a spark of honor or honesty. It is truly degrading that any should be found to justify or even palliate it.

The man who was intended to be injured did not know of the prosecution. Such an attempt to destroy his fame is a public crime, and as such it was prosecuted. All considerate men must feel their deep interest that our distinguished ornaments should not be wantonly attacked, to assist an election. They will judge rightly of a cause which seeks support by such means, and will distrust their stories of plots, conspiracies, treasons, &c. which so abound before our elections.

Salem, March 21st, 1812.

Another Plot! The Heat of the Election Hatches a Brood of Plots and Falsehoods (n.d., ca. March 1812), a Federalist broadside reporting the arrest of Timothy Joy and alleging a plot to influence the outcome of pending state elections in Massachusetts. (Photograph courtesy of Peabody Essex Museum, Salem, MA, PEM# 34083.)

(facing page) "Fireboard: View of Court House Square, Salem, 1810–1820." (Photograph courtesy of Peabody Essex Museum, Salem, MA, PEM# 108,499.)

BEWARE OF IMPOSTORS.
OR "SLANDER DETECTED."

On Friday 20th inst. a transient person calling himself Nathl. Emery, dined at Kendall's tavern in Haverhill. He passed himself off for a Lieut. in the British service. Stated that he was a nephew of Col. James Hamilton ; Commander of the 67th Regiment British light dragoons, stationed at Quebec. That he was a Lieut. in the 4th company in said regiment, and that he was on his way through Salem to Boston, whence he intended to take passage to England. the course of conversation led him to remark, that there were *traitors* in every Country—that we had them in *this*—that by reason of his intimacy with his uncle, Col. Hamilton, he was knowing to a correspondence between Timothy Pickering and the said Hamilton, wherein the said Pickering had expressed an opinion that a separation of the States would take place, expressed his approbation of such an event, and manifested his wishes that it *might* take place. This statement he made *voluntarily & unhesitatingly.* The name of Mr. Pickering was not even mentioned till introduced by him in the above manner. He was then questioned strictly and critically as to his knowledge of the above facts, he again boldly declared it to be the truth, and on being requested, consented without hesitation or reluctance to reduce it to writing and sign it ; he accordingly did, left it with a gentleman of this town, and soon afterwards proceeded on his journey.

I Stephen Crooker, testify and say, that I was present when the above conversation took place, that the person denominating himself Nathaniel Emery made the above statement and gave the above account of himself voluntarily and without the instigation of any person present, & that when it was reduced to writing, he was not prompted to state any fact whatever, nor did any person present appear desirous to pervert, distort or change his meaning STEPHEN CROOKER.

Essex fs. Haverhill March 21st, 1812.

Then the above named Stephen Crooker personally appeared and made oath to the truth of the foregoing statement by him subscribed
Before me MOSES WINGATE, Justice of the peace.

I Moses H. Elliott do testify and say, that I was present when the above conversation and statement took place, that the observations which fell from the person CALLING HIMSELF Nathaniel Emery, were voluntarily made and without any solicitation whatever, that the observations contained in the sTATEMENT WRITTEN & SIGNED by him, were precisely the same as were made by him at the House of Mr. Kendall ; and I do further say, that when requested to make oath to the above statement, he observed that he could DECLARE before GOD and the witnesses present, that the said instrument contained the TRUTH which could be substantiated by him.

sinuation that the Republicans have stooped to abject and contemptible arts for electioneering purposes ? Whence the necessity of printing hand bills, posting them up at public houses and in the corners of streets, to contradict slanders, which had but a very limited verbal circulation unless extended by *federalists* themselves ! Why are the REPUBLICANS denounced as *Demagogues and Scoundrels* for the exertion of rights and the performance of duties, dictated by the most pure and patriotic motives ? The measures taken by them, were such, as were calculated the most surely and most expeditiosly to test the truth or falshood of the report.

The proceedings had by them in regard to it, were such as have been approved by the most respectable Federalists in this town, one of whom has been heard to say that it was no more than he should have done in a similar situation. In fact, what *honest man* in the community, what patriot who loves his *country*, can condemn or disapprove of an attempt to expose treason, or detect the authors of a calumny. The Federalists affect to believe that the vile slanderer, who has imposed upon an upright and unsuspecting public, was unworthy of notice, and of course his statement ought to have been disregarded. It is sufficient, *on this subject*, to say, that the degree of credit which they attached to his statement, may be appreciated by the irritation they manifested, and by their *dogging* him to Salem.

Honest Federalists, honest Republicans, honest men of all parties, are requested to point out wherein any Republican is culpable in this transaction. By the affidavits of Doctor M. H. Elliot and Mr. Stephen Crooker, two very respectable young men, in this town, against whose integrity the breath of calumny never dared whisper a slander, and who were present during the whole transaction, it appears " that the statement made by this self-called Nathaniel Emery, was made by him voluntarily, and without the instigation of any person whatever—that it dropped from him in the course of conversation, and that the statement by him written and signed was specisely the f........ wish the versation."

The vile and scandalous by certain individuals to .... that the gentleman who w......... in procuring this statem........ prompted the man to.......... ment, may now b...........

Beware of Imposters or Slander Detected (n.d., ca. March 1812). Eager to deflect criticism of their party, Massachusetts Republicans countered with their own version of Joy's allegations and subsequent arrest. (Photograph courtesy of Peabody Essex Museum, Salem, MA, PEM# 34084.)

Durham, New Hampshire, 1805. (Adapted by Dr. Claudia Walters from an 1805 map of Durham by D. Smith, Milne Special Collections, University of New Hampshire, Durham.)

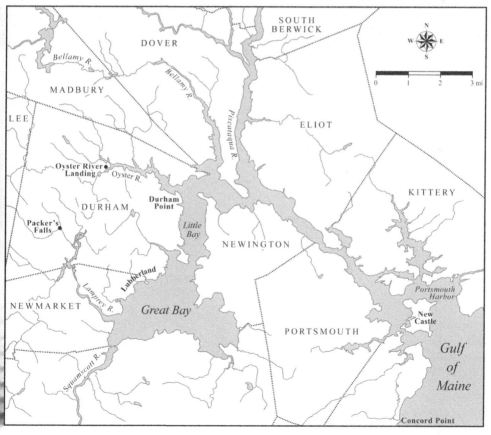

The Piscataqua region. (Created by Dr. Claudia Walters.)

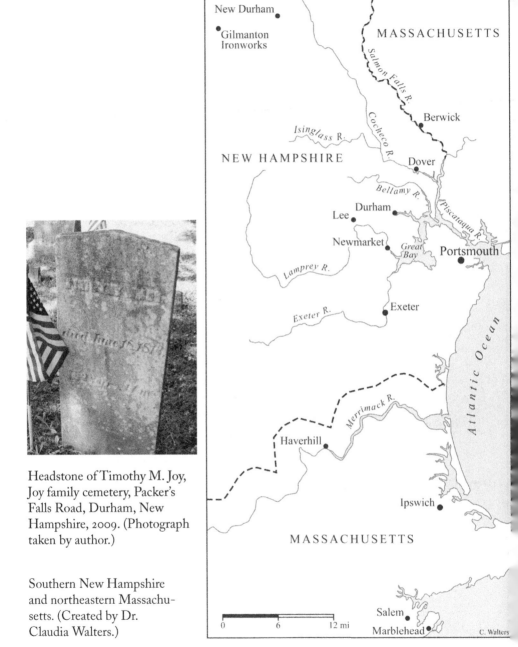

Headstone of Timothy M. Joy,
Joy family cemetery, Packer's
Falls Road, Durham, New
Hampshire, 2009. (Photograph
taken by author.)

Southern New Hampshire
and northeastern Massachusetts. (Created by Dr.
Claudia Walters.)

Chapter 5

"ADIEU YE DAMP SOLITARY WALLS"

Sleep likely came sparingly for Timothy Meader Joy on the night of June 1–2, 1812. Tormented by the "little black Gentry" who had "taken up their abodes in [his] straw," and with his mind swimming in thoughts of home and family, the restless Joy fitfully tossed and turned in his cool, dark cell, anxiously awaiting the first glimpse of the morning sun that would announce the arrival of the day of his release from Ipswich Prison after seventy-three days behind bars. Certainly, his mind also wandered to his economic plight, to his responsibilities as a father and husband, to the damage done to his family name, and to the imperative need to find a way to provide a competence for his family. Joy also, undoubtedly, as he had on so many other nights in prison, turned to God: thanking him for "keeping and bringing [him] through so many trials & perils in safety," and praying for guidance and support in setting his life right.[1]

As daylight broke, Joy hastily gathered his things, including his journal, and eagerly paced the floor in his cell, waiting for the familiar sound of footsteps echoing in the corridor and the grating sound of the key being turned in the lock that separated him from freedom and those he loved. After what must have seemed like an eternity, the moment he had been longing for finally arrived, and his cell door swung open. Awash in emotions, Joy, gaunt and frail as a result of his recent bout of illness, would have bid his cell mates a hurried good-bye. Hastening into the corridor, he made his way to the prison's gate and freedom. There, choking back tears, Timothy, one can readily imagine, lingered momentarily to thank, for their kindness and unflagging support, Sheriff Robert Farley and jailer J. Sandford and his daughter

Margaret, her cheeks wet with the tears streaming from her eyes. Basking in his renewed freedom, Joy turned and gave his brother Eben, who had arrived in Ipswich on Monday, June 1, a long, warm embrace. Mounting their horses, the two men turned to give a last farewell to those who had meant so much to the young prisoner while he was incarcerated and to cast a last look at the cold, gray stone prison. With a brisk pull on the reins and a kick of their heels, they then set off for their homes in New Hampshire. As they traveled, perhaps retracing some of the very route Timothy had followed during his March flight from Middleton, the two brothers undoubtedly had much to say—Eben filling Timothy in on family and Durham news, Timothy expressing his sincere gratitude for all that his brother had done for him and his family and eagerly soliciting Eben's counsel about his future plans.

It is unknown exactly when Joy arrived home, but his reunion with Mary and the children was certainly an extremely emotional one, especially in light of the family's extended separation and the suddenness of Joy's March 17 departure. Catching her first glimpse of her emaciated and pallid husband, Mary's emotions spilled forth in a mix of euphoria and heartbreak. Likewise, the ever-demonstrative Joy, swarmed by his wife and young children and reeling from the obvious signs that Mary was again with child—the baby, who the couple would name Ebenezer in honor of Joy's altruistic and noble brother, would be born on November 30—sobbed uncontrollably and begged his family for forgiveness, struggling, with every breath, to regain his composure. Steeled by his recent experience and by the new revelation about his expanding family obligations and buoyed by his renewed religious assurance, Joy, with a clarity of mind that he had not felt in some time, solemnly pledged to do better by his family and to never leave them on their own again.[2]

True to his word, Timothy Meader Joy immediately went to work to set things right. His first order of business was to find a way to extricate himself from his credit woes and, if at all possible, to repay his brother Eben for his generous financial assistance. Accordingly, on June 17, just two weeks after his release from prison, Joy sold, for $17.50, the Middleton "shop" that he had constructed after his purchase of the Buzzell property in late 1811, to Joseph Goodwin, a Middleton blacksmith. Determined to put an unhappy chapter of his life behind him, Joy agreed, on the following day, to sell his Middleton residence (and the initial location for his trading business) to Elijah

Goodwin, a local cordwainer, for eighty-five dollars. That same day, though certainly unknown to Joy (given the nation's poor communications), the Madison administration declared war against Great Britain. News of war spread rapidly throughout New England, and military recruiters stepped up their efforts to build an army to meet the crisis. Joy needed steady employment, especially with a third child on the way, and his recent highly politicized exposure to the partisan run-up to war and the selfless actions of such Revolutionary heroes as Robert Farley had bolstered his determination to stamp out treason and the numerous threats (which he had come to see as very much connected) facing his beloved country. These factors motivated Joy, on July 2, to enlist at Middleton for service as a private in Captain John Wingate Gookin's Third Regiment of Artillery at a pay of seven dollars per month.[3]

At some point between the sale of his Middleton properties and his departure for service in early July, Timothy relocated his family to Durham, most likely to the Joy homestead. Initially, the move might have been considered a temporary expedient until the young father regained his financial footing. Or perhaps Joy, on learning of his country's declaration of war, had already determined to enlist and thus moved his family to Durham believing that Mary and the children would there be safer and well cared for, with the unmarried Eben and Timothy's parents, Deacon Samuel and Hannah, at hand (not to mention the nearby French relatives in neighboring Newmarket). Secure in the belief that his life was now moving in the right direction and that his family had a solid and comprehensive support system in place, Joy, his health still not fully restored from his prison illness, bid his family a tearful good-bye once again and marched off to war.[4]

The precise movements of the Third Regiment of Artillery and particularly of the specific company in which Timothy Joy served, during the early phases of the War of 1812, are difficult to pin down. The unit was, at the time of his enlistment, a relatively new entity, having only been formed, along with a Second Regiment of Artillery, under a congressional act in January 1812. Because of their status as part of the nation's "additional military force" cobbled together in the face of a looming war, service in the Second and Third Regiments was generally considered less prestigious than service in the First Regiment, which was part of the "permanent" military establishment. The lack of prestige did not seem to deter Joy from enlisting, however. Initially under the leadership of Alexander Macomb, who went on to become general-in-chief of the army, the unit was attached to the command led by Major General Henry Dearborn operating along the northeastern New York frontier. After an aborted move north toward Montreal in British-held Canada in November 1812, Dearborn's soldiers, Timothy Joy among them, settled into winter camp outside of Plattsburg, New York, to wait for spring and the beginning of a new campaign season.[5]

Early the following spring, Dearborn's force was ordered to Sackett's Harbor, New York, on Lake Ontario, where the general was to link up with Commodore Isaac Chauncey, whose men had been occupied over the cold, snowy winter constructing a small fleet of ships. The vessels were to be used to transport Dearborn's men across the lake for an assault on Kingston, Ontario, Canada. From there, Dearborn was to march his men overland and take York (present-day Toronto) and then move against the British forts on the Niagara frontier. Rumors of reinforcements to the British garrison at Kingston, however, led Dearborn to revamp this plan. Leaving a token force of regulars, militia, and elements of the Third Artillery (though it is unclear precisely which elements) behind to defend Sackett's Harbor, Dearborn loaded the bulk of his force (again, including portions of Timothy Joy's regiment) on Chauncey's transport ships and set out directly for York. There, on April 27, his army, temporarily under the command of Zebulon Pike (Dearborn was ill), successfully defeated the smaller British force defending the city. Dearborn's continued absence and Pike's death as a result of the explosion of a powder magazine left the army without a recognized commander, and discipline among the men quickly broke down, leading to the looting of the town and the burning of its public buildings. Having accomplished his goal of taking York, Dearborn once again loaded his men onto Chauncey's ships and took them back across Lake Ontario, marching them overland to the Niagara frontier for a planned assault on that region's British forts.[6]

With Dearborn's force on the western end of the lake, the governor-general of Canada, Sir George Prevost, set his sights on the small American force defending Sackett's Harbor. On May 26, 1813, Prevost landed his force at Sackett's Harbor. The town's defenses, under the command of Brigadier General Jacob Brown of the New York state militia, consisted of two forward lines of infantry (mostly comprised of militia) set in front of a fortified battery made up of the rump elements of the Third Artillery. Repeated British assaults drove back the American defenders, first one line and then the other. But in the end, Brown's men behaved nobly under fire and, with the support of the artillery, fell back into previously prepared defensive positions that proved effective in turning back the British assault and in securing an American victory.[7]

Unfortunately, the spotty historical record makes it impossible to trace, with any precision, Timothy Joy's whereabouts during much of this time. It is known, due to the existence of a dated written order, that he was present in Sackett's Harbor on March 10, 1813, but whether his unit accompanied Dearborn's invasion force for its attack on York or remained behind and played a role in the defense of Sackett's Harbor is uncertain. Indeed, there is a distinct possibility, given that we find Joy back in Durham in early June suffering from some unidentified disease that he contracted in camp, that he did not participate in either action, that he had already departed for home before either portion of the Third Artillery went into battle. If Joy did participate in one of the two military engagements, it seems much more plausible, given its closer proximity to Durham (and thus the greater likelihood that he would be able to make his way home in the window of time available), that Joy's company had been left behind to defend Sackett's Harbor. What is altogether certain, though, is that Timothy Joy, his constitution already in a weakened state from his lengthy illness the year before and taxed further by the effects of a long winter, his close quarters with a large number of other men, and the rigors of a Spartan army life, was stricken with some sickness in the spring of 1813 and that this illness brought the young man back home to Durham for a final time.[8]

Sometime between late March and early June in 1813, in the Durham home of his childhood, Timothy Meader Joy was reunited with his family. That now included his youngest son, Ebenezer, who, in all likelihood, Timothy had never seen before that moment. Surrounded by his loved ones, Joy, despite his condition, felt relief and calm. For the assembled family members, however, the young man's homecoming was unquestionably bittersweet. While certainly overjoyed to have their loved one with them once again, Joy's family could not have helped but to have felt deeply worried about his obviously failing health. Putting him to bed, the family set about trying to restore Timothy's health, and Mary, Hannah, and other female relatives, friends, and neighbors began the long vigil known as "sitting in." As historian Jane Nylander relates, in the early nineteenth century, "it was customary for sick people to be confined to bed for long periods of time—months, or even years." The women charged with "sitting in" with the patient—an often long, laborious, and draining exercise—bore responsibility for keeping the patient comfortable, clean, and nourished, for providing medicines and poultices as necessary, for offering prayer, and for watching for signs of a sudden change in the patient's condition. We do not know the length of Timothy's confinement to bed, but one can well imagine the toll that such an arduous, around-the-clock vigil took on Mary, who also had to care for her three young children, and on Joy's sixty-seven-year-old mother, Hannah. Despite their best efforts, Timothy's condition continued to worsen.[9]

On Friday, June 18, 1813, as the New England spring prepared to give way to summer, the members of Deacon Samuel Joy's household gathered together at the bedside of Timothy Joy. A month short of his twenty-fourth birthday, Joy, his health now failing rapidly, found himself surrounded by his sobbing wife, Mary; his three, very frightened and scared small children, Alfred Timothy, Mary, and the babe Ebenezer; his stoic parents, Deacon Samuel and Hannah; and his ever-faithful brother and confidant, Eben. With the faces of his loved ones fading in and out of view, Timothy mustered what strength he had and joined, in his mind, with his father, then engaged in prayer with the family, in giving thanks to God. At peace with his maker and warm in the loving embrace of his family, Timothy Meader Joy exchanged a last glance with those he loved. Finally succumbing to the illness ravaging his young body, he took his final breath and closed his eyes. His earthly travails were over.[10]

It was well-established custom in New England at the time that someone stay with the body of the deceased and "watch" until the body was interred. One can readily imagine the distraught Ebenezer Joy, ever the protector over his younger sibling, assuming that somber responsibility upon his brother's death. Eben's "watch" would not have lasted long. As bodies were not then embalmed, funerals for the deceased followed soon after death, particularly in the warmer months. In preparation for burial, Timothy's body would have been cleaned by Eben, his father, and/or perhaps his elder brother Samuel, and then dressed in a loose, long-sleeved, white cotton gown, made by a local woman for the deceased and known as a shroud, or, in terms beginning to occur at that time, in "grave clothes." Timothy's body would then have been set into an open coffin (also made quickly after death) and displayed on a bed or table or on sawhorses inside of the house, so that family and friends could pay their last respects. Additionally, "the paintings and looking glasses throughout the house were themselves shrouded with white fabric out of respect," and "herbs such as rosemary and tansy would be set out in the room to counteract the smell of the corpse."[11]

On the morning appointed for Timothy's burial, friends, family, and neighbors prepared themselves for the funeral. Hannah, Mary, and Joy's young daughter, Mary, along with the other female funeral goers, donned mourning dress—"black garments, veils, ribbons, and other tokens of their grief"—hurriedly made for them after Timothy's demise. Deacon Samuel, Ebenezer, Alfred Timothy, and other male family members and friends also dressed for mourning, though their garments would have been the black clothing worn on an everyday basis, perhaps now embellished by a black armband. The purposes served by the wearing of mourning dress were many.

> By wearing mourning, bereaved family members could communicate their loss to the community without having to repeatedly explain the details, and at the same time protect themselves and others from the embarrassment of thoughtless or unknowing remarks. The return to regular clothing then signaled the end of the deepest period of grief and the mourner's return to a normal routine. The mourning period generally lasted six months to a year, depending on the relationship of the deceased to the mourner. Men were not expected to follow mourning etiquette as closely as women were. They lived more active public lives and were allowed to resume their normal routine shortly after the funeral . . . Women, on the other hand, were under heavier obligations. Defined as the moral and emotional centers of their families, they were required to express their grief more elaborately and for a longer time.

Now properly dressed, the mourners somberly assembled at the Joy farm.[12]

The Durham Congregational Church had no established minister at the time, and no record of the funeral exists. We can only guess as to who gave the funeral service on that somber day. It is possible, for instance, that Curtis Coe, Timothy's childhood minister, who was now residing in nearby South Newmarket (Newfields), was prevailed upon to perform the service. It would not be much of a stretch, however, to suggest that the Reverend John Osborne of the nearby Lee church most likely presided over the funeral service, given his connection to Mary and Timothy. After leading those assembled in prayer and allowing each to bid Timothy a final farewell, the reverend offered his blessing and stepped back from Joy's body, and the coffin lid was put in place and nailed shut. With audible sobs surrounding them, Ebenezer, Samuel, Deacon Samuel, cousin James Joy, Valentine Smith, and other male friends and neighbors, such as the junior Curtis Coe, stepped forward to carry Timothy to his grave. After placing a black cloth pall over the coffin, the men lifted it from its resting place, hoisted it to their shoulders, and moved slowly out into the yard. There, behind the pallbearers, Hannah, Mary, and Mary's now fatherless children, along with other members of the family, assumed their places at the head of the funeral procession. Behind them, neighbors and friends lined up in turn—usually in an order that reflected their relative social ranking. With the bright June sun beating down on them, the men solemnly marched Timothy's body, accompanied by the train of mourners, the short distance to the family burial plot situated in a copse of trees across the road from the Joy homestead, where Timothy was to join in eternal sleep with his grandparents Samuel and Mary Burley Joy, his sister Polly and her young son Ebenezer Smith, and his three brothers who died in infancy.[13]

After a final prayer by the reverend, those assembled stood in pained silence as Timothy Meader Joy's body was lowered into its grave and as the first shovelful of soil—the same soil that he had worked as a young man and the very same soil on which three generations of Joys had staked their claim to respectability and security—was thrown, with a dull thud, onto the coffin. Though he was never able to fully claim the mantle of respectability for himself, none of those gathered at his graveside had any doubt that Timothy Meader Joy had given his all, including his life, in pursuit of that goal.

Now on her own with her three small children and no known assets, Mary Joy faced a very uncertain future. It is quite likely that she and the children remained under Deacon Samuel's roof, along with Eben (who was in line to inherit the family farm), at least for the short term. Indeed, it may well have been the case that Mary was encouraged to do so and that she assumed primary responsibility for the care of the elder Joys, on top of the already tremendous burden of raising three small children, for a significant portion of 1814, when Eben, as a member of the local militia, was twice called into active service due to mounting fears of a British assault on nearby Portsmouth. It appears very unlikely, however, that the young widow stayed in the deacon's household much beyond 1814, if she remained there at all after her husband's death. On January 16, 1815, the twenty-nine-year-old Eben Joy ended his bachelorhood and married a fellow Durhamite, Nancy Watson (ten years his junior). The addition of a new member to the already crowded Joy household, the now looming prospect of additional children in the house, and perhaps the fear of being viewed as a potential rival—Mary was, after all, just five years older than Eben's new wife and undoubtedly had a close relationship with her brother-in-law—likely convinced Mary that the time had come for her to leave Durham and to return to her own French family relations just down the road in Newmarket. That she did so is certain. In the account book that he maintained from 1816 on, Eben Joy includes entries for the "widow Mary Joy" and gives her residence as Newmarket. The 1820 federal census confirms her relocation to that town, listing a Mary Joy who resided next door to a Reuben French, very likely her father.[14]

The scanty evidence indicates that life for the widowed Mary Joy and her three children was not easy. Though Mary never took another husband, she apparently did occasionally use her French surname, as suggested by her gravestone, which identifies her as Mary French (she died, according to her headstone, in 1887, though many family genealogists list her death as 1869). It is unknown what trade, if any, Mary engaged in to support her family. The one source of income that is certain, at least early on, was the widow's pension of $3.50 per month (half of Timothy's monthly pay) that she drew commencing in late November of 1813 and running for a course of five years. This money enabled Mary to rent a small house from Paul Chapman for six dollars per year and to make payments on the firewood, grain, and cash advances she obtained on account from Ebenezer Joy. That the pension was adequate for meeting all of Mary's and the children's expenses seems unlikely. Undoubtedly, any shortfall was covered through some form of paid work and/or the largesse of Mary's French and Joy relations. The burden of raising children on this meager, temporary income was indisputably daunting.[15]

Certainly this difficulty, along with her determination to provide something better for her children, induced Mary to send fourteen-year-old Alfred Timothy to Portsmouth to learn a trade. There he was apprenticed to Langley Boardman, a master cabinetmaker. Given the cost associated with such a position, it is clear that the young man's apprenticeship was planned and subsidized in some manner by the boy's extended family (or, perhaps, was made possible by the small sum bequeathed to him after his grandfather's death in 1824, detailed later in this chapter). After learning the cabinet trade, Alfred Timothy established himself as a furniture dealer (in partnership with Edmund Brown) on the second and third stories of 44 Market Street, near the busy intersection with Hanover Street (a business he operated, according to family history, for thirty years—though his business was burned to the ground in a devastating fire in May of 1846). Alfred learned his trade well, and his work earned him material success (in 1860, the value of his real estate holdings was put at four thousand dollars and that of his personal estate at two thousand dollars), a circumstance that put him in a position to later assist his nephew William, his brother Ebenezer's oldest son, in his start in the cabinet trade. Beyond the material comfort that financial success brought, though, Alfred Joy was also able to achieve what his father, despite his best efforts, was never able to achieve in his all-too-brief life—respectability. Alfred served as chief engineer for the Portsmouth Fire Department and treasurer for the city's Mechanics Association and was elected twice (in 1859 and 1869) to serve in the New Hampshire state legislature—an accomplishment that his very political father would certainly have appreciated—thus earning the sobriquet the Honorable Alfred Timothy Joy.[16]

It appears that Mary and her relations followed a similar course of action for her youngest son, Ebenezer. Kept close to home, the young Eben was apprenticed out to learn the trade of cordwainer (shoemaker). He married Mehitable Doe at age nineteen and settled down in Newmarket near his mother and sister and among Burley and Meader kin, earning a living through his shoemaking and farming. By 1860, he was the head of a household that consisted of his wife, Mehitable, and six children, among them a boy named Timothy Meader, born in 1846. Eben then owned an estimated twenty-five hundred dollars worth of real estate and claimed an additional eight hundred dollars in personal wealth (these values increased to thirty-five hundred and one thousand dollars, respectively, by 1870). Two older daughters of Eben had already married and moved on to set up households on their own, and his oldest son, William, was working as a cabinetmaker, after apprenticing with his uncle, Alfred Timothy, in Portsmouth. Eben continued to ply his trade in Newmarket until his death in September of 1889.[17]

Timothy's daughter, Mary, followed a much different path from her mother's home to independence. In the issue of the Dover *New Hampshire Republican and County Advertiser* of February 13, 1827, there appeared a marriage notice for Mr. William Badger and Miss Mary Joy, posted Newmarket. Given Mary's very young age—she would not yet have been sixteen (her spouse was six years her senior)—and the 1827 birth year given for the couple's first child, who Mary would name Timothy, it is altogether likely that the marriage was precipitated by a pregnancy. Two years later, Mary gave birth to a second son, who the couple named Samuel. It appears that Mary Joy may have moved in with her daughter and her family: her name disappears from the 1830 census (she reappears in subsequent years), and there is an indication of a female above the age of forty living in the household headed by William Badger, who also happened, at the time that the census was taken, to be residing among many members of the French family of Newmarket. In 1833, the young couple rounded out their family with the birth of a third child, this time a daughter named Mary. Sadly, like her mother before her, Mary became a widow in her twenties (ironically, also with three young children), with her husband's passing in 1837. It is uncertain what happened to the new widow in the next few years. She also never remarried. By all appearances, it looks as though the elder Mary Joy, by 1840, had taken up residence in the home of her youngest son Ebenezer, the Newmarket shoemaker and farmer, with his wife, Mehitable, and three small children, Sarah, William, and Mary.[18]

Over the next decade, the widow Mary Joy seems to have improved her circumstances somewhat, as she can be found living in her own household again in the 1850 census. Residing with her were her daughter, Mary, who had personal property valued at an estimated one thousand dollars; her eldest grandson, Timothy, age twenty-three; and her seventeen-year old granddaughter, Mary. Three years later, Mary Joy, in response to a War of 1812 pension act passed by Congress in February of 1853, once again began to receive a monthly stipend of $3.50 in compensation for her husband's military service. A subsequent act of Congress in June of 1858 ensured a continuation of the payment for the remainder of her life or widowhood and increased her monthly stipend to $4.00. Mary also availed herself of an additional benefit offered to veterans by the federal government, applying for a bounty land warrant in early 1850. The warrant (number 598), which was approved the following year, entitled Mary to apply for a land patent for 160 acres of western land. Her timing in making her application was fortuitous, as such land patents were nontransferable prior to an 1852 act of Congress. It seems altogether likely, given her and her family's persistence in the seacoast area and her need for ready cash, that Mary, if she filed for the land patent, sold her land to a third party. It may, in fact, have been this money that enabled her daughter, the widow Badger, to begin business as a milliner and dressmaker. By 1860, Mary Badger's business was profitable enough to enable her to afford her own house, to double the size of her personal estate to two thousand dollars, and to allow her to take in her son Samuel (listed as a clerk) and her now seventy-year-old mother (who had a personal estate valued at three hundred dollars) to live with her.[19]

The final years of Mary Joy's life are very much a puzzle. Both she and her daughter disappear from the census in 1870, though Mary Badger, still working as a milliner, reappears in the Newmarket census listings for 1880, by which time she is listed as living alone. Likewise, the elder Mary does not appear in the households of either of her sons, Alfred Timothy or Ebenezer (Eben in the 1880 census), nor is she mentioned in Alfred Timothy Joy's 1883 obituary, which mentions both of his surviving siblings. If Mary Joy died in 1869, as some family historians suggest, that would account for her absence from the historical record in 1870 and 1880. If the 1887 date given for her death on her gravestone is correct, however, the remainder of her story is very uncertain. In the end, whenever Mary's time came, she was finally laid to rest (oddly under her maiden name) in the Joy family plot near her husband, Timothy, within sight of the spot where the young couple had, so many years before, spent their final moments together; Timothy and Mary's long separation was finally over.[20]

At the time of Mary's burial in 1887 on the southeastern edge of the old Joy farm, the Joy homestead had passed (though only very recently) from the family's hands. After Mary and her children departed from Durham in or around 1814 or 1815, Ebenezer, his new wife, Nancy, and Deacon Samuel and his wife, Hannah, busied themselves, with the assistance of hired help, attending to the many needs of the farm and, after the birth of Eben and Nancy's first child, John, in 1817, to the needs of their expanding household. Deacon Samuel also kept busy with church business, assuming a lead role in the hire in 1819 of a new minister, the Reverend Federal Burt, for the Durham church's long-vacant pastorate. The seasons passed in a gentle rhythm for the extended household, and the new couple's family grew quickly, with the birth of daughters Nancy and Sarah in 1819 and 1821, respectively.

Eben, as his account books (and subsequent will) make clear, prospered on the family's land and, following his father's path, turned his attention to his faith and to solidifying his own reputation and respectability. On August 12, 1822, the family, very likely including Mary and her children, gathered to repeat the vigil they had stood around Timothy back in 1813; this time, though, they assembled around the bed of the aged Hannah Meader Joy. Two years later, on October 31, 1824, just months after the birth of Eben and Nancy's fourth child, who they lovingly named Samuel in honor of the now frail patriarch of the family, Deacon Samuel breathed his last, joining his wife and children in eternal repose in the shaded grove he had so devotedly tended for his loved ones.[21]

The deacon's nurturing spirit was very much in evidence in the distribution of his worldly goods. Samuel's will opened with a heartfelt declaration and reminder of the critical importance of his faith: "I commit my soul into the hands of my faithful Creator through my merciful Redeemer in full faith of a future Resurrection." Thanking the Lord for the blessings he had bestowed upon him, Joy went on to bequeath to his two surviving daughters, Sally and Susanna, fifty dollars each and a full one-third share of his household goods. For his grandchildren born to his deceased daughter Polly and his son Timothy, he left one hundred dollars each. To his son Samuel, he left one dollar "in addition to what I have heretofore given him," and to Samuel's son, also named Samuel, he assigned "all my right and title in and unto the farm in New Durham whereon the said Samuel now dwells on the express condition that my said grandson Samuel Joy maintain and support his honored father and mother for and during their natural lives." The remainder of his property, including the family's Durham homestead, he left to Eben.[22]

Sadly, within three years time, grief would once again prevail over the Joy household, as first Eben (on August 8) and then Nancy (on October 1) passed away, leaving behind their five small children (another son, Henry, was born in April of 1826), the oldest of whom was but ten years old. Blessed with a large estate (valued at nearly six thousand dollars), Eben's children, who became wards of his brother-in-law, Judge Valentine Smith, faced a far more secure future than had their cousins Alfred Timothy, Mary, and Ebenezer. One-fifth of the Joy homestead, roughly forty-two acres, would eventually make its way to Eben's oldest son, John (though he sold the land and left Durham sometime between 1870 and his death in Manchester, New

Hampshire, in 1875), with the remainder of the family's acreage passing to the first of his daughters to marry (in 1846), Sarah, and her husband, David Griffiths, who also happened to be the son, by a second
marriage, of Edward Griffiths, a Packer's Falls neighbor and one of the
committee members appointed to determine the distribution of Eben
Joy's estate (the remaining assets were divided among the remaining
three children).[23]

Like the marriage of her parents, the bond between Sarah and
David ended prematurely, with David's untimely death in 1857. The
Griffith's short marriage was also cursed with the loss of two small children, Martha Frances and Martha Ann, both before the age of three.
Though she retained possession of the property for another thirteen
years, it is unclear whether Sarah actually lived on the farm. She undoubtedly associated with the homestead the plethora of tragic deaths
that she had experienced in her relatively short life (the loss of both
parents, a husband, and two daughters, which she would have been reminded of constantly with the proximity of the family plot). Indeed,
when she sold the property in 1870, she listed her address as Newmarket, Rockingham County, as opposed to Durham, Strafford County.[24]

When Sarah Griffiths decided to sell the farm that had been in her
family for four generations, she found a ready and able buyer in the
person of Alfred Timothy Joy, Portsmouth cabinetmaker, member of
the state legislature, and eldest son of Timothy Meader Joy, whose remains now lay at rest in the shaded plot across the road from the
homestead. On November 10, 1870, Sarah Griffiths transferred title of
the family farm over to her cousin for the sum of seventy-three hundred dollars. Interestingly, but perhaps not surprising, given the centrality of death in her life to date, Sarah spelled out, in great specificity,
her wishes for the Joy burial place. She declared that the plot, which
she insisted be known henceforth as the "Joy Family Burying
Ground," was to be "reserved for . . . any and all of the Joy family who
may here desire to bury their friends, and keep the plot they occupy in
good repair at the expense of those living of the nearest of kin each so
desiring and not to be used for any other purpose whatsoever." In addition, the signed deed included an agreement by Alfred to expand the
burial plot by seventy-five feet on both its northern and eastern sides.
Sometime shortly after purchasing the farm, Alfred Timothy Joy,
along with his wife, Sarah, and his daughter Mary, left their
Portsmouth home and relocated to the Packer's Falls neighborhood in
Durham, where, according to family history, Alfred Timothy "pulled

down the old buildings and erected a larger house." There Joy experienced life as a gentleman farmer, employing, by 1880, at least one hired hand to assist him in his endeavors. The irony that he, the orphaned son of the failed trader and convicted slanderer Timothy Joy, would come to own the family's hard-won patrimony, that he would stand on the same land as that paragon of dignity Deacon Samuel without anyone questioning his right to claim the mantle of respectability and success that the deacon had so selflessly toiled to bestow on the Joy name, could not have been lost on Alfred Timothy as he surveyed the well-worn fields and as he wandered among the mossy gravestones, his father's among them, in the shaded glen across the road. What tremendous comfort he must have felt knowing that yet another generation of Joys had been sustained by this farm and by the hard work of the many Joys who had toiled on this land before him. Though he would be the last Joy to live in the old family homestead and to work the Packer's Falls farm begun by his great-grandfather Samuel (he died of pneumonia in the house that he had built to replace the old family homestead, on the same plot where his father had died seventy years before, in early May of 1883, and the property passed from the family), Alfred Timothy could go to his grave with the satisfaction of knowing that he had brought his father's legacy full circle. Timothy Meader Joy— through his struggle and sacrifice, through his successes, through his humility in accepting his failures, and through his indomitable will to begin anew—had instilled within his children the value of hard work, humbleness, and perseverance. Because of their achievements and successes, he would not be rendered a failure.[25]

Chapter 6

DIARIES, DEAD ENDS,
AND DISCOVERIES

I became familiar with Timothy Meader Joy entirely by accident and was moved to write about his life and times through sheer coincidence and good fortune. In the process of conducting research for my dissertation at the Bentley Historical Library at the University of Michigan, I was drawn to the correspondence of James F. Joy, a Michigan railroad attorney and politician of the Civil War era, whose papers were part of a larger collection of manuscripts gathered by his son, the Detroit industrialist Henry Bourne Joy, one of the founders of the Packard Motor Car Company. After having finished reading a box of correspondence related to James Joy's railroad interests and local politics, I requested the retrieval of additional materials from the collection housed in the archive's stacks. Hoping to find something of interest to fend off the boredom attendant with what might be a lengthy wait, I took one last look in the box I had just been working in and noticed a file labeled "genealogy." Sensing that the file might provide an interesting diversion while I waited for my new materials to arrive, I removed it from the box. There, appropriately enough tucked inconspicuously away amid numerous pedigree charts and other ordinary documents prepared by a genealogist hired by Henry Joy to compile his family's ancestry, was an eighty-four-page, unbound, handwritten journal. The heavy, yellowed, unlined pages, stood in stark contrast to the brighter, typescript documents immediately surrounding it and possessed a, by then, very familiar musty smell. While a bit tattered around its edges, the pages were covered with the neat copperplate script that we associate with a formal education. Attached to the manuscript was a simple receipt documenting the purchase of the diary—

written in 1812 by Timothy M. Joy (who, it turns out, was a cousin of Henry Joy's grandfather, also named James, mentioned in the journal)—by the Joy family genealogist from a New England antiques shop. Curious, I began to read, "Ipswich Prison, March the 20th, 1812. Confined in a dismal awful Prison. . . ."

The timing of my discovery of Timothy Joy's prison journal could not have been better if planned, as it came at a point in my professional training where I had become enamored with a relatively new and somewhat controversial mode of historical analysis known as microhistory. As a history student, I was, by this point in my training, very familiar with the ever-growing body of books written by social historians exploring the lives of everyday folk. But as much fuel for my imagination as I found in Paul Johnson's meticulous description of the collective experience and religious awakening of early nineteenth-century shopkeepers in Rochester, New York, or in Thomas Dublin's sweeping exploration of the lives and experiences of the Lowell Mill operatives (to cite but two examples), I desperately desired more; I wanted to be able to bore down into individual households and into the lives of these folks to understand how they, as individuals, experienced and shaped the changes outlined in these works. Imagine my glee, then, when I discovered microhistory. Here, in works such as Laurel Thatcher Ulrich's penetrating and personal recounting of the life of a simple Maine midwife named Martha Ballard or John Demos's exploration of the captivity of young Eunice Williams and her subsequent rejection of white society, historians did exactly that. "The glory" of this type of an approach, according to one of microhistory's most noted practitioners, Richard Brown, "lies in its power to recover and reconstruct past events by exploring and connecting a wide range of data sources so as to produce a contextual, three dimensional, analytic narrative in which actual people as well as abstract forces shape events."[1]

Indeed, it was my fascination with this genre of historical writing, steeped as it was in a close read of the detail and minutiae of the individual lives of ordinary people or of obscure localized events and in examination of the connections between these lives/events and broader historical trends, that had initially led me to the collection housing the journal; I was looking for information about a group of Michigan farmers who attacked railroad trains because the trains had been accidently killing their livestock. A quick scan of Joy's journal convinced me that the document was tailor-made for microhistory. First and foremost, Joy's arrest and trial for defamation offered a ready point of entrée into the hard-fought world of politics in the early republic. But as I read further, I also realized that the journal revealed a story of an ordinary person caught up in a series of rather common and yet extraordinary and transformative events in the nation's history: the foundation of a new market-oriented economy in the United States and the personal and cultural ambivalence that accompanied that shift, the intense bitterness and distrust engendered by the rise of partisan politics in the new nation, and the vertigo and uncertainty induced by the nation's spiral toward a second war with Great Britain. Joy's crushing indebtedness, his heartrending decision to leave his family, his barroom exploits, and his subsequent arrest and incarceration provided a very ready means of engaging readers and drawing them into this broader narrative. Beyond Joy's compelling story, though, this journal, by capturing Timothy Joy's own voice, provided an accessible way of gauging one person's personal thoughts and feelings about these (and many other) events. What better way to explore and explicate the "webs of significance"[2] that shaped the lived experience of a time and place, I concluded, than to examine Timothy Joy's interactions with these changes? So I set out to learn as much as possible about Timothy Meader Joy, his family, the places where he lived and visited, the things that he did, and the times in which he lived.

While employing a microhistorical model to make sense of Timothy Joy's experiences seemed perfectly logical to me, other historians do not necessarily share my enthusiasm for the genre. Critics of the approach often raise questions about the relevancy of the people or events under consideration. These people and, especially, the events they found themselves involved in, they contend, while often very interesting, are obscure because they only mattered to the individuals involved or for a fleeting moment in a particular place and time. Moreover, they often contend, the tight focus and the overwhelming level of detail that characterizes such work smacks of antiquarianism and leaves the uniformed reader mired in a good story (or, in the minds of some, a quagmire of facts) but unable to draw any broader significance from such a narrative. Beyond this, these same skeptics insist, many microhistories rely too heavily on speculation and guesswork in the face of gaps in the historical record—speculation all too often accepted as truth and certainty by readers.

Indeed, not a small number of colleagues and friends recommended that I forgo writing a microhistory altogether and that I approach Joy's journal in other ways. Some, for example, urged me to pair Joy's journal with other extant diaries from the period to construct what they believed would be a richer, more synthetic monograph exploring the era's most salient changes on a broader, macro level. Others proposed that I focus more narrowly on a single theme in the journal, such as Joy's religious struggle, in order to explore how Joy fits into the larger literature on the subject. Still others suggested that I tie Joy's writing more broadly to an emerging body of work on prisoner literature.

Certainly, these types of broad studies have added much to our understanding of the American past, and I have learned a great deal from them. In fact, they actively informed my own thinking about some of what I read in Joy's journal. For me, however, this sort of work lacks the immediacy, the complexity, the intimacy, and even—for all of its frustrations—the ambiguity of a closer, microlevel study. They fall short in their ability to explore individual and universal human concerns/experiences—in all their glorious intricacy, imprecision, and murkiness—as lived in a particular moment and place and as experienced by those who found themselves grappling with broad social, cultural, economic and political forces that were often indiscernible, hard to decipher, or completely incomprehensible to those living in that moment. Joy, for instance, knew little to nothing of globalization, markets, or the abstract workings of instruments of credit. For me, the ability to play around in this historical mud was incredibly appealing. Individual actions and decisions are never as black and white or as orderly as many historians who operate in the world of broad, observable trends might have us believe. Knowing that large numbers of Joy's contemporaries found themselves in financial difficulty in an evolving economy is useful, but knowing the details about how an individual such as Joy, who was caught up in the transformation, felt about what was happening or explained what he (and, likely, others like him) had experienced is, in my mind, inherently more interesting and useful. All of us, as unique individuals, experience our world in ways that are both similar and different from those around us. Microhistory's ability to capture this sense of contingency thus renders the past more accessible and more truthful than any other genre. It enables us to literally reach back in time and touch the past and the lives of those who lived in the past in a very real and personally intimate way.

Having settled on my approach, my next task was to decide on an organizational scheme for the book; that is, I had to determine what story I wanted to tell, how to best do that given the available evidence, and how to make clear to my readers what I perceived to be the larger significance of that story. For me, the pivotal moment in the story revealed in the journal was Timothy Joy's run-in with his creditors and his subsequent decision to flee. While it is certainly possible that my own academic interests and work on the nineteenth-century economic transformation known to American historians as the "market revolution" predisposed me to gravitate to this event, I also believed that most readers would conclude (and this desire to allow readers to participate in the process of discovery along with me led me to plan to include the journal in its entirety) that this event was indeed seminal, because had it not been for this incident, none of what subsequently happened—and what brought Joy's until-then-insignificant life into wider view—would have transpired. Obviously, I needed to know more about the circumstances surrounding Joy's flight. It followed that I would also need to know about his early life in order to be able to make any sense of what had happened to him. Was he from a family where indebtedness was a common worry? If not, what had happened to him? How much of what happened could be attributed to Joy himself, and how much was due to larger forces beyond his immediate control? What options would someone like Joy have had when faced with his circumstances? What recourse did his creditors have under the law?

The events following Timothy Joy's flight from debt were much easier to trace and describe. His three-month prison journal offered me a day-by-day accounting of his arrest, trial, fines, daily routine, visitors, and subsequent release. But, I wondered, what happened next? Did trouble continue to follow Joy? Was he ever able to make something of himself? Increasingly, I realized that I needed to undertake a larger study of Timothy Joy's life—not to attempt a biography of Joy, but, rather, to find out more about him so that I could make better sense of what led him to that fateful day in March of 1812 and to his subsequent arrest and notoriety.

Joy's journal itself posed an interesting set of questions for me. Diaries and journals are staples for those engaged in historical research and writing. The documents are particularly valued for the type of information that they often contain: detailed notations of daily occurrences, events, and weather, often for very long periods of a person's life; accounts of money owed or services rendered; introspective discussions of motivations and behavior; comments and observations about broader trends; and intimate personal thoughts. Though it is commonly assumed that diaries and journals are very private documents whose intended purpose is to serve as a vehicle for self-discovery and confession of our innermost secrets, experts who study this particular form of writing have increasingly come to see their general purpose as being much more public. Indeed, Joy himself suggests such a purpose when he acknowledges on the journal's first page, "I have thought proper to commit to paper while in my rational moments the most extraordinary circumstances which have happened to my Imprisonment, as correctly as I can remember them wishing, should I lose my reason that this paper may be carefully preserved & sent to my family." In other words, Joy's writing, while clearly offering the young prisoner a cathartic and safe outlet for his confused and vulnerable mind, was also undertaken for a broader, more public purpose. His writing was not necessarily intended to be hidden away. What does this mean for how we are to interpret Joy's writing? Is he spilling his deepest secrets in his journal? Is he filtering his feelings in the knowledge that others may be reading his words at some future date? In what ways are the public purposes for which he is writing shaping the material that he included in the work, if at all? How, in other words, is the journal shaped by broader cultural forces, and in what ways is it a reflection of those forces?[3]

This genre of publicly minded journal writing was nothing new in Timothy Joy's New England. On the contrary, generations of Puritan New Englanders maintained lengthy journals in which they detailed their spiritual ups and downs and where they worked out their personal theological issues. Certainly, these journals were intimate spaces filled with personal lamentation, confession, and grief. They also, however, stand as public testimonies to the power of God and the necessity of following a spiritual life. This dual purpose is very clear in Joy's religious writings. As introspective, personal, and often emotionally painful as those specific entries are, they were also designed to serve a higher purpose: to induce the reader to examine their own individual fate. When we read these sections and empathize with the lonely and confused Joy, we are responding exactly as he hoped his readers would—we see some of ourselves in him. We take stock of our own fate and of the human condition.

Joy's journal is also what some experts of the genre have identified as a journal of "situation"; that is, it is a journal begun specifically to report on an unusual event in an individual's life. Triggered by his arrest and subsequent imprisonment, Joy's journal recounts what was, by any account, a rather unsettling and troubling chapter in the young man's life. A common form of journal writing, situational journals offered a secure place for individuals to work through unfamiliar circumstances they found themselves confronting. The very act of keeping the diary, in fact, became a point of stability, solace, and order in what had certainly become a very chaotic period for Joy. As is common with this particular journal form, a resolution of the circumstances that triggered the journal—in this case, Timothy Joy's release from prison in June of 1812—brought about an end to the journal. Unfortunately, we do not know whether Joy packed the journal when he departed or left it behind as a cautionary tale for those who might read it.[4]

After scrutinizing the journal for many months and after many more months spent ruminating about possible chapter schemes, it occurred to me that Joy himself was suggesting an answer to my quandary through his own writing. The journal, of course, is organized chronologically by month and day. Beyond this obvious fact, however, it also became clear to me as I read the journal (you might see things differently) that the focus of Joy's writing shifts over time: from an early emphasis on his indebtedness, his flight from his creditors, and his attempts to grapple with the meaning of these events; to a more focused exploration of religion and spirituality during the middle portions of the journal; and finally, toward its end, to a more politically oriented focus. That these same themes happened to coincide with some of the most important topics under consideration within the professional historical community—the market revolution and the emergence of a cash economy, the antebellum religious revival known as the Second Great Awakening, and the political culture of the nation's nascent political party system—only brought this reality into sharper focus for me. Why not, I determined, let Joy be my guide and try to tell his story by emphasizing the very things that he deemed, as evidenced in his own words, central to his life, at least in the moment in which he was writing? I thus decided to allow what some historians might label the "provenance" of the document to guide my writing. Moreover, I also decided, given the ebb and flow of Joy's thematic focus, that it would be an easy thing to pair the themes with one of the months recorded in the journal and to thus follow a more familiar and comfortable chronological format. It seemed to me to be a natural pairing. I could then add a chapter covering what I would be able to learn about Joy's life and family circumstances prior to his flight and another that followed his life beyond his release. One additional thought occurred to me at this stage of the planning process; I determined to employ a technique in the book that I have found to be particularly effective in the classroom: find a dramatic story to encapsulate the main theme of the chapter, to build reader interest, and to reinforce the usefulness of microlevel work to explore complex and macrolevel themes. As the details of Joy's life unfolded, I discovered no shortage of dramatic moments.

There are, of course, other choices that might have been made regarding the book's structure, especially in light of the obvious limitations in the evidentiary base, which became clear over time. Timothy Joy's prison journal is an extraordinarily rich and detailed accounting of a particular series of events unfolding at a specific historical moment. To make more sense of the journal entries and to contextualize and complete Joy's story, it was necessary to immerse myself in the available historical record. First and foremost, I needed to learn what I could about Joy beyond what the journal told me. Fortunately, the Joy family genealogist had done some of the legwork for me. Through the published family history, I was able to determine some of the particulars of Joy's early years (date and place of birth, birth order, mother's and father's names and dates of birth/death, marriage date, spouse's name, names and birth dates of his children) and that Timothy went on to serve in the War of 1812 after his release from prison. I was also stunned to learn that he died within a year of his release from prison, leaving behind his wife and three small children. But what else could I learn? Where exactly did he live? Where had he attended church? What did his neighbors think of him? What factors led him to Middleton? Was he from a poor family? How large was his store? When and from whom did he purchase it? Who did he owe money to? What happened to his family after his death?

Research of this nature is tedious and slow work, entailing trips to a wide range of repositories to ensure that no potential facet of the story is ignored. Many were the dead ends and frustrations. For instance, though I knew from the journal that Joy owed money to the mercantile firm of Leigh and Ferguson (as the journal makes clear, they hear of his incarceration in Massachusetts and file suit against him there), I was never able to learn more about the nature of Joy's economic difficulties prior to his flight from Middleton. My initial queries into this issue led me first to the Stafford County Courthouse in Dover, New Hampshire, to survey records from the Court of Common Pleas (the court where writs against debtors would be issued).

Sadly, however, I arrived too late, as the records had recently been transferred to the state archive in Concord. After a quick phone call to that repository, I learned that the collection had not yet been processed and was thus unavailable to researchers. Crushed, I proceeded to Concord the next day anyway, to view some other materials. There, I was surprised to learn from the person at the reference desk (the person I had spoken to before was out for the day) that I could indeed look at the court records, though they would be completely unorganized. Knowing that this window of opportunity would close quickly (as the archivist who had told me the collection was closed was to return the following day), I immediately plowed into the boxes. The documents, still in their original-period cloth ties, were covered in dust, mildew, and rodent droppings. I plunged into them with great enthusiasm and excitement nonetheless. Alas, though I discovered many writs issued on behalf of Leigh and Ferguson, I could not locate any, even attributable to other plaintiffs, related to Timothy Joy. Tired, dirty, deflated, and with very irritated eyes, I completed the last box just before the close of business that day and headed back to my hotel room to regroup. Sadly, that piece of Joy's story remains a mystery.

Far fewer, though intensely rewarding, were the major finds. For instance, a trip (the last of many) to the Registrar of Deeds Office in Dover to explore the buying and selling of land in New Durham by Timothy's father, Samuel Joy, turned up a reference, embedded toward the bottom of a long legal document, informing me that Timothy was living in that community prior to purchasing his store in Middleton in December 1811. As I was about to depart, it occurred to me that I had not yet examined the deeds for the period between Joy's release from prison in June 1812 and his subsequent death the following year. Did he still own the store at his death? If so, what had Mary done with it? A quick review of the records revealed that Joy had sold his Middleton property immediately upon his return to New Hampshire. Had this settled his debt? I could not know, but it did help me to better understand his choice to enter the military and the reasons for his death in Durham and not in Middleton. Similarly, the chance discovery of an account book kept by Timothy's father and his brother Ebenezer for the period under consideration, held by the Baker Library at Harvard (how they obtained this book remains a mystery), revealed much about the family's efforts to assist Mary Joy and her children after her husband's untimely death.

Still, as more and more scraps of evidence came to light and as the number of sources of potential new evidence diminished, it became abundantly clear that there was much that I would never be able to know about Timothy Joy or his life. Faced with this reality, I, like virtually every other historian working in the field of microhistory, was forced to rely on the secondary literature's description of general trends and macrolevel behavior and to close gaps with reasoned speculation and conjecture, that is, to conclude that Joy's life probably mirrored the overall trends historians have been able to document for specific places at certain moments in time. In response to these gaps, some colleagues of mine, who were familiar with the work and with the shortcomings in the historical record, encouraged me to rethink my approach and to restructure the book. Scrap the family history, some said; it offers little insight into Joy. Dump the discussion of his economic struggles, others affirmed; you do not have enough there to go on. Yet others proposed a tighter focus on only two of the main themes found in the journal—religion and politics. Jettison the other material, they urged, and organize your book around Joy's spiritual journey and/or the evolution and manifestations of his Democratic-Republican partisanship. In my mind, to have pursued any of these courses of action would have been a travesty and would have left much of Joy's rich journal underutilized and unexplained. Likewise, in my mind, a simplification of the book's primary focus would not be true to Joy's own expressed priorities, nor would it have facilitated a full and complex discussion of the nuances and detail of an individual life lived in a specific moment in time, the precise elements that microlevel analysis was designed to make visible. Certainly, there are limitations to what we can say with any degree of certainty about Timothy Joy and his relevance to the many important currents swirling through America at the momentous juncture in time during which he wrote his prison diary. In the end, it is up to the individual reader to determine whether the choices I have made and the arguments I have put forward in this work are justified in the face of what we can know about Timothy Joy and his circumstances. I have shared with you what I was able to learn and what I think I was able to piece together about his life. I now invite you to read the journal for yourself. What are the stories that you see in this document? What kinds of questions would you ask of it? How would you tell this story? I hope that you find the journal to be as engaging and thought-provoking as I have found it to be, and I very much look forward to learning about how you and other historians reconstitute and refine this story.

Appendix

DIARY OF TIMOTHY M. JOY

page 1

Ipswich Prison, March the 20th, 1812.

Confined in a dismal awful Prison and sometimes so absent in mind as not to recollect the circumstances which have ocured to me since I left my home, I have thought proper to commit to paper while in my rational moments the most extraordinary circumstances which have happened to my Imprisonment, as correctly as I can remember them wishing, should I lose my reason that this paper may be carefully preserved & sent to my family. My circumstances being very much embarrassed at Middleton, N. H. I came to the resolution of quiting this ~~country~~ place for a season, & going to Salem[1] there to endeavor to get into some line of business or other to earn money to pay my debts, my family being dear to me I often before I started doubted my duty to remain but on the 17th of the present month, my creditors broke upon me and took every article I possesed in the world, except some household goods I had previously sold to my brother.[2] Thus circumstanced, I had but one alternative, to fly or go to Prison being naturly timid & by no means used to misfortunes I new not which to turn,

page 2

but, at length, my friends urg'd my departure. Oh my God, what were the feelings of my mind at that trying moment. I kised my dear wife & she sat all bathed in tears & my two helpless babes[3] lay asleep

& rush'd out of the house in a hurry, jumped into my sleigh & drove off, I hardly knew which way. In a little time however I became more rational concluded to go to Gilmanton[4] thinking by taking such a cicuitous rout to Salem I should escape pursuit. I accordingly drove on but my horse began to tire I had then drove ten miles, now I was again in trouble, was affraid of every person I met with for fear that they would give information which way I had gone, my mind was so much disturbed that I began to lose my recollection. I was sensible of it & being in a piece of wood I stoped my sleigh kneeled down by its side & poured out a humble prayr to god that he would be pleased to preserve my ————————

page 3

reason let what ~~would what~~ ever befall me, after I arose I felt more calm & composed pursued my journey, came to a place caled the Iron works in Gilmanton where I exchanged my tired horse for one young & sprightly. & here was the begining of my troubles, if I may use the expression, for previous to this the dependance I placed on the promises of God & the pleasure I felt in serving him, supported me in all my afflictions, but here I got into lively company and being off my watch, the Devil put it into some persons head to ask me my name, which before I had time to consider the consequences, I deny'd: being afraid I should be known & pursued if I owned my true name. Oh what horror did now seize upon my soul. I had told a falshood. Where now was my religion. All vanished all gone. I then began to despond. The adversury persuaded me that I never knew what it was to be regenerated and born again, that I had been deceiv'd, else I should have been kept from sining. I accordingly settled down in this dangerous opinion & concluded myself lost & undone both soul and body, that I was rejected of God, else he would not have suffered me to have fallen from affluence to

page 4

poverty, from serving him to be a subject of sin & satan. Frantic with rage & despair I left Gilmanton for Salem but my brain was so much disordered I never yet have been able to recolect which way I came to Haverill in Mass[achusetts] where I arrived about noon on fryday the 20th Inst. Thus I traveled about two days without end or aim

distrauted in my mind & not caring where I went I suppose I
traveled fifty or sixty miles in this situation when I arived at Haverill
I was more composed & enquired the way to Salem & was informed
by some young Gentlemen with whom I dined & who were
discoursing about politics at the table.[5] I having drank a considerable
quantity of spiritous liquor before sitting down became unknowingly
a disputant which drew the atention of the gentlemen towards me.[6] I
stated some circumstances respecting Timo[thy] Pickering which
excited their curiosity when they fel to asking me questions which I
answered I hardly know how for esteeming myself a lost man
deserted of God & abandoned by man I cared not what

page 5

I said. At last I was roused to sense of my situation by being
requested by one of the party, whose name I have since learned is
Frances Eaton, a Republican Lawyer, to step to his Office & attest to
what I had said. What could I do. I must either acknowledge that I
had told a falsehood or tell a greater, however I had no time for
consideration. I went with him & among other things stated I was a
Brittish subject by the name of Nathaniel Emery, that I was knowing
to a correspondence being carried on between Timo[thy] Pickering
& a Brittish Officer in Canada. He wanted me to swear to it but
thank God I was kept from sealing my destruction in that manner.
He wrote down what I had stated & requested me to copy it which I
did & came away as desperate as a man could be. There are a great
many more circumstances that I have heard of since which I cannot
now recollect being in such agitation of mind & despairing of ever
enheriting eternal life I was so desperate I cared not what I said or
did. I rode in my sleigh about six or eight miles not knowing where I
was going untill crossing a pond in the woods my horse fell through
the ice where

page 6

the water was three or four feet deep & it was with great difficulty I
got him out. After I did I took another byepath & wandered in it
some time. At last I came to a road & enquiring of two men the road
to salem was enformed I was as far from Salem as I was when I
entered the woods. These complicated misfortunes added to the

horror of my mind, put me in a complete frenzy. I drove on however at a smart rate until I found the road entirely bare. I then left my sleigh & harness at a tavern I know not where, drank a considerable quantity of wine, bought a bridle, took my saddle I brought with me & started off. I rode very fast untill I arived at Salem, about, as I have since been informed, eleven oclock at night. I enquired for a tavern of the first man I met who directed me to the Salem Hotel where I put up for the night.[7] Arived here I began to be more rational. Being asked my name by the landlord I told him my true one, viz., Timothy M. Joy. When I had done this I felt more calm, but still I was very much

page 7

out of order & varied from the truth in a number of instances this evening, but I felt determined on the morrow to refrain & endeavor to collect my scattered senses, but in the morning, Saturday, the 21st Inst., I felt a return of all the horror of mind. I thought I had fallen irecoverably falen from grace, that there was no mercy for such a wretch as I was. These thoughts drove me to despair. I thought I should see no more peace in this world & it mattered not what became of me under these impressions. I mounted my horse & rode round the City & down to the Fort or Castle & back again.[8] When I was coming back I felt a little hope that I should yet once more be brought back to the true fould of Christ. I tryed to pray & felt some comfort, but I felt as tho some heavy judgment awaited me as a correction for my past follies. but I was in a measure resigned to the will of God, let what would hapen. In this I was not deceived, for in about an hour after the above reflections passed through my mind, as I was viewing a fine new ship which was lying at the head of Derby's wharf[9] a gentleman, whose name I have since learned is John Pickering, son of Timothy Pickering, came up to me & engaged me in conversation untill a Constable, with about three hundred men & boys at his heels, came up & made me a prisoner in the

page 8

name of the Commonwealth of Massachusetts.[10] I asked what was my crime. He told me defaming the caracter of Timothy Pickering at Haverill. I had but a confused idea of what I said there, &

apprehended no great injury. I delivered myself up without the least resistance & was promised good usuage. In a few minutes along came a big belly'd Depputy Sherriff, who caut hold of me, riffled my pocket of my pocket pistol, pocket book & money & paper. The cowardly wretch not content with this dragged me into a store hard by & obliged me to strip every rag of my clothes off except my shirt. It was then I learned that I had falen into the hands of the Federalists, whose tender mercies are cruelty & that I was to expect no mercy at their hands. While they were searching me it seemed as though one spoke to me & told me that it was a mercy of God that I was so soon overtaken by Gods judgments, so that I might be brought to repentance, ere it was eternally too late. I saw God was just & merciful.

page 9

Just in bringing me to punishment for my transgression, merciful in not suffering me to go on till by my disobedience I should have sealed my own damnation. I could truly say with David Psalms 40th Chap 12 & 13th verses innumerable evils have compassed me about: mine iniquities have taken hold upon me, so that I am not able to look up: they are more than the hairs of mine head: therefore mine heart faileth me. Be pleased O Lord to deliver me: O Lord, make haste to help me, &c—my despair left me & I could not help rejoiceing to think of the Goodness of God while they were leading me along the streets to the Courthouse for examination.[11] I was escorted to the Courthouse by thousands & as they came along I heard them say one to another, he ought to be hanged. Some said, he ought to be imprisoned for life & some passed one sentence on me, some another, but through all this the Lord caried me in a wonderfull manner. I can truly say that I felt as calm & resigned to the will of God as though I had been going to Church. But my heart began to flutter after I got into the courthouse, to see so many

page 10

spectators all I believed inimical to me. I was araigned before Mr. Justice Prince[12] a Federalist who after reading the complaint & warrant asked me if I was guilty or not guilty. I then rose and told my story how I was oblidged to flee from home that misfortunes had

overcome my reason & if I had done or said wrong it must be
attributed to a disordered brain, that I meant nobody any harm, had
hardly any recollection of what had happened to me since I left
home, & threw myself on the mercy of the Court notwithstanding.
This & the examination of my papers which proved to a
demonstration the truth of my asertions the Fed[eralist] Justice
called in a cloud of Fed[eralist] witnesses & among the rest the son
of old namesake who decoyed me into the hands of the Fed[eralist]
officer, to prove what a poor unfortunate distrauted man said at
Haverill against a Fed[eralist] of windham,[13] and employ'd a
Fed[eralist] lawyer[14] to examine a man who hardly now knew how to
arrange his ideas much less how to answer one who possessed all the
art of a Fed[eralist] crossquestioner, but after a long examination
which continued about two hours, his Fed[eralist] Honour with the
advice of his Fed[eralist] Council required poor me to find bail in the
sum of five Hundred Dollars or else be comitted to

page 11

prison there to lie in dirt untill the sitting of the Supreme
Fed[eralist] Court at Ipswich which would commence its Fed[eralist]
session on the fourth Wednesday of April ensuing. Not being able to
procure bail, I was committed to Salem Jail[15] on Saturday, 21st of
March 1812, about two oclock in the afternoon, destitute of
everything except life—my great coat was at the hotel where I put up
the night before, as was likewise my mittens & all my other clothes
except what I had on. I was not allowed any fire no not enough to
light a cigar. I had but The room in which I was confined was in the
second story of the building it was very open & cold & I thought I
should have frozen before morning, having only two blankets to
cover me. My bed consisted of a sorry two cloth sack stuffed with
straw which made my bones ache again. But I am rather before my
story. After I was put in prison I was visited by many of the leading
Republicans belonging in the city whose names I shall at present
conceal, who encouraged me with assurances of friendship, told me I
owed my imprisonment to the Fed[eralist]s & not to them. This I
knew before. I shall always remember with gratitude the kind offices
of these Gentlemen to a poor prisoner who could not make them
compenceation for their trouble. The gentlemen Fed[eralist]s
likewise very often made their appearance, not contented with

insulting me out of doors they came to try to catch me in my
conversation that they might make use of my own words

page 12

against me on my tryal, at least so I thought by their conversation. Of
this I was warned by a friend, one of the first caracters in Salem, who
visited & conversed frely with me daily while I taried there, for
which he has my thanks.

I was put into a room with one Neil McCoy who ~~was~~ being in debt
to the Fed[eralist]s and refusing to vote for their candidates incured
their resentment & of course was deprived of his employ & thrown
into prison as he told me while his wife & three small children were
left to beg their bread. Oh—the humanity of the Fed[eralist]s. Who
after reading this would not be a Fed[eralist]. This man possesed a
humane heart. He took unwearied pains to comfort me in my
affliction to cheer up my drooping spirits & make me resigned to my
fate. He partisipated in my sorrows & endeavoured to sooth me in
my afflictions by recounting his own sufferings. The next day after I
was commited being the sabbath I asked for a bible that I might read
& contemplate by myself being deprived of the priviledge of going to
meeting, but was informed it was against the rules of the Prison to
allow the prisoners any books. This at first was very trying to me,
especially when I saw the people going to meeting. O how my heart
panted for liberty to join them when I thought of my dear

page 13

friends & brethen in Middleton who then were doubtless assembling
themselves together assaying to worship God, with whom I had
formerly had so many comforting seasons. It seemed as though my
heart would have burst within me. My tears flowed afresh & my head
grew dizzy. For a considerable time I hardly knew ~~not~~ where I was,
but at last God in his mercy looked in pity upon me & granted me a
good meeting. I prayed sung shouted & felt happy. I was rational &
calm in my mind. I saw that the Lord had not quite forsaken me, for
I felt the same good spirit working in me that I was wont to feel
when encompassed by the children of God at Middleton, which
made my heart leap for joy. I felt the promise of God verified where
he says in Psalms 40th 15,[16] Call upon me in the day of trouble I will

deliver thee & thou shalt glorify me. But to return to my narrative, about noon Mr. McCoy's wife came to visit him. She was a good looking woman of about twenty eight years of age. She also was very kind to me. She traveled two miles to find out a young man by the name of Pierce a native of N H who Mr. McCoy recomended to me to carry a letter to my parents, and upon hearing me wish for a bible & conveniences to write she the next

page 14

day, after consulting her husband, sent me down from Danvers where she resided her own Bible & a book entitled the beauties of the Bible, likewise a table & chair, a plate knife & fork, two mugs & some small articles to make me comfortable. Thus the Lord raised me up friends when I little expected it. He likewise recompenced them for their kindness in an unexpected manner for soon after the above named things arived two gentlemen came and bailed Mr. McCoy out of prison. As soon as this kind hearted man was at liberty he went immediately about procuring me nessesaries. I gave him some money with which he bought me some biscuit, sugar, butter, writing paper & these added greatly to my comfort, for before I was destitute of the necessaries of life. My allowance consisted only of a pint of coffe & a piece of coarse brown bread about as a cracker & this only twice every twenty four hours. I ate heartily of my new stock of provisions felt afresh'd & in a measure contented with my condition. I sat down & wrote to my father, sent off the letter by Mr. Pierce & resigned myself up into the hands of God. There was confined in the apartment above directly over me two black women named Sal & Eleanor. Sal who was confined for theft, kept continually

page 15

singing lewd songs, cursing & swearing. I talked to her of the things of the kingdom but she only mocked at it. I then hired her with a glass of spirit every morning to swear no more. She promised me she would not & kept her word while I taried. I now had my clothes sent me accompanied with my trunk & papers in a confused state. This evening just after I had laid myself down at night on my straw shivering with cold & more than usually dejected in spirit, I was rous'd by the rattling of key. In a few minutes my doors were opened & another unfortunate Republican was ushered in. I have forgotten his name. He informed me that a malicious Fed[eralist] had purchased a note against for about twenty dollars & notwithstanding two responsible men offered to be his bail had dragged him from his home & family consisting of his wife & seven children to Prison for the express purpose of keeping him from voting at the ensuing election. O Federalism, where is thy blush. I had but little rest this night on account of the cold & the nausious smell emitted from the vault. ~~Tuesday,~~ I shall now endeavor to keep a regular diary of what has occured to me daily as far as I can recollect ————

Tuesday March 24th. This morning, Anthony the negro waiter informed me that I should come out today.

page 16

I asked by what means, but he said he was not at liberty to inform me farther. Hope began to play round my heart that some of the numerous friends I had acquired in Salem had come to the determination to bail me out. As one man as I was told had the day before offered one Hundred Dollars towards paying up my bond & setting me at liberty. I had my brown bread & coffe brought me early this morning & was told I must be ready to come out in half an hour. I ate but little, pack'd up my cloths in my saddle bags & waited anxiously the moment of deliverance. But no tongue can tell, no pen describe my feelings when Ann, the black girl who cook'd for the prison, came up and told me without any preface that a Sherriff had arived from Ipswich with orders to remove me to the stone prison in that place, that I was likewise to be put in Irons like a malefactor. This piece of news overcame me quite. I sat down in my chair quite insensible of what passed until I saw the sherriff enter. I then fell out of my chair on the floor insensible. How long I laid in this condition I know not. All I recollect is that when I came to myself a little, there were many people

page 17

standing round me & the jailor, Mr. Tho[ma]s Hudson, spoke to me and asked if I knew him. I reached out my hand & he & the sheriff lifted me up & helped me downstairs. They then brought me some

spirit which I drank. I felt more calm untill he went to put on my
irons then I was again overcome. I besought him not to put me in
irons. Told him I would go with him peaceably, but he said it was
ordered so to do & it was out of his power to grant my request.
Suffise it to say I was put in irons & conveyed to Ipswich prison by
Mr. Brown,[17] a Deputy Sheriff in the County of Essex. He used me
very well but I had been so agitated I was absent & my recollection
gone during the greater part of the time we were on the road. He
shewed me the residence of Old namesake.[18] It is situated in
Windham[19] about a quarter of a mile from the post road. The house
is a large two story building, wears an ancient aspect. I suppose he
wishes in everything to represent his brethern the ole Brittish Lords
in his buildings as well as his writings. It puts one in mind of the old
feudal times. But enough of this old castle and its owner. To return
when I arived at the Prison I found the high Sherriff[20] there who
had been waiting for our arrival some. He acosted me with the
familiarity of an old

page 18

acquaintance, endeavored to calm my agitated spirits by promising
me good usuage, caused me to sit by the fire, caled for some spirit &
a dinner for me of which after I had partaken I felt greatly refreshed.
He then accompanied me to the room alloted for me but on my
requesting to be put where I could speak to some person he
immediately granted my request & conducted me to the west wing of
the Prison where was confined one Elisha Guerney a native of
Newbury Port. He had been confined in this prison nine months.
His crime was secreting some articles in his house in the time of the
great fire in N[ewbury]Port.[21] With this man was I confined. I felt
thankfull that my situation was no worse. Our room was clean &
wholesom. We had blankets enough, the light of two windows each
containing nine squares of glass, but the light was diminished
considerably by two rows of iron grating on each window, made of
bars two inches square which were let into the stone wall by means of
drills, and the windows being placed on the inside of this wall which
is three feet thick. In company with Guerny I felt quite contented.
He was a man about sixty four years of age, was

page 19

a very sensible man, serious and sober, used no profane language, read considerable in the bible & was very fond of having prayers evening & morning. He would do anything I asked him to do cherfully & endeavoured to cheer up my drooping spirits all in his power. ~~The sheriff~~

Wednesday 25. The High Sheriff, Maj. Fairlee of Ipswich came to see me this morning & taried about an hour. He was very lively in his conversation, promised to interest himself in my behalf & to befriend me all in his power. His pleasing aspect & conversation won my confidence & I related to him every circumstance I could recollect relating to what brought me into this difficulty. He was pleased I believe with my naration & gave me some good advice & left me promising to call again soon. I was better reconciled to my fate this day than I had been before. I had victuals enough & at my request the jailer, Mr. J. Standford, brought me a table to write on, likewise his daughter Margaret, a fine girl of eighteen, furnished me with many usefull & entertaining books which served to beguile many hours of time which otherwise would have hung heavy on my hands.

page 20

Thursday 26th. This morning I felt greatly refresh'd, having had a good nights rest on my straw bed. About nine this morning the sheriff made me a visit & brought me a Salem newspaper[22] in which the Gentlemen Fed[eralist]s had pretty well exausted their magazine of abuse on me, but it moved me very little, knowing as I did that the truth would soon give their assertions the lie. The sheriff, being a good staunch Republican, cautioned me against conversing much with these Brittish gentlemen, as they would catch at my words & endeavour to entrap me. I took his advice & have since been more cautious, altho' some of these Dear gentlefolks have been very anxious to pry into what they called the truth of my story. This afternoon I was in anxious expectation of hearing from, or seeing some of my folks from Durham, but after looking through my windows perhaps a hundred times I was obliged to give it up and after reading a chapter & committing myself to God in prayr went to bed as happy in my mind as ever I was in my life.

Friday 27th. This day I was very much out of order, my spirits very low on account

page 21

of my wife and children who were continually presented in immagination to my view, distressed by affairs & I here confined in Prison, could grant them no asistance. These thoughts overcame me & I was almost distracted. In this state Mr. Pierce, whom I had sent to my father with a letter, found me & the news he brought operated as a cordial to my fainting spirit. He informed me that my brother Eben[eze]r Joy, upon hearing of my Imprisonment had dismissed his school & was on his way to see me accompany'd by my Cousin James Joy of Durham, that they ~~procured the necessary~~ had procured certificates ~~from~~ of my birth & caracter from the selectmen of Durham & other respectible inhabitants of the town together with a letter from Judge Wingate of Farmington[23] to Mr. Pickering in my behalf & that they would be here tomorrow, but brot no tidings of my wife & family after whom I enquired with great eagerness, but could learn no news of them. I took up my bible & read awhile & found much comfort therein as likewise I did in prayr. After which I lay down for the night. As we have no fire allowed us we are obliged to go to bed as soon as it is dark.

page 22

Saturday 28th. This morning I felt calm wrote several pages in my journal & anxiously waited the coming of my brother. Towards noon I quited writing & traveled the cell at every turn looking out of the windows in expectation of seeing my friends arrive. Thus I exercised myself untill about two oclock in the afternoon when I saw them arive. O how my heart palpitated. My wonted serenity was gone. My head grew dizzy & I hardly knew which end of me was downwards. I laid down on the bed & on Margaret coming to inform me my friends were below desired her to request them to postpone their visit untill I was better prepared to receive them which they did. In about three quarters of an hour they made their appearance. My resolution to be calm when they came forsook me. As soon as I heard their footsteps on the stairs, my head grew dizzy & I knew not who was near me for some time. At last I recovered from the first shock &

found my brother sitting near me in tears. He tenderly embraced me entreating me to compose

page 23

myself & converse with him which after some time had elapsed I was able to do. He told me he had done & would still continue to do for me all in his power, that he would attend my tryal & if I was fined he would pay the fine & liberate me, that he would immediately on his return, visit my family & befriend them all in his power. In fact he said all a tender & affectionate brother could to alleviate my sorrows—my friend the High Sheriff likewise said everything to console & comfort me. He told my brother in a jesting manner that if he let my family suffer when he came into N[ew] Hampshire he would make use of his authority to make him suffer for it. Cousin James offered his assistance likewise if necessary on tryal—after conversing some time on the distracted state of my affairs I concluded to sell my brother my horse which I did for about thirty dollars. I then sat down & wrote a letter to my wife which my brother promised to carry himself. After I had done writing it I handed it to the Sheriff who read it. As soon as he had finished it he said returning it to me, you have been a schoolmaster, but I did not know before that you were a minister

page 24

aluding to the style in which the letter was written. My brother & friend then left me & I felt resigned to my fate, but before my brother went away he gave orders for me to have anything the house afforded, either victuals or drink in addition to my allowance—May God recompense him for all his labours of love towards me & mine, for I fear I never shall be able to. I felt very much out of order this evening on account of the great agitation of spirits I had undergone: but my heart was full of love to God for his kindness in raising me up so many loving & powerful friends in the time of my trouble. After I had committed myself to him, the Almighty in humble prayr, in which I found great comfort, I retired with my fellow prisoner to rest ————

Sunday 29th. This day I felt uncomonly dark in my mind. I was in a wilderness of doubts & fear respecting my future state almost all day,

but at last the Lord appeared for me when I little expected him &
granted me a comfortable season in prayr in the evening, after which
I went to bed with a light heart meditating on the goodness of God
to us mortals.

page 25

Monday 30th. This day we suffered much with the cold. It snowed all
the forenoon. About eleven oclock the Circuit Court for the County
of Essex commenced its session in the Courthouse about thirty rods
from the jail. The Courthouse is a fine two story building with a
cupola but no bell. It was really laughable to see so many fools
capering through the storm & snow, merely to be allowed the
priviledge of giving their money to a clan of Idle Lawyers, & in
return be made greater fools by them, if possible, than they were
when they went. I had no company to see me today, it being stormy. I
took advantage of my brothers direction today & had a quart of coffe
& two biscuits for supper, which was a great luxury—two meals only
being allowed by the jailor. After eating a good supper & attending
prayr as usual went to bed —————
Tuesday 31st. Rose greatly refreshed by a good nights rest. After
breakfast the right side of my face began to swell and pain me in an
extraordinary manner. This day I had a great deal of company some
of them very polite others impudent & saucy—one asked me if I was
the Pickering man. I answered that my name was not Pickering. He
called me a comical fellow

page 26

and asked me if I expected to be able to prove what I had asserted to
be true. I told him I could form a better oppinion after tryal when if
he wished I could inform him. He then left me muttering curses.
Another looked into the room & said, damn you, you ought to be
hanged. I replyed thank God you are not to be my judge Sir. Another
soon came & said to me I wish I were a Judge & had power. I would
set you at liberty & admonish you to do better in future. which of the
three would make the best judge. This day two new prisoners were
brought in ~~by the~~ for debt by the Gentle Fed[eralist]s who now begin
to hunt out all they can of the oposite party & if they owe them they

148

must pay, vote for them, run away or go to Jail. After what I have
seen, I ~~should~~ shall not wonder if Massachusetts gets shackled with a
Fed[eralist] Governor the ensuing year.[24] My face continued to swell
all day. At night it was very painfull. After supper felt very much out
of order, my mind harrassed by the many questions which had been
put to me in the course of the day, my face very much swollen & very
painfull.[25] O, thought I, could I but be this night with my dear
family, have my wife to soothe my sorrows &

page 27

dress my face, how happy should I be. The thought almost overcame
me & I did not recover my wonted serenity untill sleep closed my
eyelids————
Wednesday April 1. This morning the sheriff paid me an early visit
accompanyed by a young gentleman I did not know. He discoursed
frely, sometime after which he took his leave, promising to call again
as soon as possible. This day I had very little company. My face
continued swollen & pained me very much.
Thursday 2nd. The swelling increased in my face which was very
painfull. Now did I long to be at home, but the thought only added
to my distress. I found great comfort in reading & meditating on the
scriptures. In them I have a large field for contemplation. The
lamentations of Jeremiah & the Psalms are my favorite books. There
I find comfort & consolation. If ever my heart leaped for joy it was
when I read the 18th, 19th, 20th & 21st verses of the 31 Chap. of
Jeremiah. I opened to them when I was involved in darkness & dwelt
upon them until my soul was enlightned. I could say with the
Psalmist, I will hope in the Lord, for with the Lord there is mercy &
with him there is plenteous redempsion.

page 27 ¼

Friday 3rd. This day my face began to grow better & the swelling
abated. Felt very low in my mind, read considerable, but the bible
seemed like a sealed book. The sheriff visited me this afternoon,
renewed his protestations of friendship & endeavored to cheer up my
spirits. He came again just as night & seemed sorry to see me so dull,
but my thoughts were exercised about my ~~future &~~ future state & the

prospect appeared so gloomy I was almost again in despair. I prayed God to relieve me & bring once more to see his face & favours & this state went to bed.

Saturday 4th. The swelling being gone down in my face I felt much better. The sheriff never weary of administering comfort to one paid me an early visit accompanyed by Mr. David Cumings, the County solicitor. This Gentleman came every day to see me when I was confined in Salem Prison. He now bid me cheer up, said he did not think the Grand Jury would find a bill against me, that I was committed out of spite & that after election it would be forgotten. This revived my spirits considerably. Afternoon. Another prisoner just brot in—another Republican put in by a Fed[eralist] for debt just before election,—thats all the news I have today.

page 27 ½

Sunday 5th. My face continued to grow better, but my hands swell but do not pain me. I conclude it is for want of exercise. It being rainy our room is very dark. Can hardly see to read or write & how I long to have my liberty so that I may go to meeting. To see others go & to think had I never doubted, I might still have enjoyed the same liberty overcomes me. I shed tears but they avail nothing. I mourn & cry to God but find no comfort. When O lord will thou apear for my soul.

Monday 6th. I slept very little last night. My thoughts strayed to my dear family. I beheld the situation my worthy partner was in & I was the unhappy cause of her misfortunes, afraid she would sink under them, then again it seemed as tho I could hear her chide me for giving way to sorrow & exorting me to put my trust in God who alone was able to deliver me. O my God remember the widow & the fatherless. I have just had a disagreeable visitor. Mr. Sheriff Dutch[26] of Salem came just now & served a writ on me in behalf of Leigh & Ferguson, of Berwick, Maine, the debt 31.45 cts.[27] I wonder when the Gentlemen Fed[eralist]s will leave off persecuting me. How can I pay money confined as I am in jail. I now must lay here the lord knows how long to gratify these fellows malice. If I get clear on tryal for deffamation I will set down & write to my brother, perhaps he may help me out of this hobble. O my wife my

page 28

Children shall I never more be allowed to embrace you. O why did I leave you. But it is useless to repine. It is so, but for why, God only knows. I submit ———

I have written a long letter to my brother Eben & have wept all the time like a child, but now I will leave off for I am quite overcome, once more the dismal sounding Town Clock strikes six. I can see to write no longer. Oh that I could banish my thoughts with my pen but I cannot. God be merciful to me for thou art alone able to help me—

Tuesday 7th. My face continues to grow better but my hands swell, my fingers so stiff I can hardly write. I sent off my letter this morning which I wrote yesterday to my brother. I feel more calm than I did yesterday & more resigned to the will of him who governs all things, knowing that he oversees all the actions of man & without his consent not a sparrow shall fall to the ground.

Wednesday, 8th. I sat up reading last night untill the bell rang for nine, being furnished with a candle by Margaret who likewise furnishes me daily with books. I found sweet consolation in the scriptures & had a remarkable refreshing season in prayr. I went to bed happy. I waked up several times in the night praying. I felt my soul lifted up

page 29

above the things of time. I seem to partake of the joys of the blessed. This morning I still felt resigned & calm, but when I think of my dear wife & prattling babes my heart bleeds afresh. I divide my time thus. After eating breakfast I usually walk around my cell for the space of half an hour, sometimes longer, then sit down & read two or three chapters in the Bible & draw from them all the comfort possible, which supports me until after dinner. I usually set down the occurrences of the day just before night. & I write on other subjects about two hours in the day, when I am dull & melancholy I go to writing or reading, but sometimes these fail to amuse & my tears mark the pages as they turn. In looking to God I find the greatest comfort & in my Bible a continual feast to my hungry soul ———

Thursday 9th. Having sat up late last night I slept late this morning & felt quite unwell. My hands continue swollen & painful. As it is fast day the people already begin to assemble for public worship. —— night — the day is past & I left alone. About eleven oclock today our doors were opened, the jailer came in & bid my fellow prisoner Elisha Gurney prepare to leave the Prison immediately. These welcome orders to the old man who had been in close confinement nine months & twelve days

page 30

and suffered everything from the cold during the winter, at which season the inside of the Prison is one uninterrupted cake of ice & the windows block'd up with snow ~~renders~~ makes the rooms very cold & gloomy. Without any fire has he brav'd it out emtomb'd in this coffin of stone & ice—he was so overjoy'd he could hardly bid me farewell as he hurried out of the room. But it was otherwise with me. The thoughts of being left alone in this gloomy place overcame me to such a degree that it was sometime before I could speak & after I recovered who had I to speak to, alas none. I sat down brooding over my misfortunes till I wept, then a thought darted through my mind that I must not depend on man but on God for help & assistance. I fell on my knees & beseeched him to support & comfort me & felt my petition granted before I rose from the floor. The heavenly crum I then receiv'd from my fathers table sustained my drooping spirit in a remarkable manner. I found great comfort in reading the scripture. Sometimes when I found a blessed promise to the afflicted I should shed tears of joy over & over would I read it untill I could retain it in my memory. Being thus comforted I do not feel so lonesome as I expected I should, having God for my friend what more do I want.——

page 31

Friday 10th. I rose this morning with a mind more at ease than usual. I felt resigned to the will of God, but not so lively as I ~~was~~ did last night. I have never since I have been in Prison felt the presence of the Lord in such a degree as I did last night. Before I went to bed I tryed to pray & it seemed as though my mouth was sealed up at first but I cryed unto the Lord & he heard me & had compassion on me

& sent the comforter. I felt so happy I hardly knew what to do with myself. I prayed, sang, shouted, laughed, wept, prayed again & then after setting my candle at the head of my bed, went to bed & read in my bible until after nine oclock. Oh the comfort & satisfaction there is in serving God, the God of love—the God who condescends to visit the poor backsliden prisoner. O may I never more swerve from the path of the riteous which leadeth to true hapiness & felicity. The weather is stormy & my room so dark I can hardly see to write or read, but I can contemplate on the goodness of God & that is a great priviledge, when I think how good the Lord has been to me in restoring me my reason my heart often swells with gratitude & my eyes betray its feelings. I am determined by the help of God to serve him the rest of my days having a hope of a blessed Immortality after I shall quit this troublesome world. It is not from this world that any ray of comfort can proceed

page 32

to cheer the gloom of the last hour: but futurity has still its prospects; there is yet hapiness in reserve sufficient to support us under every affliction. Hope is the chief blessing of man & that hope only is rational, of which we are certain it cannot deceive, this hope if grounded on belief is sufficient for every creature, for the King on his throne, for the prisoner in his dungeon, for the aged & the youth, for the poor & likewise for the rich, for the sick & the healthy, for the [illegible], lame, & blind. O may I never give up this hope during life and I am sure it will stand by me in death ——
Saturday 11th. After a good nights rest rose greatly refreshed, but felt more than usually dull & melancholy, but found relief in prayr. How good is our God to condescent to notice such a wretch as me who has once deny'd him after being made acquainted with his excellencies. This weighs me down, when I think how great the sin I have committed I shudder to think what an abys I have escaped through the interference of divine providence. Another prisoner arrived today, a debtor. There are now six in prison. One, Colby, formerly lived in Middleton, N. H. & is acquainted with ~~most~~ many of the inhabitants. We converse some times through the windows. Although he is confined in the cell directly over mine, we cannot hear each others voices until we shove up our windows & put our faces as close to the

page 33

grates as possible. There is confined with him one Jordan for debt. He has been a trader in Kenebeck but absconded, was taken & put in prison. Here he is as he says going to swear out soon. But a circumstance hapened this morning which it is thought will hinder him. It was this—Feeling dull & melancholy I went to my windows & after taking it down, caled to them above. Jordan opened his window to answer me when two small pieces of paper flew out & fell in the jail yard. He immediately missed them & asked me if I saw them pass my window. I told him I did. He then requested Stewart, a prisoner who has the liberty of the house, to go down and pick them up, which he did. On examining them they proved to be two Notes of hand for seven hundred dollars made payable to him, Jordan, in about six months. On handing them into him he was much agitated & asked if anyone had examined them.—from this circumstance it is supposed that he is a man of considerable property & intends by taking a false oath to swindle his creditors out of their just dues which however the sheriff is taking measures to prevent

page 34

Sunday 12th. I rose this morning with a heavy heart which is generally the case with me on the sabbath which is occasioned by thinking of the blessed priviledge I once enjoyed of looking to God in prayr surrounded by my family, & considering the priviledges which are enjoyed by those of the brethren who have their liberty, of meeting together for public worship, whilst I by reason of sin am debarred meeting with them. But God who knoweth all things is capable of meeting with me in prison as well as with those who assemble in his house.

Monday 13. Having spent a very restless night feel very much out of order this morning. I got no sleep last night untill after twelve oclock, when I was disturbed by a frightful dream. I dreamed that my wife had gone distracted, that I went home & saw her, that she did not know me & soon after I got home she died. I then awoke in great distress, but falling into a doz I again dreamed the same. I thought I saw her in her coffin in her fathers house, that her face was so disfigured I hardly knew her, that I leaned over the coffin & wept it seemed as real as tho it had been the case. I was in such distress that I awoke, weeping. After the day dawned I went

page 35

to sleep again & had the same vision. I thought the people were assembled to attend the funeral that I ~~could~~ would not be removed from the corps. I thought as my conduct had been the cause of her death I would die too & be buried with her. I thought some told me that she had her reason before she died & was anxious to see me, & went out of the world praising God. It seemed to me as if my heart strings were breaking & that I was dying. The thoughts of death did not seem to daunt me I felt considerably calm & resigned to the will of God & when the bystanders told me I could live but a few minutes, I thought I was rejoiced to think I should go to heaven & join my wife in praising God it seemed. In imagination I still stood by the head of the coffin my relations & friends weeping round me when after recomending my children to my brother Eben. & exorting the assembly to believe in the Lord Jesus & being sensible I was going began to sing praises to God & sang so loud that I awaked. The Idea is still so impressed on my mind that I can think of nothing else. O if when I come to die I am so well prepared as I thought I was last night Death will be only desirable. But my heart forbodes

page 36

something ill which is about to befall my family. I do not often notice dreams but this seems so remarkable that I should dream the same three times, that I cannot help mentioning it. I feel unusually dull & mellancholly. I count the days and hours with impatience, but hope of better days keeps me from sinking quite. My family seems dearer to me than ever. O why did I leave them. I might have known that I had not fortitude sufficient to sustain a separation, but it is useless to repine. It is as it is & Gods will be done ————
Tuesday 14th. I have passed The day is spent & the dismal sounding bell anounces that it is time to retire to rest, but it might as well be silent, my disturbed thoughts have no rest. The day & evening have been charming to those who have their liberty, but to me they have

lost their influence. I once could enjoy the cool breeze of evening surrounded by my dear family & friends & with sublime delight contemplate the wonderful beauties of the Creation, but alas: the scene is changed Oh how changed, myself shut up in a tomb of stone, far distant from those I love, cheered by the rays of the sun not more than two hours in the day, while my worthy partner is many miles distant mourning

page 37

my unhappy fate & my children. O my God, my children. I can write no more my heart is ready to burst my eyes brimful of tears. I will now begin again. I am more calm. I have been hearkening to the sweet sounds of distant music which gently floats through the air, the shrill sounds of the fife & Clarionet, the plaintive notes of basson, the rattling of drums or the mallancholly toll of the bass drum enliven not heart of the prisoner. The feelings of my heart I have endeavored to describe in the following rude composition

> Oppres'd with every anxious woe
> A mortal can sustain,
> While with the day my sorrows grow
> And life wears out in pain.
> Where shall I ease, or comfort find,
> Oh! how relieve my care?
> What can preserve my tortur'd mind
> From sinking In despair.
> Thou canst, religion, whose bright beam
> Oer my benighted soul
> A smiling ray of comfort gleams
> And all my fears controul

page 38

> From earth my boundless wishes soar
> And thy bright tract pursue,
> The worlds false joys can please no more
> When heav'nly are in view.
> The frowns of partial fortune here
> The virtuous may despise,

They're only happy who can fear
Not poverty, but vice.

My eyes grow dim, the lonesome hour of twelve finds them still
open. I have spent a malancholly day my whole system is out of
order, my hands & face swollen very much, pains wrack my body in
almost every part, my burning flesh creates a thirst unquenchable, I
dread being sick here in Prison, but God knows all my distress to
him I will cry mayhap he will have mercy. ——
Wednesday 15.

Another day is gone & past, the evening shades are spreading.
Oh will my sorrows ever last, till the cold earth's my bed.
I vainly sigh for liberty, but no relief I find
Inclosed in stone in vain I cry, Oh that I was resigned
Unto the will of a just God, Who justly punishes
Those who have cleans'd by his blood, And then believed lies.
I would be calm & kiss the rod. Ceace all my mur'mring ceace,
I'll slay my cause before the Lord, 'Tis he can send me peace.

page 39

Now my poor body's rack'd with pain, My limbs are swol'n &
    sore
I hardly can my weight sustain, My thirst can quench no more.
Oh that my dear & lovely Wife, could now my nurse become
What would I give, Ah! but my life, To see that dearest one.
From her fair hands I willingly would nauceous med'cine take.
Oh could I in her bossom lie, my pains would me forsake,
But Oh my God 'tis all in vain, For me to mourn & weep
Misfortunes have rent us in twain, Oh that my thoughts would
    sleep.
The clock strikes nine & I must go, and stretch me on my
    straw
There may my tears in rivers flow, Oh that I'de kept Gods law.
Oh mighty God, I pray draw near, and pity my sad case
Oh banish that fell fiend Despair, and fill my soul with Grace.

Thursday, 16. I have spent a day of woe. My disorder increases
surprisingly I can sit up but little, my face swells very fast & is very

painfull, the onside of my lips is raw, the roof of my mouth to a blister, my body rack'd with pain, my apetite all gone, my thirst unquenchable My feet & hands swolen & covered with blisters, this is a faint sketch of my unhapy situation. The medicine I have taken does not operate at all. Indeed I should be quite disconsolate if it were not for the extreme kindness of this family with whom I am. One will bring me a hot brick to put to my feet, another will bring me tea or medicine, some one thing, some another. Everyone seems to want to do something towards restoring me to health. Margaret has just brought me an orange which she had given her a few days since & would take nothing for it. Thus the Lord raises up friends

page 40

to comfort me in my affliction. I think I never felt more resigned than I do now. I do not know but this sickness will bring me to the grave, the house appointed for all the living. Oh may I be prepared to die that I may reign with Christ forever. Religion is my only support & I have many happy seasons in prayr more especially since I have been left alone. I feel myself more confirmed in the blessed doctrine of perseverance of the saints[28] than ever. Oh that I had always believed as I do now. If I had I should not have been here. But I trust my hope is now built on that foundation which the gates of hell shall not prevail against. But I am overcome by sitting up too long & must lay by my pen. Feeling some better I resume my narative to notice that the Judges of the Court of Sessions have just paid me a visit accompanyed by a number of gentlemen. They enquired minutely into everything which concerned my treatment by the prison keeper & wether I had proper attention paid me in my sickness, all which questions I answered in the afirmitive. After they had conversed some time on the issue of my tryal they gave it as their opinion that I should be cleared. This revived hope once more in my heart & my thoughts run continually on the distant prospect I have of being permitted once more to embrace those I love, if I should recover my health, on this side of boundless Eternity.

page 41

Friday 17th April, consumed by pain & sickness it cannot be expected that I have spent this in rejoicing but the contrary, my disorder increases fast. I can but just reach the scuttle to take in my medicine. The inside of my mouth is to a blister & my face swolen to an enormous size. I hardly know myself when I view my face in the glass. My teeth are every one loose & my gums swolen. I can chew nothing. Indeed I have but little inclination to for my apetite is all gone. Tea & some times a little broth constitutes my living, my situation is truly pitiable. I almost despair of ever coming out of this Prison alive, yet I am wonderfully supported by the hope I have of a blessed immortality, but I long to see my dear wife & Children, Parents & friends & sorely lament the unfortunate sircumstances which serv'd to part us.

> My Lamentation, in this stormy night,
> Black night o'er the concave is spread.
> Hoarse winds thro' the grates how they roar
> In vain do I lie in my bed,
> While the sea rolls its surf on the shore.
> Hail scene of terrific dismay!
> Thy horrors compare with my own,

page 42

> 1 As fill'd with deep anguish I lay,
> As bursts from my bosom the grown.
> 2 I once knew the pleasures of peace,
> And Innocence dwelt in my heart,
> Fair Friendship gave rapture to ease,
> And love could its transport impart.
> 3 What extacy dwelt in my soul,
> When my Mary with hapiness smil'd.
> What Joys thro' my bosom oft stole,
> When her tear soft compassion beguil'd.
> 4 Alass! now how chang'd is the scene,
> In Prison I languish & mourn.
> My heart torn with anguish so keen,
> Oh I would I had never been born:
> 5 The sport of Dame Fortune to be,
> And the child of affliction and woe;
> Given up to the passions a prey,
> I down to the Grave soon shall go.

6 Methinks on the crags of the rock,
Swift destruction some shattered ship seeks?
How its timbers are torn with the shock,
How the agoniz'd passenger shreiks.
7 Compar'd with my anguish how faint,
Are the horrors that fill him with care;
His fancy destruction may paint
But he knows not the woe of despair.

page 43

What waves on the vessel are driv'n,
How the surf throws its foam on the deck!
What thunders roll dreadful thro' heav'n!
What lightnings illumine the wreck!
But soft—see the storm dies away
The beams of the morning appear,
Hope to him may a promise display
But my bosom she never can cheer!

Saturday 18th. I have lived to see another day pass away, and a long one it has been to me. My disorder continues to rage with unabated vigour. I can sit up but little & grow weaker every moment. Sometimes I am almost discouraged, when I think of my destitute situation, sick & in Prison & no friend or acquaintance near me to sucour me in my distress, but I would wish to be resigned to will of him who governs all things, to him I commit myself, trusting that in the midst of Judgment he will remember mercy ————
Sunday 19th. My disorder increases and I am too weak to write.
Monday 20th. I have been some better today than usual. My pains abate, but my mouth is so sore that if I had a good appetite I must go hungry the best I could. I have sat up two or three hours today & am in good hopes I shall soon be able to sit up all day, for when I am in bed the little black Gentry who have taken up

page 44

their abodes in my straw muster their forces and attack me with great bravery in front flanks & rear & if repuls'd they hardly stop to take breath, but renew the charge thirsting for my blood, tho' some have

paid for their temerity with their lives, it does not discourage the rest
& I see no other way to get off with honour than by making a retreat
and leaving the rascals in possession of the field of battle, which I
hope to be able to effect in a few days. Great as my afflictions are I
cannot help sometimes giving way to the natural gaiety of my
temper. In some of these sallies I have written some piecss of poetry
ridiculing the Fed[eralist]s which while they please my Republican
friends, they cause me to receive many inverted blessings from the
opposite party. Some even take pains to come to the prison for that
purpose. But enough of them. It grows late & my eyes grow heavy &
as I have rested very little lately I gladly embrace the drowsy God.
Tuesday 21st. My body has this day been free from pain, but I am still
very weak & low. I have had considerable company today. Even the
young ladies seem anxious to alleviate my distresses all in their
power, frequently visiting me & bringing books for me to peruse.
Two married ladies came today to see me. They conversed some time
with me & after I had given them a sketch of my history &

page 45

misfortunes, at their request I sung the lines I pened when I was sick,
which are inserted in the 41st page. They stood in the entry and wept
all the time I was singing & after I had done they very politely
thanked me & requested a copy of the verses, which I promised
them. They would have given me money if I would have accepted it
but I refused, one of them, Mrs. Bishop is a Proffessor of Religion.
She at parting gave me very good advice, exorted me not to despair
but to put my trust in God, wished she could see my wife,
acknowledged that she felt interested in my fate, wished me well and
departed. One of the prisoners informed me that after she went
down stairs she would have sent me up money, if it had not been for
the interference of Mrs. Standford, who told her I should be
mortified by such a transaction. The kindness of these two ladies
affected me so much that I did not recover my wonted serenity of
mind the whole day after. My wife & children destitute of the
comforts of life, left alone amongst an ignorant insolent race of
beings, whose delight it is to distress the distressed, myself confined
in prison many miles distant from them & the rest of my relations &
friends, my fate uncertain, consumed by sickness & sorrow, almost in
despair, was continually agitating my thoughts. A young Miss

Colwell made me a visit this afternoon accompany'd by two other young ladies of her acquaintance. She was on a visit to this family when I was brot from salem thither. Then I was very much agitated expecting severe usuage. She conversed very familiarly with me, inquired how long I had been ill, said she hoped I had been agreably disappointed in respect to the treatment I expected, which I answered her was the case. Her companions stood aloof during the conversation & appeared to eye me with as much earnestness as tho I had been an Oran Outang. If I looked one of them in the face she would immediately run out of sight and then come forward again peeping to get a sight of the wonderful creature. After sometime Miss Collwell took her leave wishing that I might soon regain my liberty. I thanked her for her good wishes, & mine followed her.

page 47

Wednesday 22nd. I have undergone a great deal of pain today. My mouth is so sore I am obliged to cover my teeth with lint to keep my lips, which are raw, from touching them. I can eat nothing which needs chewing, so content myself with drinking broth & porridge. But notwithstanding all the difficulties under which I labour, I have at times heavenly seasons. Here alone in Prison I can praise him in whom I trust & who in his own due time will deliver me out of the hands of those who seek my soul to destroy it.

> Kindly he opens me his ear
> And bids me pour my sorrows there
> And tell him all my pains:
>
> Thus while I ease my burden'd heart
> In ev'ry woe he bears apart
> His arms embrace me & his hand my drooping
>   head sustains.

My friend the Sheriff has paid me a visit. He was very lively. Gave me a sketch of his history which was very interesting, promised to interest himself in procuring my release. He informed me that he had seen Wm. Pickering[29] and had said all he could in my favour. After assuring me

page 48

I might depend on his using his influence with the Judges in my favor he left me to visit the other prisoners. He, Robert Farlee, was born in this town about the year 1757, of respectable parents, he went to sea when a boy, being particularly attached to the profession of a seaman. On the commencement of hostilities between this country and great Brittian he immediately went aboard a privateer & made several valuable prises. His courage and good conduct procured him the good will of the ships crew & he was soon made an officer. After a long run of good fortune, by which he had gotten a handsome property together, the ship was taken after a severe action by a Brittish man of War, & the crew which amounted to one hundred and seventeen souls, put in irons & confined on board the Jersey Prison ship.[30] He there suffered all the horrors of close confinement for five months during which time eleven hundred of the Americans died aboard that ship among whom were all his ships crew except himself & the first mate. After he was liberated he again enlisted in the service of his country & continued

page 48½

the bold defender of his country & rights untill the close of the War. He then for a number of years shone conspicuous as an honest merchant, but the loss of two of his vessels which were richly laden, captured & condemned by his sworn foes, the Brittish, reduced this worthy citizen to state of dependence hitherto unknown by him. In consideration of his past services, the Hon. Governor[31] & Council last year appointed him Sheriff of the County of Essex, which station he fills with honor. He makes it his particular business to visit the Prisons inquiring minutely into everything relative to the treatment of the unfortunate prisoners & by relating his own sufferings endeavours to cheer up the spirits of others in similar circumstances. It is not to be wondered at that such a man should be unerversaly beloved, almost every day he calls at my cell to enquire after my health & bring me newspapers. I can never say too much in his praise. He shall have my thanks for his kindness to my latest breath.

page 49

Thursday 23rd. My disorder continues to abate but I am very weak
and feeble. Nothing of consequence has occur'd today with me. I
have felt very low in my mind & something seems to whisper me
that the isue of my tryal will be unfavorable, but I hope for the best. I
sincerely long to see & embrace the Wife of my youth & the dear
pledges of our mutual love, but I hardly dare to promise myself so
much felicity soon. My tears flow freely when I think of them, my
prayr's are offered up many times each day & night for their
prosperity to him who Governs all things & now to his care I
Commit myself them & all our concerns.

> Why dwell forever on the gloomy side?
> Say doth not God unerring still preside?
> Why they ungratefully presume to scan
> With Impious cavils marking every plan!
> Tho' truth and justice both surround his throne
> And mercy gems the Glory of his crown.

page 50

Friday 24th.

> Then are the shafts of disappointment barb'd
> When of her well form'd hopes the soul is rob'd.

May not these lines be apply'd to me; Indeed they may. View my
situation. Four years since, see me then, blessed with health &
strength, loving my wife & being beloved in return, earning my bread
honestly & eating it with contentment. Beloved by numerous friends
& respectable relations & loving them in return. Blest with a son and
daughter, the dear pledges of our mutual love. But alass! Those
haylcon days are flu forever. View now the other side of the carpet.
First depriv'd of health, then overwhelmed in misfortunes by losses
in trade, my property attach'd, my dear wife broken hearted, my
children weeping round me, reduced to poverty, I fly from the friends
of my heart, reason loses her seat & phrenzy siezes the reigns. See me
wandering among strangers who connive at my ruin, see me taken up

as a spy, dragg'd to prison by ruffian hands, now see despair mark'd in my war worn countenance as reason by degrees resumes her seat. View my forlorn condition confined in a stone cell shivering with the cold, no friend to speak to, no friendly hand to administer comfort to my necesities & uncertain how long I am to remain in this situation, far from the dear objects of my fond affections. Oh pity me but to whom do I cry none

page 51

answereth, all is still as the mansions of the dead. But is there no one to comfort the afflicted? Yes, the God of Paul & Silas, is ever ready & willing to administer comfort to the distressed seeking soul.

> Forgive my treasons prince of grace,
> The bloody Jews were traitors too.
> Yet thou hast pray'd for that curs'd race
> Father, they know not what they do.
> Great Advocate! look down & see
> A wretch whose smarting sorrows bleed
> O plead the same excuse for me
> For Lord, I knew not what I did.

Saturday 25th. As the day approaches which is to decide my case I feel all the horror of fear. Some times, the states prison rises in my view, then I fear again that I shall be confined here a long time, which will surely put a period to my existence, as my health is as yet but poorly reestablished. Oh my God what a wretched situation am I reduced to, what was I once, what am I now. I once was happy. I now am wretched, in every sense of the word. Yet I have an Immortal part, a soul to save or lose. Let then my thoughts be imploy'd in seeking its salvation, that when this poor lump of earth shall become inanimate, my immortal soul shall seek a shelter in the arms of the God who gave it.

page 52

Sunday 26th. I have this day heard from my dear connexions which has operated as a cordial to my agitated mind. My brother, Ebenezer & Valentine Smith, Esqr[32] arived in the afternoon & brot the glad

tidings. This fresh manifestation of their friendly regard for me quite overcame me. At first I could not utter a word, but am now more calm. I was afraid to ask my brother after the welfare of my family & waited sometime for him to inform me which at last he did. Oh how sweet did these words sound: "Your wife and children are well." He & Mr. Smith came into my cell & conversed with me some time & promised to use their utmost endeavour to ~~procure my [illegible]~~ set me at liberty. Hope once more gladens my heart. Oh may God bless their endeavours by crowning them with success ————————
Monday 27th. My brother has been to Salem to see the prosecutor in my case, but have been able to do nothing in my favor yet. But have good grounds to hope they shall be able to settle with the states attorney. If they cannot I will come to tryal. I fear I shall be hardly able to undergo the fatigue attendant on it but God's will be done.

page 53

Tuesday 28th April 1812 The long waited for day has at length arived & the Supreme Court has commenced its sitting. When the bell rang to call the Court it sounded to me as dismal as tho it was tolling for a funeral. Nothing has yet been effected by my friends except that they have employed an Attorney to plead my cause, so I must be led a criminal before the Court & the Lord have mercy on me.
Wednesday 29th. Nothing particular has occured today. My spirits are very low, but I have a secret hope of deliverance thro' the united exertions of my friends. I have had several visitors today, among the rest my old playmate Curtis Coe.[33] He spent some time with me & cheer'd me up with his lively conversation. My health is not yet reestablished. My mouth is yet very sore, but getting better.
Thursday 30th. I still remain in uncertainty. No evidence has yet come forward against me. What the reason is I do not know. I begin to hope that no one will appear. If that is the case I shall be discharged immediately. The great agitation my spirits have undergone lately has put me quite out of order & I begin to fear another fit of sickness.

page 54

May 1st 1812. My hopes are all fled & I plung'd in despair. My persecutors ever active sent of a Deputy Sheriff yester afternoon to

Haverill to procure evidence against me & this morning they throng the court house. What the result will be God only knows. My attorney Esqr Andross has been with me and gave me reason to hope that I should be liberated by paying a small fine. For want of exercise my health declines apace. My room is sixteen feet long & ten wide. The door opens into the entry way. It is made of huge iron bars riveted together lengthwise on the inside & crosswise on the outside. The bolts are secured to the door on the outside by clasps made of thick iron bars and riveted through the door. The both are as large as a mans arm & are shoved into the stone wall about a foot & fastned with two huge padlocks. In the upper part of the door is cut a hole four inches wide & three deep through which I receive my provision. There is an iron shutter staple & lock to this, & when the prisoners behave bad it is fastened up. Where the prison joins the dwelling house at the end of the entry there is another iron door, which is usually kept locked so that no person can speak to the prisoners within. The jailor has however indulged me so far as to leave it open by day since I have been here so that I have had liberty to converse with

page 55

any person who came to see me. But this priviledge has never been granted to any of my unfortunate predecessors. These doors weigh upwards of one thousand pounds. My windows are darkened by a double grating made of bars two inches square. The bars which compose the inner grating are all plated with steel so that it is impossible to saw them off. There are nineteen cells & dungeons in this Prison. The dungeons have no windows. The light is emited only through a hole in the wall five inches wide & about a foot deep. This Prison was three years in building & cost thirty thousand Dollars. It is three stories high, it is founded on a smooth solid ledge so there is no danger of its ever setting. The walls are three feet thick & the stones some of which are twelve feet in length are all dog'd together with large square iron bars. The Prison is impregnable, nothing can start it but an earthquake. The yard round the jail is eight feet high and spiked round the top. The prisoners are not allowed to have any fire. In the winter season the inside of the rooms are one continued sheet of ice so that a person confined in them must use every exertion to keep from freezing. This prison has been built five years ————

page 56

Saturday 2nd. My answers are now before the Grand Jury & there is
no doubt but they will find a bill against me. The lawyer Eaton, the
one who led me into this scrape & persuaded me to write what I did
at Haverill, came to see me this morning accompany'd by one
Wingate.[34] He just looked in then started back & looked as pale as a
sheet. He looked me in the face some time but never utered a word.
Wingate spoke a few words but was soon hurried away by Eaton. I
never saw a mans countenance show more guilt than his in my life.
He has told my brother that he expects to be indicted for his conduct
in this affair. I expect my cause on this afternoon. How it will
terminate God only knows. I however hope favorably. My spitting of
blood continues to increase & keeps my stomach continually sore.
My mouth is yet very sore, & my feet & hands swollen. I have heard
that the Grand Jury have found a bill against me & of course my
tryal will come on on monday or tuesday. Report says that there is a
bill found against Eaton.
Sunday 3rd I have this day counted forty four long days since I have
been in prison. It seems as tho it has been as many weeks. Have been
quite unwell to day & have rais'd a large quantity of blood ——

page 57

Monday 4th May 1812. The long dreaded day which witnessed my
tryal is at length past & I am thank God yet alive & in tolerable
health & spirits. About three o'clock this afternoon Sheriff Bailey
came to the Prison & conducted me from hence to the courthouse.
My indictment was then read by the Clerk, and I was asked whether
I was guilty or not guilty. I answered that I was guilty of writing the
paper mentioned in the Indictment but not with a malicious design
& that I should not contend with the Commonwealth, but this
answer did not satisfy my lord Judge.[35] He must have his own way so
poor I was obliged to plead guilty. My brother Eben Joy & N
[Valentine] Smith were called on the stand. They testify'd to my
former caracter. Then there were some dear Fed[eralist] gentry
questioned, one of whom swore to a pretty round falsehood. The
states attorney spoke but a few words, my attorney manoever'd with
skill & my Lord Judge was but a few minutes employed in making
up his blessed Judgement which amounted to this in toto . . . that I

should pay a fine of fifty Dollars, be imprisoned in the County Prison thirty days & pay all costs. Bravo! Fine doings, what a charming sentence this. Who would have thought that a democrat would have come off so cheaply, when he was convicted of the high crime of insanity.

page 58

I had been imprisoned only forty four days and nights, but law suz, the Judge was a Fed[eralist] thats all how it com'd to pass. Every one cried injustice & aserted that had I belonged to the black fraternity fiends, yclep'd Federalists, I should have been discharg'd, but thank fortune its no worse, that is to say thank the laws which brail up the power of these fat faced gentry, for if they were allowed their full scope there would be many an honest democrat made headless by the guilotine, but the old adversary knows his bounds & so do they. Huzza for democracy, if I spend my days in Prison I still will be a democrat. I glory in my sufferings knowing as I do that everybody knows the cause of my detention, that it now is merely for my political principles. But to be serious I am more contented than I was before I knew what was to become of me & I mean to keep up my spirits all in my power so as to be able to show the malicious Fed[eralist]s something more than skin and bones at the end of the thirty days. Hope once more cheers my heart. I now contemplate with pleasure the day when if it please God I shall once more embrace the dear objects of my fond affections.

page 59

Tuesday May 5th 1812. One day of the thirty is passed away & a long one it has been to me. If the Honorable Fed[eralist] Judge knew by experience the blessings of close confinement he would I think have shewed me some mercy but I am a democrat & no democrat ought to live so say some folks. Now for instance today a man was arraigned at the bar for beating a poor sick man untill he was almost dead. He was so much hurt that he has been under the doctors hands ever since. Now when this inhuman wretch was asked whether he was guilty or not, he answered that he should not contend with the Commonwealth, which was not pleading guilty nor yet exonerating himself from blame, well Mr. Judge Sewal said not a word against it.

Now let us look back a little yesterday. I made the same plea, but Mr. Powerful would not have it so but drove my words down my throat again and commanded me to use the usual forms of Guilty or not Guilty. Now if any of my children should live to read this they may perhaps wonder why the Judge should make this difference. I'le tell you children this man who was so highly favored by the Judge is a Federal, the man who was beaten was a democrat, and as he

page 60

the Fed[eralist], is thought by the Judge to be a very suitable person to beat bruise & wound the honest supporters of their country's fredom & their own liberty, it would be highly detrimental to their cause to suffer him to be dealt by as justice demands, so he came off very light he might plead as he pleased, but because I was a democrat I must plead just as Mr. Powerful saw fit. Well much good may it do them. They wont get much by keeping me in prison. The high sheriff has just left me, he says that every person who says anything about my case says that had I been a Fed[eralist] I should have been discharged, said that had I been his own brother he could have done no more for me than he had, that he had conversed with the Judge & states attorney & had endeavored to make my cause appear as favorable as possible,—here is the picture of a friend of humanity. He might with propriety kept aloff from me. He might have left me to have starved in Salem Jail, but no, having suffered himself he knows how to sympathize with others. Scarcely a day has passed since I have been in prison but what this friend of men, this hero who has fought for his country & who has groan'd in irons on board one of the Brittish prison ships, to finish the picture, this true Republican, has personally visited the prison & administer'd comfort to the unfortunate prisoners and

page 61

may God bless him for it. A prisoner by the name of Mussel was brot in last night. He was taken up for stealing two hundred Dollars from a widow woman in Manchester. He was indicted and tryed today & on pleading guilty was sentenced to remain fifty days in close confinement & then be sent to the States Prison for three years. Sal a mulatto woman was sentenced to eight days close confinement & one year imprisonment in the States Prison for stealing eighteen Dollars—so much for stealing. But as it is very late in the evening and cold likewise, I will close today's journal by wishing Mr. Powerfull & all his gang as good a nights rest as their guilty conscience'es will suffer them to have.

Wednesday, 6th. I have had a great deal of company today. Some came to congratulate & others to insult me, but they for the most part I believe got as good as they sent. The tryal of Mr. Palfrey the editor of the Salem Gazette,[36] commenced today for publish[ing] to the world the nefarious proceedings of the Salem Selectmen at the late election, so it is a Fed[eralist] may lie with a bold face & defame the Government as often as he pleases & come off without punishment, but if a democrat dare to expose their fiend like proceedings he must be drag'd before their

page 62

Judges and is sure to suffer. Several military officers have been here today endeavoring to persuade me to enlist in the new army. One offered to make me a sergeant, but I would rather swing my hammor alongside my little wife than be trampooseing thro' the woods of Canada. I have some doubts about my courage likewise. My health grows better & my spirits revive in proportion.

Thursday 7th. I was visited at an early hour this morning by a number of my Republican friends from Salem, who have been indicted by the Fed[eralist] Grand Jury, for committing a riot as they term it at the annual town meeting holden in Salem for the purpose of voting for Governor in April last. These young men some of whoom are of the first respectability ventured to expostulate with the selectmen on the impropriety of their being deprived of their right of suffrage, in pretty plain terms, & for the audacity, have got to stand tryal before this all Powerful high & mighty Federal Court. The Editor of the Salem Gazette[37] came to see me this afternoon. He informed me that his cause was continued the Jury not agreeing, so for once Mr. Judge Sewal has got disappointed for in his charge to the jury he plumply declared that even his, the Editors, attempt to

page 63

make a defence was an aggravation of the crime, so says report. This
gentleman taryed some time with me informed me that the
Fed[eralist]s had entered into a combination to ruin him & put down
his paper. A short time since his partner was imprisoned by
Pickering & his gang two months in this Prison & when he was brot
to tryal nothing appearing against him worthy of death or of bonds
he was by the pure clemency of the Judge discharged. This is as I
heard the story, but it is useless to attempt to recount the many
instances of Federal injustice & oppression. It would require the age
of Methuselah to complete the history of one year, so I'll drop the
subject.

Friday 8th. There has been many visitors to view the Prison today, &
many of my acquaintance have visited me, among the rest Mr.
Saltmarsh, the officer who made me a prisoner in Salem. We had an
agreable conversation for some time, when he went away he
expressed his wishes that I might proffit by this lesson & never again
put myself in the power of the relentless Fed[eralist]s. The Salem riot
tryal still continues. The result is waited with anxiety by both parties.
No news worth mentioning today. My health grows better & the
swelling in my hands & feet has at last left them.

page 64

Saturday 9th. The rioters are condemned, eight of nine were found
guilty & wonderful to relate by a Federal Jury, "were there not nine
indicted up but where are the eight." They were oblig'd to procure
bonds for their appearance at the next term of the Supreme Court
holden in Salem where they must appear to receive their sentence. O
depart ye Republicans into the dungeons prepared for you by we
Fed[eralist]s. Because you dared to assert your right of suffrage—The
Sheriff paid me a visit immediately after the court rose, today &
related many things done by them that I shall not mention, which is
enough to make a beetle blush & Justice, who is ruled by a Federal
faction, mourn herself into a consumption. One gentleman, Leach,
by name, who has been deprived of his right to vote by the Salem
selectmen, is an old revolutionary officer who was several times
wounded when defending the liberty of his dear Country. He is a
man worth a handsome property in Salem, has long been an

inhabitant of the town & never dream't that his name was struck off the rolls, untill he went to put in his vote when the Selectmen forbid him because his name was not to be found on

page 65

the New list, in vain did he remonstrate, in vain did he call in evidence numerous citizens, to prove his right.[38] The answer was, it is too late now, the polls are opened, to put on any new names, why had you not apply'd before. The answer may be easily supposed, that he had not an idea, that he who had been a voter for twenty five years and still a citizen worth five thousand dollars would be struck off the list merely because he was a Republican. One of the selectmen had the impudence to insult him saying, "we shall never have any peace or good order so long as one of these seventy five's are suffered to live." Repeat those words, said the injured hero, stepping up to Mr. C——,[39] repeat those words again & I will close your jaws forever. Out of pure modesty Mr. C—— held his peace, being a little scared withall. Leach immediately commenced an action against the selectmen for depriving him of his right of suffrage in damages of fifty thousand Dollars. His conduct so displeased the hon. Mr. Powerful, that he requested him to come into Court and state what were his reasons for thus embarrasing the honorable selectmen. Agreeable to this request he appeared before the Court & his

page 66

oppressors & addressed the Judge in a speech replete with the spirit of '75. "Sire, said he, you behold in me an injured citizen, who has been deprived of his right by those very men who when babes I fought to defend, when Brittain dared to invade our rights I Sir, volunteered my services with many other heroes who in the arduous struggle for liberty exposed their persons to the shot of the enemy & their with their lives in their hands met the haughty foe at the point of the bayonet. I sir, have bled in my countries cause thrice was I wounded while fighting to secure that right which now in my old age I am deprived of by those who were then 'mewling & pewking in their nurses arms.' When I hear these men saying that they expect no peace or order so long as one of those men exist who fought & bled in the cause of freedom, I look on my scars and sigh, Oh my

ungrateful Country! But sire I will not give up my right without a
struggle. It is the first time I ever was a party in a lawsuit & nothing
but the being deprived of my right of voting, wrongfully by a faction
who wish to sway the scepter of tyrany & oppression oer the sons of
freedom should have driven me to it, so long as God spares my life
Sir, shall that life every moment of it be

page 67

devoted to the cause of liberty. 'Tis true I am old but I can yet handle
a musket & if ever my country requires the exertion of her citizens I
sir, am ready and wiling to spill my blood in her defence. Thus spoke
the hero & much more which I can not remember, it being rehear's
to me by the sheriff. But it had a different effect from what the
Fed[eralist]s desired. Their motive was to catch him in his speech,
but it was rendered abortive by the candid & solemn manner in
which he stated the extent of his injuries & his determination to seek
redress. This pathetic appeal to the feelings of the sons of Liberty
drew tears from many eyes, and while they could hardly be kept back
from embracing the knees of the old warrier they bestow'd many
inverted blessings on the heads of those who had so grossly injured
him, while they poor souls stand out of sight behind the benches &
seats fearing the just vengeance of an enraged populace. But the
Hon. Judge would not consent for the case to be tryed this term as
his clients had not had time to procure false witnesses sufficient to
prove themselves innocent, so they have until November to look
about themselves, when if they cannot hire some of their gang to
swear for them they must pay the money for their sauce—which is
the cinsere desire of their implacable friend

T. M. J.

page 68

Sunday 10th. I lived thro' another day which is set apart for the
worship of the most high, while others have been waiting on the
Lord in the usual places of public worship I have been mourning in
Prison. I have besought the Lord to look in pity upon my sufferings,
but my mind still labours in darkness, and sometimes I almost
despair of ever again enjoying any comfort, but then at some other
times I feel a gleam of hope shine into my heart which keeps me

from sinking. I have been too negligent of late in attending to the things of the kingdom. My mind has been agitated with a spirit of revenge against my persecutors & I have written what I wish I had not, for I now declare that I feel no enmity towards one son or daughter of Adam. I dare not read much in the scriptures. When I do I get a studying and it bewilders my understanding. I have therefore stinted myself to five chapters a day which affords matter sufficient for contemplation the whole day & evening. I sometimes light upon a passage which encourages me to hope & at other times drive me almost to despair. I must still hope. I am determined to search my own heart. I know that I have been very wicked but then Christ came not to call the riteous but sinners to repentance. I know that I do not feel the same relish for sin & sinful pleasures I once did. I know too that I love the servants of God. I rejoice when I sometimes feel the presence of God in prayr. I believe I have some ground for my hope.

page 69

Monday 11th.

> Why dwell forever on the gloomy side?
> Say doth not God unering still preside?
> Why then ungratefully presume to scan,
> With Impious cavils marking every plan?
> Tho' truth and Justice both surround his throne,
> And mercy gems the glories of his crown.

I would fain get rid of my melancholy, but cannot. I have been studying the scriptures til I am left in uncertainty. Oh that I could but be guided aright, I should then be happy. My head grows dizy. I wish I could drink the waters of lithe & consign to oblivion past events, the rememberance of which drives me to distraction. My peace of mind is gone, my vain hopes of happiness fled. My health ruined—my reason—Oh my God how miserable am I—since writing the above I have had a strange feeling in my head, but now I feel better. I wish I could be more resign'd to the will of divine providence & study up into the mysteries of religion. I fear it is another plan of satan to bewilder my understanding, but I hope for the best. I wish to be inform'd aright and am yet affraid to trust my

own judgment. I hope that God will enlighten my understanding, that I may disern good from evil ————
Tuesday 12th. After passing a restless night I this morning felt very much out of order. The horrors of my mind were so great that I feared I should lose my reason

page 70

entirely, but still I felt something like hope which prevented my falling again into despair. After earnestly praying God to strengthen & assist me I thought I would make one effort more & if I found no comfort this day I would give up the point & let despair take its full scope. But it pleased God to direct me to this passage of scripture which at once dispell'd the gloom which beclouded my mind, 1 Luke 6th 21st Blessed are ye that hunger now for you shall be filled. Blessed are ye that weep now for ye shall laugh. This & many more such comforting passages raised my dropping spirits. It is passing strange but so it is that those very passages which in my hours of darkness read death to my soul now speak life in all its beauty. If I was a castaway should I feel as I now do, should I find any comfort in reading the scriptures? Should I have such melting seasons in pray'r. I think not, & I think further that I have nourished false doctrine which has been the cause of all my misfortunes & darkness of mind. I mean the doctrine of falling from grace. This doctrine drove me to despair, depriv'd me of my reason, & for awhile kept my mind captive in more than Egyptian darkness, but thank God light again shines in upon my benighted Soul

page 71

I see things in a different from what I formerly did. And I feel more calm & established in my belief of Gods all protecting power than I did in the belief of his partial mercy. If those who have been regenerated, born again & cleans'd by the blood of Christ, and received into the family of the saints, can be wrested out of the hands of a savior who bled & died, that they might live, then is the power of Satan greater than the power of God & the whole plan of redemption is rendered abortive at the will of the adversary, but I am not afraid to risk the salvation of my Immortal soul on the very words of our blessed redeemer where he says in John 10th 27th &c.

My sheep hear my voice & I know them and they follow me and I give unto them eternal life, and they shall never perish, neither shall any man pluck them out of my hand. My Father which gave them to me, is greater than all: and no man is able to pluck them out of my fathers hand ———

Wednesday 13th. I have passed this day very cheerly. An heretofore unnown calmness pervades my Soul. I never in my life felt more peace of mind. I can now study without having my ~~thoughts~~ ideas entangl'd. the scriptures reads like another book to what it ever did before. I feel satisfied that I have at last got into the true channel, at least I hope I have, & pray God to direct me through.

page 72

Thursday 14th. My imprisonment sits easier upon me than ever, as my mind is more at ease. I hope I shall always be thankfull to my Maker for his goodness to me in removing the thick darkness from my mind & bringing me once more into the light of hope. This alteration is great indeed. Sometimes I can hardly believe, but it is true that I feel that comfort which for many days my fainting soul has sought in vain. When I look into my soul all is at peace. Like the sun after a storm when it becomes calm & smooth, I think of my affairs without being driv'n to distraction at their untoward state. God only knows what is best for me. If I am driv'n to poverty it is no more than I deserve, if I am separated from my dear wife & children, it is no more than I deserve, for when I enjoyed their company & conversation, I was not thankfull enough to the great giver of such inestimable blessings—all in providence is for the best & I wish to be content.

Friday 15th. My time passes away in haste. I fondly look forward to the third of June when I hope to be once more at liberty & if providence so orders it shall be permited once more to embrace my family & friends—my health has never been so good, except the raising of blood, as it is now since I have been in prison & my mind thank God is in a comfortable state.

page 73

Saturday 16th. I by the blessing of God still exist & enjoy a tolerable good state of health both in body and mind. Peaceable & calm I fear

not future evils nor repine at present afflictions. My chief study is
how I may contribute to the felicity of my immortal soul. The
scriptures of truth afford an ample field for contemplation, so that I
am not idle. When I am not reading or writing, I contemplate the
wonderful goodness of God towards me in restoring my reasoning
faculties and peace of mind. Oh! may I always remember with
gratitude the loving kindness of a saviour who kindly interposed his
friendly hand & prevented my falling into the dark abyss of despair.
Sunday 17th. While others have their liberty to go to meeting I am a
prisoner depriv'd of that priviledge. Yet tho' in close confinement my
thoughts are at liberty & sometimes I have as good meetings here
alone as ever I had when encompassed by the gazing multitude. It is
true my afflictions are many, but what is it to suffer here if we can be
happy hereafter? I think I can say with Paul: For our light affliction,
which is but for a moment, worketh for us a far more exceeding and
eternal weight of glory—

page 74

While we look not at the things which are seen, But at the things
which are not seen: for the things which are seen are temporal: but
the things which are not seen are eternal. It is true I am strip'd of
earthly property, but what then? I may perhaps earn more and if I
never do, I would not relinquish my hopes of hapiness in a never
ending eternity to be put in possession of the wealth of the whole
globe, for "What shall it profit a man ~~if he~~ to gain the whole world
and lose his own soul." Yet notwithstanding I should wish for my
family's sake to be possess'd of a competency & he who has seen fit to
take it from me once has the same power to bless my exertions with
success in recovering it again. But if it otherwise ordered I am
content, as for my wife and children, "He who tempers the wind to
the shorn lamb" is able to succour & support them.

> Let kindled fancy view the glorious morn
> When from the bursting graves the just shall rise
> All nature smiling and by angels borne,
> Mesiah's crops far blazeing o'er the skies.

Monday 18th. God is still mercifull in sparing my unprofitable life &
blessing me with a tolerable measure of health. Yet I sigh for liberty

& the society of my friends as the time draws near when I hope to be restor'd to them. I grow impatient of its delay and often count the hours of my bondage for my amusement.

page 75

Tuesday 19th. Still am I spared, tho' in Prison to enjoy hapiness. Yes I enjoy that blessed calmness and peace of mind which untill within a few days has long been a stranger to my bosom. I some times feel lifted above the world & think I shall no more suffer afflictions to overcome me or harras my thoughts. But alass! How weak is poor frail man, no sooner does my thoughts take their flight to the abode of my Wife & babes than my tears flow and all my boasted tranquility vanishes. Once was I happy surrounded by dear friends, possessed of the person and affections of her I lov'd, amus'd by the Inocent prattle of my dear babes, now depriv'd of all, yes all gone, & I in prison far from all my friends and family. What a prospect does futurity present, poverty and distress, and what embitters it is the consciousness of reducing one of the most blameless as well as the most virtuous of her sex ~~from a state of~~ to a state of wretchedness. But is there nothing to comfort, surely there is. Religion and resignation props my falling hopes. Then let me rest assured that if I lose all here, and secure my happiness in another & a better world, the exchange will be advantageous.

page 76

Wednesday 20th. This day there has been a great stir here, news having been brot that many prisoners were coming, but they have not yet ariv'd. The County is all in an uproar occasioned by the detection of a number of counterfeiters of Bills on the state Bank. The high sheriff and all his deputies are out on the scout after the culprits. Thursday 21st. At ten oclock Moses Colby, a man who was imprisoned for debt, swore out of jail. He has been closely confined 16 weeks. When he took leave of us he shed tears. He was much put to it to walk on the ground. About three oclock we were alarmed by a hackney coach, attended by the high sheriff in a chaise which came rat'ling into the jail yard, but on looking out saw three young in Irons handed out, & immediately they entered the prison. Soon the massive iron doors closed on them and they were left in darkness &

solitude to their own reflections, two of them are brothers by the name of Bennett, the others name is Wood, all taken up for passing counterfeit money. They must lay in Prison six months as the court does not sit untill November, be they inocent or guilty.

page 77

Friday 22nd. News came today that two more counterfeiters are arrested and committed to Prison, one in Salem and the other in Newburyport. These which are here have began to threaten & contrive plans for to break out but have been overheard and for their comfort have now the outside grate door lock'd continually so that none can come into the alley in which they are confined, and none are allowed to converse with them unless some of the family attends to hear the conversation.

Saturday 23rd. The High sheriff paid me a visit today almost tired to death as he said, he had been on hard service for three days and nights taking & dispersing the counterfeiters, which he said amounted in the whole to fifteen or twenty, some of whom had fled & others were lodg'd in jail. The Directors of the Bank have offered large rewards for their detention. I am still in tolerable good health. I do not raise as much blood as usual & am in hopes that I shall soon be entirely well of it. I must acknowledge my obligations to a number of Ladies in this neighborhood who visit me allmost daily whether out of curiosity or kindness I know not, but am inclined to think both, they bring me so many books that my library now consists of thirty volumes on different subjects.

page 78

Sunday 24th. Tho' yet a spared monument of Gods mercy I know not how soon I may be numbered with the silent dead, when I realize the shortness of time & the length of eternity. I am lost in astonishment to think how careless & unconcerned many waste their precious moments in vain pursuits and idel recreation which ought to be improv'd in making their peace with their justly offended maker. We have no fixed abode, but are swiftly passing through time into eternity, where we must be fixed in happiness or misery forever. Then

how great the folly of suffering our main attention to be taken up
with the present objects and seeking our chief happiness in this
world, as tho' we were settled here forever, and had no concerns with
another state. This is to too much the case with multitudes, when we
look around us, we see people engaged some in the business & others
in the trifles of time: but as for the weighty concerns of eternity, they
are by many at least put far out of mind and neglected as Idle fictions
and not treated as important realities. Oh may I never again waste
my precious time as I have heretofore, but improve every fleeting
moment in making preparation for another and a better world.
Monday 25th

> As yet lifes vital fluid flows,
> And I am spar'd to recount my woes,
> While many since the days last close
> Do now in silent Death repose

page 79

Tuesday 26th. There has been many visitors here today. Some from
Newbury Port, endeavouring to persuade one of the counterfeiters to
turn states evidence & bring out his comrades. Whether they have
been successful or not I am unable to say, but immagene they have.
My health is almost reestablished. I spit but little blood & the
distressing pains in my head have ceased. My hands and feet
continue swolen but not to such a degree as usual, my appetite is
good and I can eat my allowance without grumbling. I hope I shall
still be able to labour with my hands to support my family should it
please God once more to restore me to liberty. ————
Wednesday 27th. The old fox is caught at last, or in other words the
head man of the company of Counterfeiters has been apprehended
and is now my next door neighbor. His name is Amos Dunnels,
formerly of Rowley, where his family consisting of his wife and five
children now reside. He has been a man in considerable business, has
followed Butchering these eight years past & furnished the overseer
of this Prison when building with provision for the workmen. He has
often been here with his cart since I have been in Prison, but today
he came in high stile in

page 80

a schaise accompany'd by his honor the high Sheriff & a Deputy. He is under heavy bonds, which he cannot pay. Until within a few days he was a respectable man & nobody mistrusted him, but some of his comrades betrayed him to preserve their own Liberty. Numerous counterfeit bills of his passing come in from all quarters & it is expected he will end his days in the States Prison. They seem to have kept the proffits of their trade in the family. Dunnels & Wood are brothers in law & the Bennetts are brothers. There are more of them expected dayly. good Lord deliver me from such company. I have no peace of mind, they are continually cursing and swearing & damning their hard fate as they call it, but I hope soon to leave them for better society.

Thursday 28th. Nothing has transpired today worth mentioning. Things remain much as usual, only the prisoners are more noisey than they were before Dunnells came among them & drink more rum. The grateing door at the entrance of the alley has been continually locked since he has been here which shuts out all company & makes me more lonesome than I have ever yet been, but in a few days I hope by the help of good providence to be freed from this place which has of late grown more hateful to me than ever. My health is tolerable good & I hope to be able to go to work immediately after my emancipation if some one of my Federal friends does not take it into his head to tuck me into jail again, which God grant they may be kept from.

page 81

Friday 29th. Another long day has past away, without bringing any news to the poor prisoner worth relating only that the high Sheriff has paid us a visit & was very short in his answers to questions put by the other prisoners, but conversed freely with me some time. He said another of the counterfeiters had been apprehended & committed to prison but did not mention where he was confined. I ~~hope that~~ told him that I would willing give up my birth and be turned out of doors to accommodate any one of the gentry, but he said I was too great a prize to be wantonly thrown away, so he should take very good care of me for a few days, let who or what would come. So be it. But a day now seems as long as two did two months ago. I think continually of

home & dream about it every night, but it is now late & time I was
dreaming about something else ———
Saturday 30th. I have been very much indisposed today. I was taken
pewking soon after breakfast which continued a considerable time
attended with pains in my head & a trembling in every joint. I was
seriously allarmed lest I should be once more confined to a sick bed
in this dreary cell, but through the good providence of God I am
much better this evening though far from being well, but I am not
uneasy. He who "tempers the wine to the shorn lamb" will surely
provide for one who has lost hide and all.

page 82

Sunday 31st. This day has completed another month & a long one
too for me, who have now been in close confinement seventy one
days. But the time draws nigh when I hope to tread the verdant lawn
& praise the god of nature. It has not seemed like sunday to me
today, there has been so much company. Mrs. Dunnells and Mrs.
Sullivan have been here all day, & noice enough they have made.
Dunnells has been giving his wife instructions respecting some
hidden treasure, called counterfeit money, which was buried down in
the orchard, yet he daily asserts and calls God to witness to the truth
of his assertions, that he never had a counterfeit bill except he took it
for good money, but people sometimes take the liberty to disbelieve
him & I among the rest. I have been quite unwell all day, being sick
at my stomach not being able to keep down my victuals, but as it is to
be a very few days before I am to take the fresh air, I am in hopes by
the help of him who supports the weary & fainting traveller, to be
able to immediately fly to the bosom of my long lost family. God
grant that I may always have a proper sense of his great goodness to
me in supporting me through so many perilous scenes & that my
future days may be spent in his service.

page 83

Monday 1st June 1812 ———
I have began another month in this dreary cell. God grant I may not
see the end of it in this place. The Cannon have been roaring all day
today in honor to their famous Fed[eralist], Governor Strong,[40] who
takes his seat this day. He had but about one thousand votes majority

about which the Feds make a mighty bluster. They have a large majority in the House of Representatives but the Senate are decidedly Republican. They will serve to curb up these haughty Gentry the Fed[eralist]s. There was brought here this afternoon a young man by the name of Molton, from York, going to the States Prison. He was taken up for stealing & sentenced to the States Prison for 18 months. He shed abundance of tears, said he was innocent & was drag'd away from his wife and child wrongfully. He was in chains & whether Innocent or guilty he excited my compassion. I pity him but could do nothing for him except to give him a glass of spirit. My brother Eben has at length arived and brought the good news that my family and friends are all in good health. I now hope to be liberated on wednesday next. I am so much taken up with the pleasing prospect of regaining my liberty that I shall hardly get any sleep to night. ————

page 84

Tuesday 2nd. I have reason to hope this is the last day I shall spend within these gloomy walls. My Brother has been kind enough to pay my fine of fifty Dollars & costs of prosecution & tomorrows sun is to witness my emancipation, if nothing in providence prevents. I desire to be thankfull to almighty God for his abundant goodness in keeping me & bringing me through so many tryals & perils in safety. O may my future time be spent in an acceptable manner in the service of the most high —— Adieu ye damp solitary walls. Ye have often witnessed my sighs & groans, you have often been wetted with my tears, bear witness of me forever, that I have vow'd to serve that God, whose kind care of me has been indeed wonderfull, all the days of my life, & if I do not perform my vow, may you again receive me & inclose me forever.

NOTES

INTRODUCTION

1. "Diary of Timothy M. Joy (Written in Ipswich Prison, Salem, Massachusetts, 1812)," box 7, Henry B. Joy Historical Research Record Group, Bentley Historical Library, University of Michigan, Ann Arbor (hereafter referred to as Joy Diary), 1. The "extraordinary" circumstances that Joy alludes to are, in fact, highlighted in one scholarly piece on Timothy Pickering. See Hervey Putnam Prentiss, "Timothy Pickering and the War of 1812," *Essex Institute Historical Collections* 70 (April 1934): 105–14.

2. Robert B. Bain, "Putting the Pieces Together (Again?): History Teacher Education as a University-Wide Task" (paper presented at the National History Center conference "Reforming History Education: New Research on Teaching and Learning," June 12, 2007).

3. The work of the eminent cultural anthropologist Clifford Geertz has been particularly influential in shaping my reading of Joy's diary. See Clifford Geertz, *The Interpretation of Cultures: Selected Essays* (New York: Basic Books, 1977). Geertz's emphasis on the need for full contextualization, or thick description, has become a cornerstone of the microhistorical methodology.

4. The pioneering work in this area remains Joyce Appleby, *Inheriting the Revolution: The First Generation of Americans* (Cambridge, MA: Harvard University Press, 2000). A more thorough treatment of this topic can be found in Gordon S. Wood, *Empire of Liberty: A History of the Early Republic, 1789–1815* (New York: Oxford University Press, 2009). Wood's argument that the era witnessed the peaceful end of devotion to traditional deferential attitudes and the dawning of a more egalitarian perspective was first laid out in his seminal (and Pulitzer Prize–winning) work *The Radicalism of the American Revolution* (New York: Alfred A. Knopf, 1992).

5. For information on microhistory as a historical methodology, see Richard D. Brown, "Microhistory and the Postmodern Challenge," *Journal of*

the Early Republic 23 (Spring 2003): 1–20; Florike Egmond and Peter Mason, *The Mammoth and the Mouse: Microhistory and Morphology* (Baltimore: Johns Hopkins University Press, 1997); Jill Lepore, "Historians Who Love Too Much: Reflections on Microhistory and Biography," *Journal of American History* 88 (Spring 2001): 129–44.

CHAPTER 1

1. Curtis Coe, *A Valedictory Discourse, Delivered at Durham, New Hampshire, April 27, 1806* (Portsmouth, NH: William Treadwell, 1806), 3. Samuel Joy purchased pew 42 for his family's usage for twenty-one pounds when funding for the new Durham meetinghouse was first put into place in January 1792 ("Proceedings of Committee, Town of Durham to Build a Meeting House, 1792" [typescript], box 3, folder 6, Thompson Family Papers, 1703–1924, Milne Special Collections, University of New Hampshire, Durham). The events surrounding Coe's dismissal are thoroughly discussed in Charles E. Clark, "Disestablishment at the Grass Roots: Curtis Coe and the Separation of Church and Town," *Historical New Hampshire* 36 (Winter 1981): 280–305. Among the theological points of dispute between Congregationalists and Baptists was the issue of infant baptism. For Congregationalists such as Joy and Coe, the baptism of infants was symbolic, identifying the baptized child as a member of a covenanted community. The practice also involved baptism via the sprinkling of water on the child. Baptists rejected the idea of infant baptism and reserved the rite (in the form of full immersion) only for spiritually awakened adults who were able to profess their convictions and the principles of their faith.

The threat posed by the emergent Baptist faith was nothing new to the Durham church in 1806. In fact, Samuel Joy's first task as a new deacon in June of 1792 was to investigate (along with Dr. Robert Smith) the nonattendance of a former church member, Mrs. Temperance Pindexter. After interviewing Pindexter, Joy reported back to the church at the end of August that she "gave no reason" for withdrawing from the church "but that of a desire to be baptized by immersion." Though promising to return to the church, Pindexter did not do so, and she was eventually dismissed from the church as a "disorderly" person in October of 1801. The details of the incident are found in the "Durham Congregational Church Records" (bound volume), box 37, Thompson Family Papers, 175–77. Coe, despite his Brown training, was vehemently opposed to the principle of baptism by full immersion. His opposition, along with the Pindexter affair and the threat posed by a vigorous Baptist church in neighboring Madbury, led him to publish *A Serious Address of a Minister to His People: The Meaning of the Word Baptism Considered; Several Reasons Assigned for the Baptism of Infants, and Objections Answered* (Portsmouth, NH: Printed by John Osborne at the *Spy* printing office, 1792).

Brief sketches of Coe's personal history can be found in Daniel B. Coe and Eunice A. Lloyd, *Record of the Coe Family and Descendants from 1596 to 1885* (Cincinnati: Standard Publishing, 1885), 3–12; and J. Gardner Bartlett, *Robert Coe, Puritan: His Ancestors and Descendants, 1340–1910, with Notices of Other Coe Families* (Boston: privately printed, 1911), 128–29, 176. It is interesting to note that Coe, trained as he was at a Baptist-affiliated institution (Brown), did not embrace the strictures of that faith, though he certainly did accept its Calvinist foundation.

2. Coe, *Valedictory Discourse*, 10, 23. Samuel Joy's support for Coe and his ministry and, thus, Joy's probable attendance at the valedictory are further borne out by his signed recommendation of Coe to those seeking a minister. See the appendix to *Valedictory Discourse*. Coe family tradition (Bartlett, *Robert Coe, Puritan*, 177) holds that Coe requested at his valedictory that his Durham congregation join him in singing the Issac Watts hymn based on Psalm 120, "Thou God of Love, Thou Ever Blest":

> Thou God of Love, thou ever blest,
>> Pity my suffering state.
> When wilt thou set my soul at rest
>> From lips that love deceit?
>
> Hard lot of mine! My days are cast
>> Among the sons of strife
> Whose never-ceasing brawlings waste
>> My golden hours of life.
>
> O, might I fly to change my place,
>> How would I choose to dwell
> In some wild, lonesome wilderness,
>> And leave these gates of hell!

After his dismissal, Coe purchased a farm in nearby South Newmarket (present-day Newfields). Though declining offers for new ministerial work, Coe did participate in missionary activities throughout Maine and New Hampshire until his death in 1829 (ibid.).

3. Coe, *Valedictory Discourse*, 19, 21, 23–24, 22. The tensions between Protestant doctrine and the emerging market economy are well documented in a number of works. Among the best is Mark Noll, *God and Mammon: Protestants, Money, and the Market, 1790–1860* (New York: Oxford University Press, 2002).

4. "Durham Congregational Church Records," box 37, Thompson Family Papers, 376, 280–83.

5. On Dover's founding, see D. Hamilton Hurd, *History of Rockingham and Strafford Counties, New Hampshire, with Biographical Sketches of Many of*

Its Pioneers and Prominent Men (Philadelphia: J. W. Lewis, 1882), 758–81; John Scales, *History of Strafford County, New Hampshire, and Representative Citizens* (Chicago: Richmond-Arnold, 1914), 74–99; Charles E. Clark, *The Eastern Frontier: The Settlement of Northern New England, 1610–1763* (Hanover, NH: University Press of New England, 1983), 39–46. In 1639, Dover and its nearby neighbor, Portsmouth, successfully petitioned to be absorbed by the Massachusetts Bay Colony. The New Hampshire settlements remained a part of Massachusetts until 1692, when Britain's King William and Queen Mary established New Hampshire as a separate royal colony. The classic work on the New England town remains Kenneth A. Lockridge, *A New England Town: The First Hundred Years; Dedham, Massachusetts, 1636–1736* (New York: W. W. Norton, 1985).

6. Hurd, *History of Rockingham and Strafford Counties*, 781–83. Valentine Hill, along with a great many others, also obtained the grant to build a mill at the falls of the "Lamprell" (Lamprey) River. A brief description of Durham's early agricultural output can be found in Marjory Gane Harkness, ed., *The Fishbasket Papers: The Diaries, 1768–1823, of Bradbury Jewell, Esquire, of Tamworth, Durham, and Sandwich, New Hampshire* (Peterborough, NH: Richard R. Smith Publishers, 1963), 42. The best account of the Piscataqua lumber and mast trade is William G. Saltonstall, *Ports of the Piscataqua: Soundings in the Maritime History of the Portsmouth, N.H., Customs District from the Days of Queen Elizabeth and the Planting of Strawberry Banke to the Times of Abraham Lincoln and the Waning of the American Clipper* (New York: Russell and Russell, 1968). See also W. Jeffrey Bolster, ed., *Cross-Grained and Wily Waters: A Guide to the Piscataqua Maritime Region* (Portsmouth, NH: Peter E. Randall, 2002). According to historian Robert W. Lovett, the gundalow (also spelled "gundelow") was, prior to about 1800, "a dumb barge or square-end scow, propelled by poles and ores, with no rudder or deck"; after 1800, many of the vessels, modified in response to the Piscataqua region's evolving commercial economy, included a fixed rudder, decking, and sails ("A Tidewater Merchant in New Hampshire," *Business History Review* 33 [1959]: 66). For more on the gundalow and its evolution, see Courtney MacLachlan, "The Piscataqua Gundalow," *Maritime Life and Traditions* 30 (Spring 2007): 66–73.

7. Hurd, *History of Rockingham and Strafford Counties*, 616–20. A very detailed account of Durham's founding and early history can be found in Everett S. Stackpole, Lucien Thompson, and Winthrop Meserve, *History of the Town of Durham, New Hampshire (Oyster River Plantation), with Genealogical Notes*, facsimile of the 1913 edition, with 2 vols. bound in a single edition (Somersworth, NH: New Hampshire Publishing, 1973), vol. 1.

8. James R. Joy, *Thomas Joy and His Descendants in the Lines of His Sons Samuel of Boston, Joseph of Hingham, Ephraim of Berwick: A Portfolio of Family Papers* (New York: privately printed, 1900), 9–37. Thomas Joy's difficulties with Winthrop revolved around Joy's endorsement of "Dr. Child's Memorial," a petition denouncing the colony's policy of restricting suffrage to male

members of the Puritan Church. Joy's support of the petition eventually landed him in jail. After his release, he exchanged some of his Boston property for land in Hingham. See ibid., 14–16.

9. Ibid., 35–36. More information on the Eastman family can be found in David W. Hoyt, *The Old Families of Salisbury and Amesbury, Massachusetts* (Somersworth, NH: New England History Press, 1981), 143, 145.

10. The standard account of the Indian/Anglo violence in the Durham region is Stackpole, Thompson, and Meserve, *History of the Town of Durham*, 1:85–106. Also see Scales, *History of Strafford County*, 293–300; Russell M. Lawson, *The Piscataqua Valley in the Age of Sail: A Brief History* (Charleston, SC: History Press, 2007), 48–50. That tensions with local natives were still very much on the minds of Joy and his neighbors is further reinforced by the existence of the Pendergast garrison house in the Packer's Falls community. The fortified house, built by Stephen Pendergast, was constructed in 1735 and sat on land contiguous to Joy's. The size of the Joy farm is estimated at eighty-eight and one-half acres in the original deed to the land (New Hampshire State Archives, Rockingham County Deeds, 25:243–44). When the farm passed to the children of Samuel's great-grandson Ebenezer Joy (who inherited it in 1824), the division of the estate noted that the Joy farm had grown to roughly 181 acres, largely through the efforts of Ebenezer's (and Timothy's) father, Deacon Samuel ("Division of Ebenezer Joy Estate," September 17, 1838, Strafford County Probate Records, 53:255–57).

Accounts vary regarding the size of Samuel and Mary's family. The Joy family genealogy lists three children (Samuel, Hannah, and Jacob). See Joy, *Thomas Joy and His Descendants*, 36–37. The authoritative history of Durham, however, lists five children. See Stackpole, Thompson, and Meserve, *History of the Town of Durham*, 2:236. I have chosen to follow the town history, in light of its documentation of the marriages of the two children (Sarah and Susanna) not mentioned in the Joy family genealogy. Stackpole documents that Susanna married Ebenezer Meader (brother of Hannah, the wife of her older brother Samuel) in 1773 (ibid., 2:277). Another possible lure for Samuel's move to the Piscataqua region was that he had some distant family (the children of his granduncle Ephraim Joy) living in what is today South Berwick, Maine, located directly across the Piscataqua River from Dover.

11. Samuel Joy's legal travails can be traced in the Provincial Court Records at the New Hampshire State Archives. The following court files involved Joy (an asterisk denotes that Joy was a defendant in the case): 13077, 13079, 14759*, 13075, 13078, 10899*, 11759*, 14914*, 14928*, 16176*, 5942*, 22362*, 27582, 10591*, and 10900*. Also see Maine State Archives, Maine Court Records, 1695–1854, Provincial Court Records, 12-550-6926-YORK, 13-127-7250-YORK. An excellent account of the workings of the late colonial and early American court systems as they relate to debt is Bruce H. Mann, *Republic of Debtors: Bankruptcy in the Age of American Independence* (Cambridge, MA: Harvard University Press, 2002).

12. Nathaniel Bouton, comp., *Documents and Records Relating to the Province of New Hampshire, from the Earliest Period of Its Settlement* (Concord, NH: George E. Jenks, state printer, 1867), "Early Town Records," 11:577; New Hampshire State Archives, Probate Records, vol. 18 (1750–54), 274; Scales, *History of Strafford County*, 497. Information on Jacob Joy is derived from Joy, *Thomas Joy and His Descendants*, 38. No document of an actual apprenticeship contract exists, but given the nature of training in the skilled crafts at the time, it is likely that such a contract was drawn up.

13. The widowed Mary was designated the administrator for Samuel's estate (valued at 2,833.70) by the Rockingham County Probate Court (Durham was part of that county until 1769, when it was placed under the jurisdiction of Strafford County) shortly after Samuel's death in 1752 (New Hampshire State Archives, Probate Records, vol. 18 [1750–54], 274). Unfortunately, no copy of the inventory of his estate exists. Mary lived the rest of her life in Durham and died around 1805, presumably under the roof of her son Samuel. She was buried next to her first husband, Samuel, in the Joy family plot on the family farm. The cemetery still exists today and is located on Packer's Falls Road in Durham, just north of the Newmarket town line.

14. Joy, *Thomas Joy and His Descendants*, 37.

15. Samuel and Ebenezer Joy Records, 1807–32, Baker Library Historical Collections, Harvard University. The New Durham purchases are detailed in New Hampshire State Archives, Rockingham County Deeds, 64:78–80. It is unknown whether Deacon Samuel inherited any New Durham land from his father. Joy's Durham purchases are recorded in New Hampshire State Archives, Rockingham County Deeds, 79:150, 84:71. Joy also sold one small plot of salt marsh on the Lamprey River in Durham during this same period (ibid., 70:63).

16. Stackpole, Thompson, and Meserve, *History of the Town of Durham*, 1:187.

17. William Kidder, ed., "The Diary of Nicholas Gilman" (MA thesis, University of New Hampshire, 1972), 241–43. Gilman's devotion to evangelicalism is deftly recounted in Douglas L. Winiarski, "Souls Filled with Ravishing Transport: Heavenly Visions and the Radical Awakening in New England," *William and Mary Quarterly* 61 (January 2004): 3–46. A more critical view of Gilman can be found in Stackpole, Thompson, and Meserve, *History of the Town of Durham*, 1:191–95. For background information on why Gilman and the residents of Durham responded to the Awakening's evangelical thrust, see Clark, *Eastern Frontier*, 273–79. Information on John Adams can be found in Stackpole, Thompson, and Meserve, *History of the Town of Durham*, 1:197–200. In brief, the term "Old Light" refers to those who clung to traditional Calvinist theology delivered in the traditional manner—via learned sermons delivered by college-trained ministers. "New Lights," while sometimes adhering to standard Calvinist orthodoxies, adopted an evangelical, emotion-driven style of preaching intended to provoke individual awak-

ening through the heart rather than through the head. For a full account of such differences and of the origins and impact of the Great Awakening, see Thomas S. Kidd, *The Great Awakening: The Roots of Evangelical Christianity in Colonial America* (New Haven, CT: Yale University Press, 2009).

18. Durham Congregational Church Records, box 37, folder 16, Thompson Family Papers. No record exists in the Durham church records for Samuel's baptism. It seems unlikely, given her handling of Samuel's siblings, that Mary would not have had him baptized somewhere (perhaps in nearby Newmarket).

19. The road past Joy's farm is documented in "Road and Highway Layouts, Durham," binder 14, New Hampshire State Archives. Hannah Meader was the descendant of one of Durham's oldest families. The family's ancestry is outlined in notes found in "Genealogical Notes (Meader Family)," box 27, folder 22, Thompson Family Papers.

20. Joy, *Thomas Joy and His Descendants*, 38. The infant—Jacob Joy—was buried by the Reverend Curtis Coe on October 26, 1783. "Durham Congregational Church Records," box 37, Thompson Family Papers, 136. The death of Elizabeth, at age two, is not mentioned in the existing church records.

21. Durham's role in the Revolution is recounted in Stackpole, Thompson, and Meserve, *History of the Town of Durham*, 1:116–50. Population figures were obtained from the state of New Hampshire at http://www.nh.gov/oep/programs/DataCenter/Population/1767-1820.htm. Other circumstantial evidence exists to suggest that the Joys were perhaps supportive of the Revolutionary cause. Timothy Joy's namesake, for instance, Hannah's brother Timothy Meader, was an active participant in the Durham meeting to form a Committee of Correspondence in November of 1774, and he was also a signatory to a local agreement penned after the battles of Lexington and Concord to defend America against British aggression. See Stackpole, Thompson, and Meserve, *History of the Town of Durham*, 1:118, 128.

22. The classic work on the Revolution's impact at the local level is Robert A. Gross, *The Minutemen and Their World* (New York: Hill and Wang, 2001). For the broader implications of these changes, see Gordon S. Wood, *The Radicalism of the American Revolution* (New York: Knopf, 1992); Gary Nash, *The Unknown American Revolution: The Unruly Birth of Democracy and the Struggle to Create America* (New York: Viking, 2005). A compelling exploration of those who foundered in the face of the Revolution's liberal promise can be found in Seth Rockman, *Scraping By: Wage Labor, Slavery, and Survival in Early Baltimore* (Baltimore: Johns Hopkins University Press, 2009).

23. Though dated, Saltonstall's *Ports of Piscataqua* remains the best account of economic conditions in the greater Durham area for the period under consideration. In particular, see pp. 117–48.

24. Ibid., 122–23, 140.

25. Scales, *History of Strafford County*, 325. Information on Durham's postwar economic boom can be found in Lovett, "Tidewater Merchant in

New Hampshire." Durham's shipbuilding industry is briefly documented in "A Considerable Branch of Business: Shipbuilding in Durham, New Hampshire, 1756–1950," http://www.izaak.unh.edu/exhibits/shipbld/. Among those reported to be engaged in shipbuilding in Durham were members of the Coe family and Timothy Joy's cousin James Joy, the son of Deacon Samuel's brother Jacob. A blacksmith (like his father) by trade, James Joy established what the family history describes as "a promising ship building enterprise" in Durham that, the same source alleges, was ruined by the Embargo Act of 1807 and the War of 1812 (Joy, *Thomas Joy and His Descendants*, 41). Information on the Piscataqua Bridge can be found in Saltonstall, *Ports of the Piscataqua*, 128–29. Also see M. J. White, "A Historical Study of Old Durham" (unpublished manuscript in the possession of the New Hampshire State Library, n.d.), 15–17. Another commodity offered for sale by local farmers was stone. The area's granite was particularly coveted. See Harkness, *Fishbasket Papers*. Despite its promising eighteenth-century growth, however, Durham "remained an agricultural community in the 19th century, falling far behind Dover, its industrial neighbor to the north. In fact, its population fell after 1830, and by 1920, Durham's population was half of what it had been a century earlier" ("Introduction to Durham's 250th," special issue, *Historical New Hampshire* 36 [Winter 1981]: 254).

26. On the activities of the Ffrost family, see Lovett, "Tidewater Merchant in New Hampshire." The Coe family's business ventures are described in Bartlett, *Robert Coe, Puritan*, 253–55. See also "A Considerable Branch of Business: Shipbuilding in Durham, New Hampshire, 1756–1950."

27. "Durham Congregational Church Records," box 37, Thompson Family Papers, 165, 173.

28. Deacon Samuel appears in the Strafford County Register of Deeds a total of twelve times in the Grantee (Purchaser) Index, all between the years 1785 and 1809 (6:193, 9:119, 9:185, 11:302, 13:509, 16:153, 17:46, 19:228, 22:230, 42:461, 55:333, 61:390*—denotes book number and page), and seven times in the Grantor (Seller) Index, all between 1784 and 1815 (5:282, 28:142, 39:288, 53:512*, 61:390*, 67:232, 86:200). Some of Joy's land purchases and sales are for lands in Alton (see asterisked entries). Alton was originally part of the town of New Durham. It became an independent town in 1796. A brief history of the town of New Durham can be found in Hurd, *History of Rockingham and Strafford Counties*, 658. Joy's sale of timber to Durham is recorded in "Durham Town Records, 1792 Acct," box 2, folder 5, Durham (N.H.) Selectmen's Records, and "Durham Town Records, 1800" and "Durham Town Records, 1803," box 3, folders 11 and 1, Durham Town Records, 1732–1993, Milne Special Collections. Joy's account book is located in the Samuel and Ebenezer Joy Records, 1807–32.

29. The inventories and tax records used in this analysis come from "Durham Town Records, Town Inventory, 1784," and "Durham Town

Records, 1784, Tax Rates for Town," box 1, folder 12, Durham Town Records, 1732–1993; and "Counterpart of Rate List in Durham for 1790," box 38, folder 26, Thompson Family Papers. The two samples used include the most complete data sets for the town as a whole for this period and thus allow for a fuller comparison of Joy's personal position in contrast to that of his fellow townsmen. The Dover *New Hampshire Republican* ran an obituary for Joy on November 2, 1824. See William Edgar Wentworth, *Vital Records, 1790–1829, from Dover, New Hampshire's First Newspaper* (Camden, ME: Picton, 1995), 255. Samuel's will can be found in the Strafford County Probate Records, 32:34–35. No actual value is affixed to Samuel's estate at that time. However, three years later, Ebenezer Joy, the executor of Samuel's estate and the inheritor of the Joy farm, also passed away. The inventory for his estate places its value at four thousand dollars (Strafford County Probate Records, 38:94–99).

30. The source of this quote and the chapter's title is from *Another Plot! The Heat of the Election Hatches a Brood of Plots and Falsehoods* (n.d., ca. March 1812), "Broadsides," Phillips Library, Salem, MA. Joy's selection as fence viewer is reported in "Durham Town Records, 1800," box 3, folder 11, Durham (N.H.) Selectmen's Records. As no inventory for Samuel Joy exists, one can only speculate about the types of things that might have been found in his home. The list included was derived from the published inventory of Ebenezer Joy's estate and thus, given that Ebenezer inherited much of his father's estate, likely approximates some of what might have been found in Deacon Samuel's home. Payments to hired help are recorded in Samuel's account book in the Samuel and Ebenezer Joy Records, 1807–32. Ebenezer's teaching career can be traced through his account book in the Samuel and Ebenezer Joy Records, 1807–32, especially on pp. 2–4; and in "Durham Town Records, 1812," box 4, Durham (N.H.) Selectmen's Records. Timothy claims to have been a teacher in his prison diary (23). Given the veracity of the materials included, there is no reason to doubt his claim.

31. "Descendants of Thomas French of Ipswich, MA, and Others," http://awt.ancestory.com/cgi?bin/igm.cgi?op=GET&db=figtree1&id=12096 2&ti=5535. Joy's connection to Osborne also raises some interesting questions about Timothy's later religious confusion while in prison. According to John Scales, Osborne was early on a Congregationalist but later switched to the Freewill Baptist faith ("Lee, NH—250th Anniversary of Settlement of the Territory, 150th Anniversary of Incorporation of the Town" [address, August 23, 1916]). Unfortunately, Scales does not disclose when this shift occurred. Still, it is possible that Joy was exposed to some of the Arminian principles that he later struggled with as a result of his attending Osborne's services.

32. Ebenezer's account book notes all of the activities listed, albeit for a latter period of his life (Samuel and Ebenezer Joy Records, 1807–32). It does, however, seem plausible that he was recording a pattern of work established much earlier on in his life span.

33. "Descendants of Thomas French of Ipswich, MA, and Others," http://awt.ancestory.com/cgi?bin/igm.cgi?op=GET&db=figtree1&id=12096 2&ti=5535. Excellent information about the nature of courtship in New England at the time that Timothy courted Mary can be found in Lisa Wilson, *Ye Heart of a Man: The Domestic Life of Men in Colonial New England* (New Haven, CT: Yale University Press, 1999), though that book is primarily focused on the period leading up to the Revolutionary War. Mary's signature is confirmed in the documents she filed to request a widow's pension related to Timothy's later service during the War of 1812. See "Pension Application Files, War of 1812, Death or Disability," file 13557, National Archives, Washington, DC. The specific date for the couple's marriage is also found in the pension application file, as well as the birth dates and places of birth for their children. The couple's young age at marriage was not typical for New England, though the one-year span between their marriage and the birth of their first child indicates that the marriage was not forced on the couple. For more on marriage in early New England, see Jack Larkin, "Historical Background on Growing Up in Early 19th-Century New England," OSV Documents—Historical Background on Growing Up in Early 19th-Century New England, 2002, http://www.osv.org/explore_learn/document_viewer.php?Doc ID=1992.

34. The federal census of 1810 lists three heads of household with the French surname in New Durham. It is unknown what, if any, relation they bore to Mary. Timothy Joy can be found in the United States Federal Census, 1810, New Durham, Strafford County, New Hampshire, p. 857. An excellent description of "going to household" and of the items that a young couple might have when doing so, can be found in Jane C. Nylander, *Our Own Snug Fireside: Images of the New England Home, 1760–1860* (New Haven: Yale University Press, 1993), 54–73. The baby Mary's birthplace is listed as Middleton, with the source given as a family Bible, in the Bounty Land Grant Warrant Application of Mary Joy, dated October 21, 1850, "Bounty Land Files," can 306, bundle 97, National Archives.

35. Joyce Appleby, *Inheriting the Revolution: The First Generation of Americans* (Cambridge, MA: Harvard University Press, 2000).

36. "Diary of Timothy M. Joy (Written in Ipswich Prison, Salem, Massachusetts, 1812)," box 7, Henry B. Joy Historical Research Record Group, Bentley Historical Library, University of Michigan, Ann Arbor, 13; Scales, *History of Strafford County,* 449–52; census data for Middleton found at http://www.nh.gov/oep/programs/DataCenter/Population/1767-820.htm.

37. Inventories, Durham and Middleton, 1811, New Hampshire State Archives; "Buzzell to Joy," Grantee (Purchaser) Index, 70:46, Register of Deeds, Strafford County Records; "Description of Middleton on July 1, 1814," *Collections of the Massachusetts Historical Society,* vol. 3 of the 2nd ser. (Boston: John Eliot, 1815), 120–21.

CHAPTER 2

1. The narrative of Joy's difficulties in Middleton and his subsequent flight is culled from the materials in the "Diary of Timothy M. Joy (Written in Ipswich Prison, Salem, Massachusetts, 1812)," box 7, Henry B. Joy Historical Research Record Group, Bentley Historical Library, University of Michigan, Ann Arbor (hereafter referred to as Joy Diary). That Mary was expecting a third child is confirmed by James R. Joy, *Thomas Joy and His Descendants in the Lines of His Sons Samuel of Boston, Joseph of Hingham, Ephraim of Berwick: A Portfolio of Family Papers* (New York: privately printed, 1900), 40–41. My search of the records of the Strafford County Court of Common Pleas at the New Hampshire State Archives did not turn up any record of the details of Joy's debt. He does not appear in the case index for 1812, and my own perusal of the collection (which is still being processed) did not turn up any record of cases against Joy. We do know, however, that on April 6, 1812, while he was incarcerated in Ipswich Prison, he was served with a writ issued on behalf of the firm of Leigh and Ferguson of Berwick, Maine (then part of Massachusetts), for a debt of $31.45 (Joy Diary, 27½). We also know, as the newspapers later reported, that in support of his testimony regarding his true identity and circumstances, Joy produced "writs served upon him at Middleton, and sundry small notes and accounts dated there" (*Boston Gazette,* March 23, 1812). E. A. Holyoke is quoted in Joseph B. Felt, *Annals of Salem,* 2nd ed. (Salem, MA: W. and S. B. Ives, 1849), 2:106.

2. Joy Diary, 1. A highly readable account of the mounting tensions between the United States and Great Britain and of the various trade policies adopted by the two sides in the years before the War of 1812 can be found in Gordon S. Wood, *Empire of Liberty: A History of the Early Republic, 1789–1815* (New York: Oxford University Press, 2009).

3. Joy was, as one would expect, highly agitated when he left home. He writes, "I kised my dear wife & she sat all bathed in tears & my two helpless babes lay asleep & rush'd out of the house in a hurry, jumped into my sleigh & drove off, I hardly knew which way." Shortly thereafter, he regained his composure and set a course for Gilmanton, New Hampshire, hoping that, he wrote, "by taking such a cicuitous rout to Salem I should escape pursuit" (Joy Diary, 2). Joy had apparently already been considering a sojourn to Salem—"for a season" (ibid., 1)—in the days before the incident with his creditors. The threat of arrest apparently finalized the decision for him.

4. Ibid., 4–5. The name of the tavern is identified in a newspaper article written after Joy's arrest in Salem. See *Salem Gazette,* March 27 and 31, 1812. The owner, Asaph Kendall, is identified in George Wingate Chase, *The History of Haverhill, Massachusetts, from Its First Settlement, in 1640, to the Year 1860* (Haverhill, MA: privately printed, 1861), 596. The location of Kendall's Tavern is described in Albert LeRoy Bartlett, *Some Memories of Old Haverhill*

(Haverhill, MA: privately printed, 1915), 56. Bartlett's account notes that the tavern later became a private dwelling known as the Smiley House and was relocated to the west corner of Pleasant and Winter Streets. Elm Corner was named for the large elm tree that grew there. A few rods east of the elm was a spring known as Kendall's Spring. Elm Corner is known today as White's Corner, a name it received in 1861. See *Haverhill Gazette*, August 27, 2008. The names of the men who engaged in conversation with Joy are reported in the *Essex Register*, March 28, 1812.

5. A succinct account of the Henry Affair can be found in Walter R. Borneman, *1812: The War that Forged a Nation* (New York: HarperCollins, 2004), 42–45. See also Donald R. Hickey, *The War of 1812: A Forgotten Conflict* (Champaign-Urbana: University of Illinois Press, 1990), 37–39. More generalized accounts of the era's intense partisanship (which is discussed at greater length in chapter 3), include Richard Buel, Jr., *America on the Brink: How the Political Struggle over the War of 1812 Almost Destroyed the Young Republic* (New York: Palgrave Macmillan, 2005); Joanne B. Freeman, *Affairs of Honor: National Politics in the New Republic* (New Haven, CT: Yale University Press, 2001; Paul Johnson, *The Early American Republic, 1789–1829* (New York: Oxford University Press, 2007); John C. Miller, *The Federalist Era, 1789–1815* (New York: Harper and Row, 1960); and James Roger Sharp, *American Politics in the Early Republic: The New Nation in Crisis* (New Haven, CT: Yale University Press, 1993).

6. Joy Diary, 5; *Merrimack Intelligencer*, March 28, 1812. I discuss Timothy Pickering at greater length in chapter 3. The standard biography of Pickering remains Gerard H. Clarfield, *Timothy Pickering and the American Republic* (Pittsburgh: University of Pittsburgh Press, 1980).

Joy's conversation with Eaton and company did not go unheard, though the precise details regarding exactly what happened remain a point of conjecture. At one point in the afternoon, someone from the tavern apparently reported the nature of the conversation to the prominent Haverhill Federalist Bailey Bartlett, a former member of the U.S. House of Representatives and the high sheriff of Essex County until 1811 (he would regain this post in late June of 1812). Bartlett later claimed to then have visited Kendall's Tavern, where he found "Mr. Wingate and Mr. Eaton, and . . . one or two others, who appeared to be engaged in private conversation with a man who I was told was the man from Canada." A brief time later, Bartlett asked Wingate whether he intended to depose Joy, alias Emery, and was told "no." Bartlett replied that if a deposition was taken, he wished to be present. Wingate did not, however, inform Bartlett when the deposition was drawn up in Eaton's office. Learning of its existence soon after it was drawn up, Bartlett sent immediate word to Salem "in order that a further inquiry might be made" (*Salem Gazette*, March 31, 1812). On Bartlett, see Cecil Hampden Cutts Howard, ed., "Sketch of Mrs. William Jarvis of Weathersfield, Vermont," pt. 1, *Historical Collections of the Essex Institute* 24 (April–June, 1887): 123–39.

Subsequent newspaper accounts of the incident report that Joy did indeed sign the deposition. See *Salem Gazette,* March 31, 1812, and Moses Wingate's testimony as reported in the *Essex Register,* March 28, 1812. Wingate's uncle, Paine Wingate, was married to Timothy Pickering's sister, Eunice. See Charles E. L. Wingate, *History of the Wingate Family in England and America* (Exeter, NH: James D. P. Wingate, 1886), 152, 158. The details surrounding the activities in Haverhill quickly became a source of major partisan conflict, and I discuss them at greater length in chapter 3.

7. News of Joy's allegations was immediately dispatched (at 5:00 p.m.), via letter, to the Pickering family in Salem. See John Varnum to John Pickering, March 20, 1812, "Letters to Son John, 1786–1829," box 2, Timothy Pickering Papers, Phillips Library, Peabody-Essex Museum, Salem, MA. Varnum was a Federalist attorney and a former member of the Massachusetts Senate, from Haverhill. A Harvard graduate, Varnum had been a classmate of the noted Unitarian minister William Ellery Channing and the future U.S. Supreme Court justice Joseph Storey. He would later go on to serve three terms in the U.S. House of Representatives. See John Marshall Varnum, *The Varnums of Dracutt (in Massachusetts): A History* (Boston: David Clapp and Sons, 1907), 90–91.

8. Joy Diary, 6–7; *Haverhill Merrimack Intelligencer;* March 28, 1812. The location of the Salem Hotel is identified in Irving K. Annable, "Historical Notes of the Crombie Street Congregational Church, Salem, MA," *Essex Institute Historical Collections* 77 (July 1941): 207. The report of "chilly" weather at the wharf is found in the March 21, 1812, entry of the Ezra Northey Diaries, 1800, 1810–16, Phillips Library. Northey notes, "Chilly at the wharf. A man taken up who had been reviling Tim Pickering."

9. Good accounts of Salem's rise as an international port include Margaret B. Moore, *The Salem World of Nathaniel Hawthorne* (Columbia: University of Missouri Press, 1998); Dane Anthony Morrison and Nancy Lusignan Schultz, *Salem: Place, Myth, Memory* (Boston: Northeastern University Press, 2004); National Park Service, *Salem: Maritime Salem in the Age of Sail* (Washington, DC: Department of the Interior, 1987); Daniel Vickers, *Farmers and Fishermen: Two Centuries of Work in Essex County, Massachusetts, 1630–1830* (Chapel Hill: University of North Carolina Press, 1994); and Daniel Vickers with Vince Walsh, *Young Men and the Sea: Yankee Seafarers in the Age of Sail* (New Haven, CT: Yale University Press, 2005). The allegation about Joy repeating his story regarding Pickering comes from the *Essex Register,* March 28, 1812. That story was later included in the brief recounting of the Joy affair that appeared in Hervey Putnam Prentiss, "Timothy Pickering and the War of 1812," *Essex Institute Historical Collections* 70 (April 1934): 110.

10. An excellent brief account of Elias Hasket Derby, his wharf, and the bustling East Indies trade in Salem can be found in National Park Service, *Salem: Maritime Salem in the Age of Sail.*

11. Joy Diary, 7–8. Saltmarsh's identity was gleaned from an arrest warrant

dated March 21, 1812, found in *Commonwealth v. Joy,* Essex County Supreme Judicial Court, 1812 April term, docket no. 183, Massachusetts Supreme Judicial Court Archives and Records Preservation. Later in his journal, Joy mentions a visit from the constable who arrested him on Derby's Wharf. He confirms that the arresting officer was indeed a man named Saltmarsh (Joy Diary, 63).

12. Joy Diary, 9; *Commonwealth v. Joy.* The description of the Salem Courthouse is taken from Frank Cousins and Phil M. Riley, *The Colonial Architecture of Salem* (New York: Courier Dover, 2000), 219–21; and Robert Booth, "Salem as Enterprise Zone, 1783–1786," in Morrison and Schultz, *Salem: Place, Myth, Memory,* 75.

13. Joy Diary, 9–11, 1; *Another Plot! The Heat of the Election Hatches a Brood of Plots and Falsehoods* (n.d., ca. March 1812), "Broadsides," Phillips Library; Portland *Eastern Argus,* April 9, 1812. At least one account of the hearing indicates that the county solicitor, David Cummings, a Democratic-Republican who had recently lost the election for town clerk to Prince, also supported the high bail (*Greenfield Franklin Herald,* March 31, 1812). More than likely, Cummings's recommendation stemmed from Federalist allegations that Joy was part of a larger plot to discredit the party on the eve of state elections. I explore these allegations in greater length in chapter 3. Salem's "gaol" was built in 1638 and sat on the corner of Federal Street and St. Peter Street, across from St. Peter's Church. Joy would be among the last inmates housed there, as the facility was closed the following year, when a new jail was constructed a short distance away. See C. B. Gillespie, *Illustrated History of Salem and Its Environs* (Salem, MA: Salem Evening News, 1897), 177. Joy would later, on March 24, be relocated to the new stone prison in nearby Ipswich, Massachusetts (*Portland Eastern Argus,* March 24, 1812).

14. The market revolution was by no means limited to New England in the immediate post-Revolutionary period. On the contrary, portions of the South and Mid-Atlantic regions also experienced this transformation. Later still, in the years following the War of 1812, the marketplace would leave its imprint on the areas west of the Appalachian Mountains. A great many historical works examine the market revolution and its far-reaching consequences. Among the most important are Christopher Clark, *The Roots of Rural Capitalism: Western Massachusetts, 1780–1860* (Ithaca, NY: Cornell University Press, 1991); and Charles Sellers, *The Market Revolution: Jacksonian America, 1815–1846* (New York: Oxford University Press, 1992). The connections between the market revolution and Jacksonian politics are especially well developed in Harry Watson, *Liberty and Power: The Politics of Jacksonian America* (New York: Hill and Wang, 1990). On the religious ramifications of the transformation, see Whitney Cross, *The Burned-Over District: The Social and Intellectual History of Enthusiastic Religion in Western New York, 1800–1850* (Ithaca, NY: Cornell University Press, 1950); Paul Johnson, *A Shopkeepers' Millennium: Society and Revivals in Rochester, New York, 1815–1837,* 2nd ed. (New York: Hill and Wang, 2004).

15. Bruce H. Mann, *Republic of Debtors: Bankruptcy in the Age of American Independence* (Cambridge, MA: Harvard University Press, 2002), 35–36.

16. Though Rockman's work focuses on wage laborers and the working poor in early national Baltimore, his observations about the correlation between control over other's labor and material success and mobility are also applicable to Joy's circumstances; that is, the success of the coastal merchant elite was predicated on their ability to successfully "assemble, deploy, and exploit" capital and credit, along with the labor of lesser traders and other suppliers. Joy's inability to do the same ensured his failure. See Seth Rockman, *Scraping By: Wage Labor, Slavery, and Survival in Early Baltimore* (Baltimore: Johns Hopkins University Press, 2009), 2–3.

17. "Buzzell to Joy," Grantee (Purchaser) Index, 70:46, Register of Deeds, Strafford County Records. The "shop" built by Joy is mentioned in "Joy to Goodwin," Grantor (Seller) Index, 71:456–58, Register of Deeds, Strafford County Records.

18. As previously noted, Joy records that he was served with a writ (likely of execution) for $31.45 on behalf of Leigh and Ferguson while he was incarcerated in Ipswich Prison (Joy Diary, 27½). One can safely assume that Joy owed money to additional creditors as well. Newspaper accounts of his arrest, for example, indicate that he was carrying multiple bills and notes that he offered up as evidence of the veracity of his true accounting of his circumstances (*Boston Gazette*, March 23, 1812).

Biographical information on Thomas Leigh was taken from Elaine Chadbourne Bacon, *The Chadbourne Family in America: A Genealogy* (North Waterboro, ME: Chadbourne Family Association, 1994), http://www.chadbourne.org/Gen5.html; Annie Wentworth Baer, "The Landing Mill and Its Time, March 1914," http://www.oldberwick.org/index.php?option=com_content&view=article&id=376:-the-landing-mill-and-its-time&catid=77:histories-a-articles&Itemid=126 and "Old Fields Burying Ground," http://www.oldberwick.org/index.php?option=com_content&view=article&id=415:old-fields-burying-ground&catid=50:cemeteries&Itemid=149. It is also known that Leigh had a partnership with Captain John Bowles of Portsmouth. Described as the "landside partner and manager," Leigh and Bowles "ran a profitable freight business carrying harnesses, bridles, saddles, and other leather products [presumably obtained from Philadelphia given the context in which this is found] to be sold in New Hampshire." Bowles is most famous for transporting George Washington's fugitive slave Ona Judge Staines from Philadelphia to freedom in New Hampshire in 1796. It is unclear whether Bowles did so knowingly (or whether his business partner, Leigh, had any knowledge of the event). See Evelyn Gerson, "Ona Judge Staines: Escape from Washington," http://www.seacoastnh.com/blackhistory/ona.html#1.

19. For background information on Timothy Ferguson, see "South Berwick's Historic Cemeteries"; "Portland Street Cemetery Tour,

http://www.oldberwick.org/index.php?option=com_content&view=arti cle&id=241:portland-street-cemetery&catid=50:cemeteries&Itemid=96; *New England Historical and Genealogical Register* 55 (July–October 1901): 375; Baer, "The Landing Mill and Its Time"; Sarah Orne Jewett, "The Old Town of Berwick," ed. Marion Rust, http://www.public.coe.edu/~theller/soj/ una/otb-wb.htm, 17.

Later in life, the two men both served as directors (Leigh as president) of the newly formed South Berwick Bank in 1823 (*Portland Eastern Argus,* October 14, 1823). After the War of 1812, Ferguson also became active (if he was not active already) in coastal (cotton) and transatlantic shipping and shipbuilding ("Ships built 1700–1847 in South Berwick area," http://www.oldber wick.org/index.php?option=com_content&view=article&id=251:ships-built-1700–1847-in-south-berwick-area&catid=52: trades-a-occupations& Itemid=256). After Leigh's death in 1831, Ferguson helped to administer the sale of his former partner's river property to the Quamphegan Manufacturing Company as a site for textile mills (Baer, "The Landing Mill and Its Time"). Ferguson also partnered with Isaac P. Yeaton, in 1837, to build his own woolen mill in Berwick. The mill was subsequently destroyed by fire in 1843 or 1844.

20. The dissolution of the firm of Leigh and Ferguson was reported in the *Portsmouth Oracle* on December 24, 1814. An example of the type of ad placed by Leigh, Ferguson, and Palmer is found in the *Portsmouth Oracle* edition of July 31, 1813.

21. Toby L. Ditz, "Shipwrecked; or, Masculinity Imperiled: Mercantile Representations of Failure and the Gendered Self in Eighteenth-Century Philadelphia," *Journal of American History* 81 (June 1994): 51–53. A thorough and highly readable account of American credit instruments during this period can be found in Mann, *Republic of Debtors.* Another excellent work on the subject is Stephen Mihm, *A Nation of Counterfeiters: Capitalists, Con Men, and the Making of the United States* (Cambridge, MA: Harvard University Press, 2007).

22. The threat of a second American trade embargo (the first having been imposed during Thomas Jefferson's second term, 1807–9) came to pass in early April of 1812, as President James Madison, with the approval of the Republican-dominated Congress, implemented a ninety-day cessation of trade to enable American ships to return to safety before the potential commencement of hostilities between the United States and Great Britain. See Buel, *America on the Brink,* 141–42.

23. The standard works on early American bankruptcy law are Edward J. Balleisen, *Navigating Failure: Bankruptcy and Commercial Failure in Antebellum America* (Chapel Hill: University of North Carolina Press, 2001); and Mann, *Republic of Debtors.*

24. Mann, *Republic of Debtors,* 24–25. New Hampshire's state laws relative to debtors and creditors are also outlined in Peter J. Coleman, *Debtors and Creditors in America: Insolvency, Imprisonment for Debt, and Bankruptcy, 1607–1900* (Madison: State Historical Society of Wisconsin, 1974), 53–64. Ac-

cording to New Hampshire state law at the time, Joy's creditors, had they secured his person, would have had to levy final execution within thirty days of his arrest; otherwise, they would have had to release him for one year, thus granting a temporary stay on the execution of the debt. Joy notes in his April 24 journal entry that his property had been attached (Joy Diary, 50).

Other useful works on debt in the early republic include Balleisen, *Navigating Failure;* Ruth Wallis Herndon, *Unwelcome Americans: Living on the Margin in Early New England* (Philadelphia: University of Pennsylvania Press, 2001); Carla Gardina Pestana and Sharon V. Salinger, eds., *Inequality in Early America* (Hanover, NH: Dartmouth University Press, 1999); Seth Rockman, *Welfare Reform in the Early Republic: A Brief History with Documents* (Boston: Bedford/St. Martins, 2003); Scott A. Sandage, *Born Losers: A History of Failure in America* (Cambridge, MA: Harvard University Press, 2005); and Billy G. Smith, ed., *Down and Out in Early America* (University Park: Pennsylvania State University Press, 2004).

25. Joy Diary, 2; Karen Haltunnen, *Confidence Men and Painted Women: A Study of Middle-Class Culture in America, 1830–1870* (New Haven, CT: Yale University Press, 1983).

26. Historians have been relatively late in taking up the meaning of failure in the nineteenth-century United States. Two excellent studies that attempt to rectify this gap are Mann, *Republic of Debtors;* and Sandage, *Born Losers.* A clear articulation of the attribution of business failure to "personal character flaw" can be found in Ditz, "Shipwrecked," 58.

27. Joy Diary, 1. The concept of "lived religion" has been the focus of much contemporary work in the fields of religious studies and religious history. My own understanding of the concept is drawn from David D. Hall, *Lived Religion in America: Toward a History of Practice* (Princeton, NJ: Princeton University Press, 1997).

28. Joy Diary, 3–4; *Hallowell American Advocate,* March 31, 1812; *Merrimack Intelligencer,* March 28, 1812.

29. Joy Diary, 72; Curtis Coe, *A Valedictory Discourse, Delivered at Durham, New Hampshire, April 27, 1806* (Portsmouth, NH: William Treadwell, 1806), 3; Joy Diary, 38, 74.

30. Mann, *Republic of Debtors,* 3.

31. Ditz, "Shipwrecked," 54; Joy Diary, 1, 10, 21, 27½. A very good and comprehensive account of the concept of manhood as it played out in early New England is Lisa Wilson, *Ye Heart of a Man: The Domestic Life of Men in Colonial New England* (New Haven, CT: Yale University Press, 1999). Also see T. Walter Herbert, *Dearest Beloved: The Hawthornes and the Making of the Middle-Class Family* (Berkeley: University of California Press, 1993).

32. Joy Diary, 42; J. G. A. Pocock quoted in Mann, *Republic of Debtors,* 121; Joy Diary, 42, 50, 10, 27½.

33. Joy Diary, 45, 50, 74.

34. Ibid., 74–75.

CHAPTER 3

1. "Diary of Timothy M. Joy (Written in Ipswich Prison, Salem, Mass-achusetts, 1812)," box 7, Henry B. Joy Historical Research Record Group, Bentley Historical Library, University of Michigan, Ann Arbor (hereafter referred to as Joy Diary), 26–27¼.

2. Joy Diary, 27; *Salem Gazette,* April 7, 1812.

3. *Salem Gazette,* April 7, 1812.

4. *Essex Register,* April 8, 1812; *Salem Gazette,* April 11, 1812; William Bentley, *The Diary of William Bentley, D.D., Pastor of the East Church, Salem, Massachusetts,* vol. 4, *January, 1811–December, 1819* (Gloucester, MA: Peter Smith, 1962), 91–92.

5. *Essex Register,* April 8, 1812; *Salem Gazette,* April 11, 1812.

6. *Essex Register,* April 8, 1812; *Salem Gazette,* April 7, 1812. The "very riotous" election was also noted by local diarists: see *Diary of William Bentley,* 4:92; and the April 6, 1812, entry of the Ezra Northey Diaries, 1800, 1810–16, Phillips Library, Peabody-Essex Museum, Salem, MA.

7. *Essex Register,* April 8, 1812; *Salem Gazette,* April 7 and 11, 1812. Caleb Strong captured 928 of the votes cast in Salem in the governor's race, as opposed to Elbridge Gerry's 785. All three Federalist candidates for the state senate from the region, including Bailey Bartlett, one of the Haverhill complainants in the Joy case, were also elected.

8. *Essex Register,* April 1, 1812.

9. Gordon S. Wood, *Empire of Liberty: A History of the Early Republic, 1789–1815* (New York: Oxford University Press, 2009), 3. The incipient political culture of American democracy is well documented in Simon P. Newman, *Parades and the Politics of the Street: Festive Culture in the Early American Republic* (Philadelphia: University of Pennsylvania Press, 1997); and David Waldstreicher, *In the Midst of Perpetual Fetes: The Making of American Nationalism, 1776–1820* (Chapel Hill: University of North Carolina Press, 1997). See also Andrew W. Robertson, "Voting Rites and Voting Acts: Electioneering Ritual, 1790–1820," in Jeffrey L. Pasley, Andrew W. Robertson, and David Waldstreicher, eds., *Beyond the Founders: New Approaches to the Political History of the Early American Republic* (Chapel Hill: University of North Carolina Press, 2004), 62.

10. An extensive body of literature traces the origins of what many historians and political scientists have come to label the "first American party system." Among the best are Morton Borden, *Parties and Politics in the Early Republic* (Arlington Heights, IL: Harlan Davidson, 1967); Stanley Elkins and Eric McKitrick, *The Age of Federalism: The Early American Republic, 1788–1800* (New York: Oxford University Press, 1993); John C. Miller, *The Federalist Era, 1789–1801* (New York: Harper and Row, 1960); Pasley, Robertson, and Waldstreicher, *Beyond the Founders;* Norman K. Risjord, *Jefferson's America* (New York: Rowman and Littlefield, 2002); James Roger Sharp, *American Politics in*

the Early Republic: The New Nation in Crisis (New Haven, CT: Yale University Press, 1993); and Wood, *Empire of Liberty.*

A number of excellent works examine the critical roles played by Alexander Hamilton and Thomas Jefferson/James Madison in the formation of this party system. See Ronald Chernow, *Alexander Hamilton* (New York: Penguin, 2004); Joseph J. Ellis, *American Sphinx: The Character of Thomas Jefferson* (New York: Vintage Books, 1998); Joseph J. Ellis, *Founding Brothers: The Revolutionary Generation* (New York: Alfred A. Knopf, 2000); Drew McCoy, *The Elusive Republic: Political Economy in Jeffersonian America* (Chapel Hill: University of North Carolina Press, 1996); and Wood, *Empire of Liberty,* 95–173.

11. Waldstreicher, *In the Midst of Perpetual Fetes,* 219; Kevin M. Gannon, "Escaping 'Mr. Jefferson's Plan of Destruction': New England Federalists and the Idea of a Northern Confederacy, 1803–1804," *Journal of the Early Republic* 21 (Fall 2001): 432. A wonderful account of the rampant antipartyism that characterized the early years of the American republic is included in Gerald Leonard, *The Invention of Party Politics: Federalism, Popular Sovereignty, and Constitutional Development in Jacksonian Illinois* (Chapel Hill: University of North Carolina Press, 2002). See also Gordon Wood, *The Creation of the American Republic, 1776–1787* (Chapel Hill: University of North Carolina Press, 1998). Perhaps the most famous articulation of this sentiment was President George Washington's warning against the "baneful spirit of faction" when he delivered his farewell address in 1797.

12. Pickering was actually dismissed by Adams because of his opposition to Adams's efforts to negotiate peace with France. Two very readable accounts of the buildup to the War of 1812 are Richard Buel, Jr., *America on the Brink: How the Political Struggle over the War of 1812 Almost Destroyed the Young Republic* (New York: Palgrave Macmillan, 2005); and Paul Johnson, *The Early American Republic, 1789–1829* (New York: Oxford University Press, 2007). Buel's account, in particular, offers a very detailed examination of the centrality of Massachusetts' politics to the national debates on the events leading up to the War of 1812. The best account of Pickering's role in the 1803–4 separation movement is Gannon, "Escaping 'Mr. Jefferson's Plan of Destruction,'" 413–43. A handful of biographies on Pickering exist. One of the best remains Gerard H. Clarfield, *Timothy Pickering and the American Republic* (Pittsburgh: University of Pittsburgh Press, 1980). Massachusetts and New Hampshire mirrored one another in the political realm very closely. Federalists controlled the Massachusetts governorship between 1800 and 1807, in 1809–10, and then again after the spring election of 1812. In New Hampshire, Federalist governors were in place between 1800 and 1805, and in 1809–10.

13. Russell M. Lawson, *The Piscataqua Valley in the Age of Sail: A Brief History* (Charleston, SC: History Press, 2007), 88–93; Donald B. Cole, *Jacksonian Democracy in New Hampshire, 1800–1851* (Cambridge, MA: Harvard University Press, 1970), 17–19.

14. Cole, *Jacksonian Democracy in New Hampshire,* 17–19, 21.

15. Ibid., 21; John Jay Knox, *A History of Banking in the United States* (New York: Bradford Rhodes, 1909), 337. It is interesting to consider whether this change in the political current had any relation to the forces afoot in Durham that were responsible for the removal of the Reverend Curtis Coe.

16. Cole, *Jacksonian Democracy in New Hampshire*, 22-23; *New Hampshire Patriot* quoted in Edwin D. Sanborn, *History of New Hampshire, from Its First Discovery to the Year 1830; with Dissertations upon the Rise of Opinions and Institutions, the Growth of Agriculture and Manufactures, and the Influence of Leading Families and Distinguished Men to the Year 1874* (Manchester, NH: John B. Clarke, 1875), 251; Buel, *America on the Brink*, 82. The town meeting movement, the Topsfield Caucus, and the Federalist opposition to the Enforcement Bill are discussed in Buel, *America on the Brink*, 54-84. Also see Robert S. Rantoul, "The Essex Junto, the Long Embargo, and the Great Topsfield Caucus of 1808. A Paper Read at the Field Meeting in Topsfield, Aug. 30, 1882," *Essex Institute Historical Collections* 19 (1882): 226-40. In Massachusetts in 1809, the state's outgoing Republican governor, Levi Lincoln, was censured for sedition by the incoming Federalist administration of Christopher Gore for carrying out the Enforcement Act.

17. Newman, *Parades and the Politics*, 6-7.

18. Newman, *Parades and the Politics*, 44-45; Susan Davis, *Parades and Power: Street Theater in Nineteenth-Century Philadelphia* (Philadelphia: University of Pennsylvania Press, 1986), 156-59. The best account of Washington's visit to Portsmouth and of the town's celebration of that visit is J. Dennis Robinson, "Washington's Seacoast Tour," http://www.seacoastnh.com/Famous_People/Tobias_Lear/George_Washington%27s_Seacoast_Tour/. An excellent account of how the politics of the street helped to spawn a national identity is Waldstreicher, *In the Midst of Perpetual Fetes.* The Portsmouth Jay's Treaty riot was described in the *New Hampshire Gazette*, October 13, 1795.

19. "Vote Tally, 1804," box 4, folder 2, Durham (N.H.) Selectmen's Records, Milne Special Collections, University of New Hampshire; 1810 Election Returns, "Misc. Records," box 4, folder 5, Durham (N.H.) Selectmen's Records; Inter-university Consortium for Political and Social Research, UNITED STATES HISTORICAL ELECTION RETURNS, 1788-1823 [Computer file], 5th ICPSR ed. (Ann Arbor, MI: Inter-university Consortium for Political and Social Research [producer and distributor], 1995). doi:10.3886/ICPSR00079. For 1811-12 New Hampshire voting returns broken out by town see *Haverhill Merrimack Intelligencer*, March 21, 1812.

20. Robertson, "Voting Rites and Voting Acts," 57 (voter participation rates for 1808-14); Joy Diary, 20.

21. Joanne B. Freeman, *Affairs of Honor: National Politics in the New Republic* (New Haven, CT: Yale University Press, 2001), xv, xix-xx.

22. Buel, *America on the Brink*, 107-17.

23. Ibid., 125-47. In regard to a widely circulated political cartoon depicting the gerrymander as an immense monster, Salem's William Bentley, a Re-

publican, wrote, "the division of this county into districts has given an opportunity for a Caracatura stamped at Boston and freely circulated here called the Gerrymander. The towns as they lie are disposed as parts of a monster whose feet and claws are Salem and Marblehead. It is one of those political tricks which have success as far as they go. This division favors much the hopes of retaining a republican senate, and therefore must be a sure object of party vengeance" (*Diary of William Bentley*, 4:91–92).

24. Buel, *America on the Brink*, 147. Also see Hervey Putnam Prentiss, "Timothy Pickering and the War of 1812," *Essex Institute Historical Collections* 70 (April 1934): 105–14.

25. Buel, *America on the Brink*, 23; *Beware of Imposters or Slander Detected* (n.d., ca. March 1812), "Broadsides," Phillips Library.

26. *Another Plot! The Heat of the Election Hatches a Brood of Plots and Falsehoods* (n.d., ca. March 1812), "Broadsides," Phillips Library; "Complaint on Oath," March 21, 1812, *Commonwealth v. Joy*, Essex County Supreme Judicial Court, 1812 April term, docket no. 183, Massachusetts Supreme Judicial Court Archives and Records Preservation. A wonderful account of the broader concern about liars and charlatans is Karen Haltunnen, *Confidence Men and Painted Women: A Study of Middle-Class Culture in America, 1830–1870* (New Haven, CT: Yale University Press, 1983).

27. *Salem Gazette*, March 31, 1812; *Another Plot! The Heat of the Election Hatches a Brood of Plots and Falsehoods*. The broadside was widely published in Federalist papers across the country.

28. *Beware of Imposters or Slander Detected; Portland Eastern Argus*, March 24, 1812; *Essex Register*, March 25, 1812; *Diary of William Bentley*, 4:91. Joy reportedly asked what he was paid by the Haverhill Republicans for making his disclosures and was told that it was they, not him, who should be punished (*Portland Eastern Argus*, March 24, 1812). The *Essex Register* also denounced the actions of Putnam and the Salem Federalist machine. "Mr. Putnam," the paper wrote, "adopted a most outrageous and unprecedented course—He dishonourably and artfully attempted to criminate (in their absence) Mr. Wingate and Mr. Eaton, two respectable gentlemen of Haverhill, by the evidence of this confessed liar." Unable to receive the response he was looking for, Putnam continued to press Joy until David Cummings, the county attorney, "interfered to put a stop to this unprecedented course" (*Essex Register*, March 25, 1812).

29. Joy Diary, 10–11.

30. Ibid., 12.

31. Ibid., 15, 27½. Joy comments on the arrest of another Republican for debt just two days before the April election as well (27¼).

32. Ibid., 17.

33. Ibid., 57–59. One Republican paper, commenting on the verdict against Joy for libel, wrote, "What in the name of Heaven could be said against Tim Pickering that honest impartial men would construe into a libel,

unless he was called *an honest* politician" (*New Hampshire Gazette,* May 19, 1812).

34. Joy Diary, 48, 48½, 60. Additional biographical information on Robert Farley was gleaned from Joseph B. Felt, *History of Ipswich, Essex, and Hamilton* (Cambridge, MA: Charles Folsom, 1834), 183–88; and Thomas Franklin Waters, *Ipswich in the Massachusetts Bay Colony,* vol. 2, *A History of the Town from 1700–1917* (Ipswich, MA: Ipswich Historical Society, 1917), 247, 351–52, 363, 603–4, 813. Farley went on to serve in the War of 1812 as well (ibid., 421–22).

35. Joy Diary, 62–64.

36. Ibid., 64–65.

37. Ibid., 65–67.

38. Ibid., 63, 58.

CHAPTER 4

1. "Diary of Timothy M. Joy (Written in Ipswich Prison, Salem, Massachusetts, 1812)," box 7, Henry B. Joy Historical Research Record Group, Bentley Historical Library, University of Michigan, Ann Arbor (hereafter referred to as Joy Diary), 68–71.

2. Patricia Caldwell, *The Puritan Conversion Narrative: The Beginnings of American Expression* (New York: Cambridge University Press, 1983).

3. A very large body of historical writing examines the vital role that religion played in helping early nineteenth-century Americans to adjust to their rapidly changing world. Joy's story is situated on the cusp of what historians have come to call the Second Great Awakening, and Joy is certainly not an evangelical, but his particular reliance on religion for answers in an environment replete with new questions clearly embodies the well-documented correlation between rampant social change, social flux, and religious enthusiasm/revival.

Among the best works on these varied connections are Jon Butler, *Awash in a Sea of Faith: Christianizing the American People* (Cambridge, MA: Harvard University Press, 1990); Whitney Cross, *The Burned-Over District: The Social and Intellectual History of Enthusiastic Religion in Western New York, 1800–1850* (Ithaca, NY: Cornell University Press, 1950); Nathan Hatch, *The Democratization of American Christianity* (New Haven, CT: Yale University Press, 1991); Nathan Hatch, "The Second Great Awakening and the Market Revolution," in David Thomas Konig, ed., *Devising Liberty: Preserving and Creating Freedom in the New American Republic* (Stanford, CA: Stanford University Press, 1995); Daniel Walker Howe, *What God Hath Wrought: The Transformation of America, 1815–1848* (New York: Oxford University Press, 2009); Mark A. Noll, ed., *God and Mammon: Protestants, Money, and the Market, 1790–1860* (New York: Oxford University Press, 2002); Randolph A.

Roth, *The Democratic Dilemma: Religion, Reform, and the Social Order in the Connecticut River Valley of Vermont, 1791–1850* (Cambridge: Cambridge University Press, 1987); Charles Sellers, *The Market Revolution: Jacksonian America, 1815–1846* (New York: Oxford University Press, 1992); William R. Sutton, *Journeymen for Jesus: Evangelical Artisans Confront Capitalism in Jacksonian Baltimore* (University Park: Pennsylvania State University Press, 1998); and Harry L. Watson, *Liberty and Power: The Politics of Jacksonian America* (New York: Hill and Wang, 1990).

4. Daniel B. Shea, Jr., *Spiritual Autobiography in Early America* (Princeton, NJ: Princeton University Press, 1968), 111. Two excellent works that examine the psychology of conversion among Calvinists such as Joy are Charles Lloyd Cohen, *God's Caress: The Psychology of Puritan Religious Experience* (New York: Oxford University Press, 1985); and John Owen King III, *The Iron of Melancholy: Structures of Spiritual Conversion in America from the Puritan Conscience to Victorian Neurosis* (Middletown, CT: Wesleyan University Press, 1983).

5. Joy Diary, 1, 3; Cohen, *God's Caress*, 11. An excellent account of Puritan theology is Edmund S. Morgan, *Visible Saints: The History of the Puritan Idea* (Ithaca, NY: Cornell University Press, 1963).

6. Joy Diary, 5, 7–9; Curtis Coe, *A Valedictory Discourse, Delivered at Durham, New Hampshire, April 27, 1806* (Portsmouth, NH: William Treadwell, 1806), 8. Charles Cohen (*God's Caress*, 205) identifies this initial conviction of sin as the first phase of a standard formula for conversion among those individuals adhering to orthodox Puritanism.

7. Joy Diary, 12–13. The scripture Joy included is actually Psalm 50:15 (*The Holy Bible, Authorized King James Version* [n.p.: Thomas Nelson Bibles, 2001]).

8. Joy Diary, 13–14. Joy's relocation to Ipswich prison took place on Tuesday, March 24. It appears that the items that the McCoy's loaned to Joy were returned to them at that time, as Joy later recounts that his new jailer, "Mr. J. Stanford," provided him with a writing table and that Stanford's eighteen-year-old daughter, Margaret, furnished him with "many usefull & entertaining books," among which was presumably a Bible (Joy Diary, 19).

9. Joy Diary, 29; Cohen, *God's Caress*, 204; Joy Diary, 20, 24, 27; King, *Iron of Melancholy*, 33, 24.

10. John Bunyan, *The Pilgrim's Progress from This World to That Which Is to Come*, ed. N.H. Keeble (New York: Oxford University Press, 1998).

11. Joy Diary, 27; Coe, *Valedictory Discourse*, 14; Jeremiah 31:18–21 and Psalm 130:7 (*The Holy Bible, Authorized King James Version*); Joy Diary, 27.

12. Joy Diary, 27¼, 27½.

13. Ibid., 28; Coe, *Valedictory Discourse*, 9–10. An 1885 reminiscence of life in early nineteenth-century Salem described Daniel Dutch as "the funny little old constable in short breeches, knee and shoe buckles and queue" ("Leverett Saltonstall's Reminiscences of Salem, Written in 1885," *Essex Institute*

Historical Collections 81 [January 1945]: 65). The critical acceptance stage is well described in Cohen, *God's Caress,* 207–8.

14. Joy Diary, 18–19, 11, 54–55. Joy also notes that the prisoners were not allowed to have any fire and that in the winter months, "the inside of the rooms are one continued sheet of ice" (55). An account of the damage done by the Newburyport fire can be found in the *Boston Gazette,* June 3, 1811. The fire burned over sixteen acres of the city's downtown and destroyed over 250 buildings. Additional details about the prison can be found in Joseph B. Felt, *History of Ipswich, Essex, and Hamilton* (Cambridge, MA: Charles Folsom, 1834), 113; and Thomas Franklin Waters, *Ipswich in the Massachusetts Bay Colony,* vol. 2, *A History of the Town from 1700–1917* (Ipswich, MA: Ipswich Historical Society, 1917), 107, 419. Joy's description of the prison contrasts starkly with that of the *Salem Gazette* (January 25, 1814) when it later described the conditions of British soldiers who were being confined in Ipswich's "gloomy stone gaol" in 1814.

15. Details surrounding Elisha Gurney's release can be found in Essex County Court of Common Pleas Docket (1812), Phillips Library, 384; and Essex County Court of Common Pleas Records, March 1812, Phillips Library, 341.

16. Joy Diary, 30.

17. Ibid., 31–32.

18. 2 Corinthians 12:8–10 (*Holy Bible, Authorized King James Version*); Joy Diary, 30, 32, 40; Coe, *Valedictory Discourse,* 12.

19. Joy Diary, 38–39.

20. Coe, *Valedictory Discourse,* 12; Joy Diary, 38. A cogent and accessible description of the New Haven theology can be found in E. Brooks Holifield, *Theology in America: Christian Thought from the Age of the Puritans to the Civil War* (New Haven, CT: Yale University Press, 2003), 341–69. The redefinition of success in spiritual terms is discussed in Cohen, *God's Caress,* 16.

21. I thank Dr. Sean Kesterson of the University of Michigan Health System for his assistance in diagnosing Joy's condition. Scurvy, a condition brought on by vitamin C deficiency, was common during this period of time. Joy's ability to obtain the necessary dosage of vitamin C to maintain his health would have been rendered all the more difficult by his late winter/early spring incarceration—a season in which fresh produce would have been nearly impossible to obtain. Many of the symptoms described by Joy, particularly the sore and bleeding gums and loose teeth, are characteristic of the disease. It seems that Margaret Stanford, the jailer's daughter, recognized Joy's condition as well. On April 16, Joy, in the throes of agonizing pain, writes, "Indeed I should be quite disconsolate if it were not for the extreme kindness of this family with whom I am. One will bring me a hot brick to put to my feet, another will bring me tea or medicine, some one thing, some another. Everyone seems to want to do something towards restoring me to health. Margaret has just brought me an orange which she had given her a

few days since & would take nothing for it. Thus the Lord raises up friends to comfort me in my affliction" (Joy Diary, 39–40).

22. Ibid., 41–42.

23. Joy Diary, 52. A brief biography of Valentine Smith can be found in Everett S. Stackpole, Lucien Thompson, and Winthrop Meserve, *History of the Town of Durham, New Hampshire (Oyster River Plantation), with Genealogical Notes*, facsimile of the 1913 edition, with 2 vols. bound in a single edition (Somersworth, NH: New Hampshire Publishing, 1973), 1:296–97.

Smith married Timothy's sister Polly in 1804. She died in October 1810, leaving Valentine with three small children (James R. Joy, *Thomas Joy and His Descendants in the Lines of His Sons Samuel of Boston, Joseph of Hingham, Ephraim of Berwick: A Portfolio of Family Papers* [New York: privately printed, 1900], 40).

24. Joy Diary, 53–54.

25. Ibid., 56. The grand jury's indictment labeled Joy "a person of envious, evil, and wicked mind," who "wickedly and maliciously [intended] as much in him lay to injure, oppress, aggrieve, and vilify the good name, fame, credit, reputation of the Honorable Timothy Pickering, Esquire" ("Indictment of Timothy Meader Joy alias Nathaniel Emery," in *Commonwealth v. Joy*, Essex County Supreme Judicial Court, 1812 April term, docket no. 183, Massachusetts Supreme Judicial Court Archives and Records Preservation). It is interesting to note the grand jury's inclusion of the potential damage done to Pickering's "credit." This speaks to the point made about one's reputation as a factor in determining creditworthiness.

26. Joy Diary, 57–58. Sewall's congressional biography can be found at http://bioguide.congress.gov/scripts/biodisplay.pl?index=S000259.

27. Joy Diary, 68.

28. Ibid., 69.

29. Ibid., 69–70.

30. Luke 6:21 (*Holy Bible, Authorized King James Version*); Joy Diary, 70–71; John 10:27–30 (*Holy Bible, Authorized King James Version*). Joy's decision to employ the term *castaway* is tantalizing. It is easy to assume, for instance, that this choice was influenced by the popularity of Daniel Defoe's Calvinism-laced novel *The Life and Strange Surprising Adventures of Robinson Crusoe of York, Mariner* (New York: Oxford University Press, 1998). In this particular work, Crusoe, like Bunyan's Christian, sets off on a voyage of spiritual discovery (in this case, on the sea), only to find himself hopelessly lost after a shipwreck. Crusoe's subsequent trials, adventures, discoveries, and eventual redemption thus stand as allegorical parallels to the pilgrimage undertaken by Christian and would have clearly resonated with the despondent Joy. A succinct account of the final stage in the conversion process can be found in Cohen, *God's Caress*, 208.

31. Coe, *Valedictory Discourse*, 12. A cursory discussion of the ebb and flow of this debate, along with numerous others, can be found in Holifield, *Theol-*

ogy in America, passim. Historical accounts of Osborne's ministry note that he began his work as a Congregationalist but shifted to Freewill Baptist doctrine later in life (John Scales, "Lee, NH—250th Anniversary of Settlement of the Territory, 150th Anniversary of Incorporation of the Town" [address, August 23, 1916]).

32. Joy Diary, 71–72, 78. The exact trajectory of Joy's new path and whether he was exposed to any of Osborne's Freewill evolution cannot be determined, but the shift is certainly intriguing.

33. Ibid., 84.

CHAPTER 5

1. "Diary of Timothy M. Joy (Written in Ipswich Prison, Salem, Massachusetts, 1812)," box 7, Henry B. Joy Historical Research Record Group, Bentley Historical Library, University of Michigan, Ann Arbor (hereafter referred to as Joy Diary), 43–44, 84.

2. Mary had, as evidenced by the absence of this important news in Timothy's journal, kept her pregnancy secret from her already distraught husband while he was in prison. See James R. Joy, *Thomas Joy and His Descendants in the Lines of His Sons Samuel of Boston, Joseph of Hingham, Ephraim of Berwick: A Portfolio of Family Papers* (New York: privately printed, 1900), 40–41.

3. "Joy to Goodwin" (*bis*), Grantor (Purchaser) Index, 71:456–58, 436–37, Register of Deeds, Strafford County Records. Joy's decision to enlist might strike one as surprising. After all, as late as May 6, Joy, approached by recruiters, writes, "[S]everal military officers have been here today endeavoring to persuade me to enlist in the new army. One offered to make me a sergeant, but I would rather swing my hammer alongside my little wife than be trampooseing thro' the woods of Canada. I have some doubts about my courage likewise" (Joy Diary, 62). This statement, of course, was made before Joy knew about his impending child and before the nation was actually in a state of war. Joy's place of enlistment is found in Bounty Land Grant Warrant Application of Mary Joy, dated October 21, 1850, "Bounty Land Files," can 306, bundle 97, National Archives, Washington, DC. There is some evidence to suggest that Joy attained the rank of sergeant while serving. See "Order Dated Sackett's Harbor, March 10, 1813," Third United States Artillery, Enlistment Register, National Archives. Joy's rate of pay is derived from statements made in Mary Joy's postwar pension application that indicate that she would receive half pay ("Pension Application Files, War of 1812, Death or Disability," file 13557, National Archives). It is unknown whether he received any local or state enlistment bounties.

4. The relocation of Joy's family to Durham is indicated by the Durham birthplace listed for his new son, Ebenezer, in family records (Joy, *Thomas Joy and His Descendants,* 46).

5. Jeanne T. Heidler and David S. Heidler, "Artillery," in David S. Heidler and Jeanne T. Heidler, eds., *Encyclopedia of the War of 1812* (Annapolis, MD: U.S. Naval Institute Press, 2004), 19. Also see Lieut. William E. Birkhimer, "The Third Regiment of Artillery," http://www.history.army.mil/books/R&H/ R&H-3Art.htm; Office of the Chief of Military History, United States Army, "The War of 1812, Extracted from American Military History, Army Historical Series," http://www.history.army.mil/books/amh/amh-06.htm, 129.

6. Office of the Chief of Military History, "War of 1812," 132–33; Eric E. Johnson, "The Battle of York," *Lake Erie Ledger* (June 2004): 243–47.

7. Office of the Chief of Military History, "War of 1812," 133.

8. "Order Dated Sackett's Harbor, March 10, 1813."

9. Joy, *Thomas Joy and His Descendants,* 40; Jayne C. Nylander, *Our Own Snug Fireside: Images of the New England Home, 1760–1860* (New Haven, CT: Yale University Press, 1993), 39.

10. Death certificate of Timothy M. Joy, State of New Hampshire.

11. Excellent accounts of New England funerary practices at the time can be found in Nylander, *Our Own Snug Fireside,* 39–40; and OSV Documents—Historical Background on Mourning Rituals in Early 19th-Century New England, 2003, http://www.osv.org/explore_learn/document_viewer .php?DocID=2043 (quotation in text comes from this source).

12. For more on mourning dress, see Nylander, *Our Own Snug Fireside,* 39–40; OSV Documents—Historical Background on Mourning Rituals in Early 19th-Century New England.

13. Nylander, *Our Own Snug Fireside,* 39–40; OSV Documents—Historical Background on Mourning Rituals in Early 19th-Century New England. After the funeral, the family and those assembled would have returned to the Joy farm for food and drink. It is easy to imagine the mourners gathered on the front lawn of the home, under the shade of a large tree, grieving with Timothy's newly filled grave in plain sight. A list of burials in Joy Falls Cemetery, as the family plot is known locally, can be found at http://files.usgwarchives.org/nh/strafford/cemeteries/durham/ joyfallscem.txt. The listing does not indicate any burials for the three Joy infants who died shortly after birth, but it is likely that they, too, were interred in the family plot.

14. Charles E. Porter, *The Military History of the State of New Hampshire, 1623–1861* (Baltimore, MD: Genealogical Publishing, 1972), 2:110, 114, 130–31, 198; Joy, *Thomas Joy and His Descendants,* 40; Samuel and Ebenezer Joy Records, 1807–32, Baker Library Historical Collections, Harvard University; United States Federal Census, 1820, Newmarket, Rockingham County, New Hampshire. No will could be located for Timothy Joy.

Eben served in Captain Vincent Meserve's militia company from May 25 to July 2, 1814, and in Captain Alfred Smith's militia company from September 11 to September 28, 1814.

15. http://trees.ancestry.com/owt/person.aspx?pid=44628394; "Pension

Application Files, War of 1812, Death or Disability," file 13557; Samuel and Ebenezer Joy Records, 1807–32. Some family trees suggest that Mary died in 1869, and some of these give her place of death as Oregon. While the 1869 death is possible, this information, especially the Oregon connection, is highly implausible, given that she can be found residing with her daughter, Mary, in Newmarket in the 1860 census and thus would have had to make such a journey at a relatively advanced age.

16. Joy, *Thomas Joy and His Descendants*, 46; United States Federal Census, 1860, Second Ward, Portsmouth, Rockingham County, New Hampshire. The fire of May 1846 is described at length in the *Portsmouth Journal*, May 6, 1846. The information about Alfred Timothy Joy's apprenticeship and the location of his store are gleaned from an obituary written for him in the *Daily Evening Times* (Portsmouth, NH), May 10, 1883.

17. Information on Timothy's and Mary's son Ebenezer (Eben) was derived from Joy, *Thomas Joy and His Descendants*, 46–47; United States Federal Census, 1860, Newmarket, Rockingham County, New Hampshire; United States Federal Census, 1870 and 1880, Newmarket, Rockingham County, New Hampshire.

18. United States Federal Census, 1830, Newmarket, Rockingham County, New Hampshire; Joy, *Thomas Joy and His Descendants*, 46; United States Federal Census, 1840, Newmarket, Rockingham County, New Hampshire. Mary's marriage announcement can be found in William Edgar Wentworth, *Vital Records, 1790–1829, from Dover, New Hampshire's First Newspaper* (Camden, ME: Picton, 1995), 303.

19. United States Federal Census, 1850, Newmarket, Rockingham County, New Hampshire; "Pension Application Files, War of 1812, Death or Disability," file 13557; Bounty Land Grant Warrant Application of Mary Joy, dated October 21, 1850; United States Federal Census, 1860, Newmarket, Rockingham County, New Hampshire. The best account of the land bounty system is James W. Oberly, *Sixty Million Acres: American Veterans and the Public Lands before the Civil War* (Kent, OH: Kent State University Press, 1990).

20. United States Federal Census, 1880, Newmarket, Rockingham County, New Hampshire. Searches under the French name also turned up no records for Mary between 1860 and 1887.

21. Joy, *Thomas Joy and His Descendants*, 37–38, 40; "Durham Congregational Church Records" (bound volume), box 37, Thompson Family Papers, 1703–1924, Milne Special Collections, University of New Hampshire, Durham, 203; Samuel and Ebenezer Joy Records, 1807–32; "Ebenezer Joy Inventory of Estate, May 19, 1828," Strafford County Probate Records, 38:94–99. Eben's pew is mentioned in his estate inventory. Town records also record the payment of fifty cents to a man named Vincent to repair Eben's pew in 1826. See "Durham Church Records (Series VI)," box 3, folder 3, Durham Town Records, 1732–1993, Milne Special Collections.

22. Will of Samuel Joy, Strafford County Probate Records, 32:34–35.

23. Wentworth, *Vital Records,* 310, 313–14; "Ebenezer Joy Inventory of Estate, May 19, 1828" and "Division of Ebenezer Joy Estate," September 17, 1838, Strafford County Probate Records, 38:94–99, 53:255–57; Joy, *Thomas Joy and His Descendants,* 40. Both Eben and Nancy are buried in the Joy Falls Cemetery. Additional details concerning Eben's estate can be found in Strafford County Probate Records, 30:409, 39:507–8, 42:368–69. On the Griffiths family, see Everett S. Stackpole, Lucien Thompson, and Winthrop Meserve, *History of the Town of Durham, New Hampshire (Oyster River Plantation), with Genealogical Notes,* facsimile of the 1913 edition, with 2 vols. bound in a single edition (Somersworth, NH: New Hampshire Publishing, 1973), 2:202–4.

24. Stackpole, Thompson, and Meserve, *History of the Town of Durham,* 2:204; "Griffiths to Joy," Grantor (Seller) Index, 248:436–38, Register of Deeds, Strafford County Records.

25. "Griffiths to Joy," Grantor (Seller) Index, 248:436–38, Register of Deeds, Strafford County Records; United States Federal Census, 1880, Durham, Strafford County, New Hampshire; Joy, *Thomas Joy and His Descendants,* 37 (note at bottom of page), 46; obituaries for Alfred Timothy Joy in *Daily Evening Times* (Portsmouth, NH), May 10, 1883, and *Portsmouth Daily Chronicle,* May 15, 1883. After a brief service at the Durham home, Alfred's body was transported to Portsmouth for a service at the Court Street Christian Church. He was then interred in that city.

CHAPTER 6

1. Richard D. Brown, "Microhistory and the Post-Modern Challenge," *Journal of the Early Republic* 23 (Spring 2003)n: 18. Examples of macrolevel social histories are far too numerous to even begin to offer an exhaustive list. The works that I reference are Paul Johnson, *A Shopkeeper's Millennium: Society and Revivals in Rochester, New York, 1815–1837,* 2nd ed. (New York: Hill and Wang, 2004); and Thomas Dublin, *Women at Work: The Transformation of Work and Community in Lowell, Massachusetts, 1826–1860* (New York: Columbia University Press, 1981). One of the first American examples in the genre of microhistory and perhaps the most quintessential of all microhistories is Laurel Thatcher Ulrich, *A Midwife's Tale: The Life of Martha Ballard Based on Her Diary, 1785–1815* (New York: Vintage Books, 1991). Another wonderful example is John Demos, *The Unredeemed Captive: A Family Story from Early America* (New York: Vintage Books, 1995).

2. Clifford Geertz, *The Interpretation of Cultures* (New York: Basic Books, 1977).

3. "Diary of Timothy M. Joy (Written in Ipswich Prison, Salem, Massachusetts, 1812)," box 7, Henry B. Joy Historical Research Record Group, Bentley Historical Library, University of Michigan, Ann Arbor, 1. Among the best works examining diaries/journals as both historical documents and as lit-

erary forms is Stephen E. Kagle, *Early Nineteenth-Century American Diary Literature* (Boston: Twayne, 1986).

4. Kagle, *Early Nineteenth-Century American Diary Literature.*

APPENDIX

1. Salem, MA.

2. The items mentioned were most likely sold to his brother Samuel Joy, who resided in the neighboring town of New Durham, New Hampshire.

3. Joy's wife, Mary (French) Joy, was born in Newmarket, New Hampshire, on February 13, 1790, and died in Newmarket, New Hampshire, in 1887. The couple was married in 1807. At the time of his flight, Timothy and Mary had two children: Alfred Timothy, born at New Durham, New Hampshire, on September 5, 1808, and Mary, born at Middleton, New Hampshire, on June 22, 1811. Mary was also, though she may not have yet known, pregnant at the time with a third child, who the couple named Ebenezer (in honor of Timothy's brother), born at Durham, New Hampshire, on November 30, 1812.

4. Gilmanton, New Hampshire.

5. The tavern that Timothy Joy stopped at in Haverhill is identified as Kendall's Tavern by the *Salem Gazette,* March 27 and 31, 1812. The tavern was located on Elm Corner at the junction of Main and Water Streets. See Albert LeRoy Bartlett, *Some Memories of Old Haverhill* (Haverhill, MA: privately printed, 1915), 56.

6. The men at the table with Joy were later identified as Francis Eaton, a Democratic-Republican attorney and the Haverhill postmaster; Stephen Crooker, an aspiring lawyer; and Dr. Moses Elliott. The men were later joined by Moses Wingate, the Haverhill town clerk. See *Essex Register,* March 28, 1812.

7. The location of the Salem Hotel (at the corner of Crombie and Essex Streets—also known as Main Street) is identified in Irving K. Annable, "Historical Notes of the Crombie Street Congregational Church, Salem, MA," *Essex Institute Historical Collections* 77 (July 1941): 207.

8. The fort Joy visited was most likely Fort Lee on Salem Neck.

9. Derby's Wharf, named for its builder and owner, Elias Hasket Derby, was Salem's longest (at one-half mile) and busiest. Its foundation has been preserved and is now part of the Salem Maritime Park complex. It is located directly across modern-day Derby Street from the Salem Custom House.

10. The arresting officer was Seth Saltmarsh. His identity was later given by Joy and is confirmed by an arrest warrant dated March 21, 1812, found in *Commonwealth v. Joy,* Essex County Supreme Judicial Court, 1812 April term, docket no. 183, Massachusetts Supreme Judicial Court Archives and Records Preservation.

11. The courthouse was situated in the middle of Washington Street near its present-day intersection with Church Street.

12. Justice John Prince, Jr. Prince had also recently been elected to the post of Salem town clerk.

13. Joy is referring to Timothy Pickering's place of residence—Wenham, Massachusetts.

14. Essex County prosecutor Samuel Putnam.

15. The "gaol" was built in 1638 and sat on the corner of Federal Street and St. Peter Street, across from St. Peter's Church. Joy would be among the last inmates housed there, as the facility was closed the following year, when a new jail was constructed a short distance away. See C. B. Gillespie, *Illustrated History of Salem and Its Environs* (Salem, MA: Salem Evening News, 1897), 177.

16. The scripture Joy included is actually Psalm 50:15 (*The Holy Bible, Authorized King James Version* [n.p.: Thomas Nelson Bibles, 2001]).

17. Amma Brown.

18. This is a reference to Timothy Pickering.

19. Wenham.

20. Sheriff Robert Farley. A brief biography of Farley can be found in chapter 3.

21. An account of the damage done by Newburyport, Massachusetts, fire (May 31, 1811) can be found in the *Boston Gazette*, June 3, 1811. The fire burned over sixteen acres of the city's downtown and destroyed over 250 buildings.

22. Most certainly the Federalist *Salem Gazette*. The paper ran a number of stories on what it came to call the "Haverhill plot."

23. This most likely is a reference to Judge Aaron Wingate, whose famous uncle, Paine Wingate, was married to Eunice Pickering, Timothy Pickering's sister. Timothy Pickering's wife, Eunice, was also a member of the Wingate family. See Charles E. L. Wingate, *History of the Wingate Family in England and in America* (Exeter, NH: James D. P. Wingate, 1886).

24. Massachusetts was immersed in a very heated gubernatorial contest at the time. The details of the election can be found in chapter 3.

25. It is likely, given some of the later symptoms that he describes, that Joy was suffering from the onset of scurvy. Scurvy, a condition brought on by vitamin C deficiency, was common during this period of time. Joy's ability to obtain the necessary dosage of vitamin C to maintain his health would have been rendered all the more difficult by his late winter/early spring incarceration—a season in which fresh produce would have been nearly impossible to obtain. Many of the symptoms described by Joy, particularly the sore and bleeding gums and loose teeth, are characteristic of the disease.

26. Daniel Dutch.

27. Additional information on the partnership of Leigh and Ferguson can be found in chapter 2.

28. The perseverance of the saints is the Calvinist belief that once an in-

dividual is saved, that person is saved forever. The principle is discussed at greater length in chapter 4.

29. William Pickering (1786–1814) was the son of Timothy Pickering.

30. The *Jersey* was a British prison ship anchored in Long Island Sound. The mortality rates for American soldiers held on such ships was very high. See http://www.newsday.com/community/guide/lihistory/ny-history-hs425 a,0,6698945.story.

31. Republican Elbridge Gerry.

32. Judge Valentine Smith, who was also Durham's town clerk, was Timothy Joy's brother-in-law through marriage to Joy's sister Polly in 1804. She died in October 1810, leaving Smith with three small children. See James R. Joy, *Thomas Joy and His Descendants in the Lines of His Sons Samuel of Boston, Joseph of Hingham, Ephraim of Berwick: A Portfolio of Family Papers* (New York: privately printed, 1900), 40. A brief biography of Valentine Smith can be found in Everett S. Stackpole, Lucien Thompson, and Winthrop Meserve, *History of the Town of Durham, New Hampshire (Oyster River Plantation), with Genealogical Notes,* facsimile of the 1913 edition, with 2 vols. bound in a single edition (Somersworth, NH: New Hampshire Publishing, 1973), 1:296–97.

33. Curtis Coe (1787–1817) was the son of Durham's Congregational minister, also named Curtis Coe. Timothy's father, Samuel, was a deacon in Coe's church. See Daniel B. Coe and Eunice A. Lloyd, *Record of the Coe Family and Descendants from 1596 to 1885* (Cincinnati: Standard Publishing, 1885), 11–12.

34. The Wingate mentioned is Moses Wingate, the Republican town clerk of Haverhill. He was at Kendall's Tavern when Joy made his allegations about Timothy Pickering. He was also one of the men present when Joy was deposed regarding his claims. See chapter 3.

35. The judge presiding over the case was Chief Justice Samuel Sewall (a descendant of the famous judge in the Salem witch trials).

36. Joy is referring to the case against Warwick Palfrey, who was the editor of the Republican *Essex Register,* not the *Salem Gazette.* The article mentioned followed on the heels of the election-day riot in Salem on April 6, 1812. The incident is covered in detail in chapter 3.

37. Here again, Joy is referring to Palfrey, the editor of the *Essex Register.*

38. Salem's Federalist selectmen purged the town's voting list of hundreds of voters after their election in March of 1812. Leach was apparently one of these individuals. This action was the cause of the election-day riot mentioned by Joy on p. 62 of his journal and discussed in chapter 3.

39. Mr. C—— is undoubtedly Philip Chase, one of the Federalist Salem selectmen (and the only one whose last name begins with the letter *C*) elected in March 1812.

40. Caleb Strong.

BIBLIOGRAPHY

A list of newspapers, archival collections, and government documents follows this listing of secondary material.

Annable, Irving K. "Historical Notes of the Crombie Street Congregational Church, Salem, MA." *Essex Institute Historical Collections* 77 (July 1941): 207.

Appleby, Joyce. *Inheriting the Revolution: The First Generation of Americans.* Cambridge, MA: Harvard University Press, 2000.

Bain, Robert B. "Putting the Pieces Together (Again?): History Teacher Education as a University-Wide Task." Paper presented at the National History Center conference "Reforming History Education: New Research on Teaching and Learning," June 12, 2007.

Balleisen, Edward J. *Navigating Failure: Bankruptcy and Commercial Failure in Antebellum America.* Chapel Hill: University of North Carolina Press, 2001.

Bartlett, Albert Leroy. *Some Memories of Old Haverhill.* Haverhill, MA: privately printed, 1915.

Bartlett, J. Gardner. *Robert Coe, Puritan: His Ancestors and Descendants, 1340–1910, with Notices of Other Coe Families.* Boston: privately printed, 1911.

Bentley, William. *The Diary of William Bentley, D.D., Pastor of the East Church, Salem, Massachusetts.* Vol. 4, *January, 1811–December, 1819.* Gloucester, MA: Peter Smith, 1962.

Bolster, W. Jeffrey, ed. *Cross-Grained and Wily Waters: A Guide to the Piscataqua Maritime Region.* Portsmouth, NH: Peter E. Randall, 2002.

Borden, Morton. *Parties and Politics in the Early Republic.* Arlington Heights, IL: Harlan Davidson, 1967.

Borneman, Walter R. *1812: The War that Forged a Nation.* New York: HarperCollins, 2004.

Bouton, Nathaniel, comp. *Documents and Records Relating to the Province of New Hampshire, from the Earliest Period of Its Settlement.* Concord, NH: George E. Jenks, state printer, 1867.

Brown, Richard D. "Microhistory and the Post-Modern Challenge." *Journal of the Early Republic* 23 (Spring 2003): 1–20.

Buel, Richard, Jr. *America on the Brink: How the Political Struggle over the War of 1812 Almost Destroyed the Young Republic.* New York: Palgrave Macmillan, 2005.

Bunyan, John. *The Pilgrim's Progress from This World to That Which Is to Come.* Ed. N. H. Keeble. New York: Oxford University Press, 1998.

Butler, Jon. *Awash in a Sea of Faith: Christianizing the American People.* Cambridge, MA: Harvard University Press, 1990.

Caldwell, Patricia. *The Puritan Conversion Narrative: The Beginnings of American Expression.* New York: Cambridge University Press, 1983.

Chase, George Wingate. *The History of Haverhill, Massachusetts, from Its First Settlement, in 1640, to the Year 1860.* Haverhill, MA: privately printed, 1861.

Chernow, Ronald. *Alexander Hamilton.* New York: Penguin, 2004.

Clarfield, Gerard H. *Timothy Pickering and the American Republic.* Pittsburgh: University of Pittsburgh Press, 1980.

Clark, Charles E. "Disestablishment at the Grass Roots: Curtis Coe and the Separation of Church and Town." *Historical New Hampshire* 36 (Winter 1981): 280–305.

Clark, Charles E. *The Eastern Frontier: The Settlement of Northern New England, 1610–1763.* Hanover, NH: University Press of New England, 1983.

Clark, Christopher. *The Roots of Rural Capitalism: Western Massachusetts, 1780–1860.* Ithaca, NY: Cornell University Press, 1991.

Coe, Curtis. *A Serious Address of a Minister to His People: The Meaning of the Word Baptism Considered; Several Reasons Assigned for the Baptism of Infants, and Objections Answered.* Portsmouth, NH: printed by John Osborne at the *Spy* printing office, 1792.

Coe, Curtis. *A Valedictory Discourse, Delivered at Durham, New Hampshire, April 27, 1806.* Portsmouth, NH: William Treadwell, 1806.

Coe, Daniel B., and Eunice A. Lloyd. *Record of the Coe Family and Descendants from 1596 to 1885.* Cincinnati: Standard Publishing, 1885.

Cohen, Charles Lloyd. *God's Caress: The Psychology of Puritan Religious Experience.* New York: Oxford University Press, 1985.

Cole, Donald B. *Jacksonian Democracy in New Hampshire, 1800–1851.* Cambridge, MA: Harvard University Press, 1970.

Coleman, Peter J. *Debtors and Creditors in America: Insolvency, Imprisonment for Debt, and Bankruptcy, 1607–1900.* Madison: State Historical Society of Wisconsin, 1974.

Cousins, Frank, and Phil M. Riley. *The Colonial Architecture of Salem.* New York: Courier Dover, 2000.

Cross, Whitney. *The Burned-Over District: The Social and Intellectual History of Enthusiastic Religion in Western New York, 1800–1850.* Ithaca, NY: Cornell University Press, 1950.

Davis, Susan. *Parades and Power: Street Theater in Nineteenth-Century Philadelphia.* Philadelphia: University of Pennsylvania Press, 1986.

Defoe, Daniel. *The Life and Strange Surprising Adventures of Robinson Crusoe of York, Mariner.* New York: Oxford University Press, 1998.

Demos, John. *The Unredeemed Captive: A Family Story from Early America.* New York: Vintage Books, 1995.

"Description of Middleton on July 1, 1814." In *Collections of the Massachusetts Historical Society,* vol. 3 of the 2nd ser., 120–21. Boston: John Eliot, 1815.

Ditz, Toby L. "Shipwrecked; or, Masculinity Imperiled: Mercantile Representations of Failure and the Gendered Self in Eighteenth-Century Philadelphia." *Journal of American History* 81 (June 1994): 51–80.

Dublin, Thomas. *Women at Work: The Transformation of Work and Community in Lowell, Massachusetts, 1826–1860.* New York: Columbia University Press, 1981.

Egmond, Florike, and Peter Mason. *The Mammoth and the Mouse: Microhistory and Morphology.* Baltimore: Johns Hopkins University Press, 1997.

Elkins, Stanley, and Eric McKitrick. *The Age of Federalism: The Early American Republic, 1788–1800.* New York: Oxford University Press, 1993.

Ellis, Joseph J. *American Sphinx: The Character of Thomas Jefferson.* New York: Vintage Books, 1998.

Ellis, Joseph J. *Founding Brothers: The Revolutionary Generation.* New York: Alfred A. Knopf, 2000.

Felt, Joseph B. *Annals of Salem.* 2nd ed. Vol. 2, Salem, MA: W. and S. B. Ives, 1849.

Felt, Joseph B. *History of Ipswich, Essex, and Hamilton.* Cambridge, MA: Charles Folsom, 1834.

Freeman, Joanne B. *Affairs of Honor: National Politics in the New Republic.* New Haven, CT: Yale University Press, 2001.

Gannon, Kevin M. "Escaping 'Mr. Jefferson's Plan of Destruction': New England Federalists and the Idea of a Northern Confederacy, 1803–1804." *Journal of the Early Republic* 21 (Fall 2001): 313–43.

Geertz, Clifford. *The Interpretation of Cultures: Selected Essays.* New York: Basic Books, 1977.

Gillespie, C. B. *Illustrated History of Salem and Its Environs.* Salem, MA: Salem Evening News, 1897.

Gross, Robert A. *The Minutemen and Their World.* New York: Hill and Wang, 2001.

Hall, David D. *Lived Religion in America: Toward a History of Practice.* Princeton, NJ: Princeton University Press, 1997.

Haltunnen, Karen. *Confidence Men and Painted Women: A Study of Middle-Class Culture in America, 1830–1870.* New Haven, CT: Yale University Press, 1983.

Harkness, Marjory Gane, ed. *The Fishbasket Papers: The Diaries, 1768–1823, of Bradbury Jewell, Esquire, of Tamworth, Durham, and Sandwich, New Hampshire.* Peterborough, NH: Richard R. Smith, 1963.

Hatch, Nathan. *The Democratization of American Christianity.* New Haven, CT: Yale University Press, 1991.

Heidler, David S., and Jeanne T. Heidler, eds. *Encyclopedia of the War of 1812.* Annapolis, MD: U.S. Naval Institute Press, 2004.

Herbert, T. Walter. *Dearest Beloved: The Hawthornes and the Making of the Middle-Class Family.* Berkeley: University of California Press, 1993.

Herndon, Ruth Wallis. *Unwelcome Americans: Living on the Margin in Early New England.* Philadelphia: University of Pennsylvania Press, 2001.

Hickey, Donald R. *The War of 1812: A Forgotten Conflict.* Champaign-Urbana: University of Illinois Press, 1990.

Holifield, E. Brooks. *Theology in America: Christian Thought from the Age of the Puritans to the Civil War.* New Haven, CT: Yale University Press, 2003.

The Holy Bible, Authorized King James Version. N.p.: Thomas Nelson Bibles, 2001.

Howard, Cecil Hampden Cutts, ed. "Sketch of Mrs. William Jarvis of Weathersfield, Vermont." Pt. 1. *Historical Collections of the Essex Institute* 24 (April–June, 1887): 123–39.

Howe, Daniel Walker. *What God Hath Wrought: The Transformation of America, 1815–1848.* New York: Oxford University Press, 2009.

Hoyt, David W. *The Old Families of Salisbury and Amesbury, Massachusetts.* Somersworth, NH: New England History Press, 1981.

Hurd, D. Hamilton. *History of Rockingham and Strafford Counties, New Hampshire, with Biographical Sketches of Many of Its Pioneers and Prominent Men.* Philadelphia: J. W. Lewis, 1882.

"Introduction to Durham's 250th." Special issue, *Historical New Hampshire* 36 (Winter 1981): 254.

Johnson, Eric E. "The Battle of York." *Lake Erie Ledger* (June 2004): 243–47.

Johnson, Paul. *The Early American Republic, 1789–1829.* New York: Oxford University Press, 2007.

Johnson, Paul. *A Shopkeepers' Millennium: Society and Revivals in Rochester, New York, 1815–1837.* 2nd ed. New York: Hill and Wang, 2004.

Joy, James R. *Thomas Joy and His Descendants in the Lines of His Sons Samuel of Boston, Joseph of Hingham, Ephraim of Berwick: A Portfolio of Family Papers.* New York: privately printed, 1900.

Kagle, Stephen E. *Early Nineteenth-Century American Diary Literature.* Boston: Twayne, 1986.

Kidd, Thomas S. *The Great Awakening: The Roots of Evangelical Christianity in Colonial America.* New Haven, CT: Yale University Press, 2009.

Kidder, William, ed. "The Diary of Nicholas Gilman." MA thesis, University of New Hampshire, 1972.

King, John Owen, III. *The Iron of Melancholy: Structures of Spiritual Conver-*

sion in America from the Puritan Conscience to Victorian Neurosis. Middletown, CT: Wesleyan University Press, 1983.

Knox, John Jay. *A History of Banking in the United States.* New York: Bradford Rhodes, 1909.

Lawson, Russell M. *The Piscataqua Valley in the Age of Sail: A Brief History.* Charleston, SC: History Press, 2007.

Leonard, Gerald. *The Invention of Party Politics: Federalism, Popular Sovereignty, and Constitutional Development in Jacksonian Illinois.* Chapel Hill: University of North Carolina Press, 2002.

Lepore, Jill. "Historians Who Love Too Much: Reflections on Microhistory and Biography." *Journal of American History* 88 (Spring 2001): 129–44.

"Leverett Saltonstall's Reminiscences of Salem, Written in 1885." *Essex Institute Historical Collections* 81 (January 1945): 55–65.

Lockridge, Kenneth A. *A New England Town: The First Hundred Years; Dedham, Massachusetts, 1636–1736.* New York: W. W. Norton, 1985.

Lovett, Robert W. "A Tidewater Merchant in New Hampshire." *Business History Review* 33 (1959): 60–72.

MacLachlan, Courtney. "The Piscataqua Gundalow." *Maritime Life and Traditions* 30 (Spring 2007): 66–73.

Mann, Bruce H. *Republic of Debtors: Bankruptcy in the Age of American Independence.* Cambridge, MA: Harvard University Press, 2002.

McCoy, Drew. *The Elusive Republic: Political Economy in Jeffersonian America.* Chapel Hill: University of North Carolina Press, 1996.

Mihm, Stephen. *A Nation of Counterfeiters: Capitalists, Con Men, and the Making of the United States.* Cambridge, MA: Harvard University Press, 2007.

Miller, John C. *The Federalist Era, 1789–1801.* New York: Harper and Row, 1960.

Moore, Margaret B. *The Salem World of Nathaniel Hawthorne.* Columbia: University of Missouri Press, 1998.

Morgan, Edmund S. *Visible Saints: The History of the Puritan Idea.* Ithaca, NY: Cornell University Press, 1963.

Morrison, Dane Anthony, and Nancy Lusignan Schultz. *Salem: Place, Myth, Memory.* Boston: Northeastern University Press, 2004.

Nash, Gary. *The Unknown American Revolution: The Unruly Birth of Democracy and the Struggle to Create America.* New York: Viking, 2005.

National Park Service. *Salem: Maritime Salem in the Age of Sail.* Washington, DC: Department of the Interior, 1987.

Newman, Simon P. *Parades and the Politics of the Street: Festive Culture in the Early American Republic.* Philadelphia: University of Pennsylvania Press, 1997.

Noll, Mark. *God and Mammon: Protestants, Money, and the Market, 1790–1860.* New York: Oxford University Press, 2002.

Nylander, Jane C. *Our Own Snug Fireside: Images of the New England Home, 1760–1860.* New Haven, CT: Yale University Press, 1993.

Oberly, James W. *Sixty Million Acres: American Veterans and the Public Lands before the Civil War.* Kent, OH: Kent State University Press, 1990.

Pasley, Jeffrey L., Andrew W. Robertson, and David Waldstreicher, eds. *Beyond the Founders: New Approaches to the Political History of the Early American Republic.* Chapel Hill: University of North Carolina Press, 2004.

Pestana, Carla Gardina, and Sharon V. Salinger, eds. *Inequality in Early America.* Hanover, NH: Dartmouth University Press, 1999.

Porter, Charles E. *The Military History of the State of New Hampshire, 1623–1861.* Vol. 2, Baltimore: Genealogical Publishing, 1972.

Prentiss, Hervey Putnam. "Timothy Pickering and the War of 1812." *Essex Institute Historical Collections* 70 (April 1934): 105–14.

Rantoul, Robert S. "The Essex Junto, the Long Embargo, and the Great Topsfield Caucus of 1808: A Paper Read at the Field Meeting in Topsfield, Aug. 30, 1882." *Essex Institute Historical Collections* 19 (1882): 226–40.

Risjord, Norman K. *Jefferson's America.* New York: Rowman and Littlefield, 2002.

Rockman, Seth. *Scraping By: Wage Labor, Slavery, and Survival in Early Baltimore.* Baltimore: Johns Hopkins University Press, 2009.

Rockman, Seth. *Welfare Reform in the Early Republic: A Brief History with Documents.* Boston: Bedford/St. Martins, 2003.

Roth, Randolph A. *The Democratic Dilemma: Religion, Reform, and the Social Order in the Connecticut River Valley of Vermont, 1791–1850.* Cambridge: Cambridge University Press, 1987.

Saltonstall, William G. *Ports of the Piscataqua: Soundings in the Maritime History of the Portsmouth, N.H., Customs District from the Days of Queen Elizabeth and the Planting of Strawberry Banke to the Times of Abraham Lincoln and the Waning of the American Clipper.* New York: Russell and Russell, 1968.

Sanborn, Edwin D. *History of New Hampshire, from Its First Discovery to the Year 1830; with Dissertations upon the Rise of Opinions and Institutions, the Growth of Agriculture and Manufactures, and the Influence of Leading Families and Distinguished Men to the Year 1874.* Manchester, NH: John B. Clarke, 1875.

Sandage, Scott A. *Born Losers: A History of Failure in America.* Cambridge, MA: Harvard University Press, 2005.

Scales, John. *History of Strafford County, New Hampshire, and Representative Citizens.* Chicago: Richmond-Arnold, 1914.

Scales, John. "Lee, NH—250th Anniversary of Settlement of the Territory, 150th Anniversary of Incorporation of the Town." Address, August 23, 1916.

Sellers, Charles. *The Market Revolution: Jacksonian America, 1815–1846.* New York: Oxford University Press, 1992.

Sharp, James Roger. *American Politics in the Early Republic: The New Nation in Crisis.* New Haven, CT: Yale University Press, 1993.

Shea, Daniel B., Jr. *Spiritual Autobiography in Early America.* Princeton, NJ: Princeton University Press, 1968.

Smith, Billy G., ed. *Down and Out in Early America.* University Park: Pennsylvania State University Press, 2004.

Stackpole, Everett S., Lucien Thompson, and Winthrop Meserve. *History of the Town of Durham, New Hampshire (Oyster River Plantation), with Genealogical Notes.* Facsimile of the 1913 edition, with 2 vols. bound in a single edition. Somersworth, NH: New Hampshire Publishing, 1973.

Sutton, William R. *Journeymen for Jesus: Evangelical Artisans Confront Capitalism in Jacksonian Baltimore.* University Park: Pennsylvania State University Press, 1998.

Ulrich, Laurel Thatcher. *A Midwife's Tale: The Life of Martha Ballard Based on Her Diary, 1785–1815.* New York: Vintage Books, 1991.

Varnum, John Marshall. *The Varnums of Dracutt (in Massachusetts): A History.* Boston: David Clapp and Sons, 1907.

Vickers, Daniel. *Farmers and Fishermen: Two Centuries of Work in Essex County, Massachusetts, 1630–1830.* Chapel Hill: University of North Carolina Press, 1994.

Vickers, Daniel, with Vince Walsh. *Young Men and the Sea: Yankee Seafarers in the Age of Sail.* New Haven, CT: Yale University Press, 2005.

Waldstreicher, David. *In the Midst of Perpetual Fetes: The Making of American Nationalism, 1776–1820.* Chapel Hill: University of North Carolina Press, 1997.

Waters, Thomas Franklin. *Ipswich in the Massachusetts Bay Colony.* Vol. 2, *A History of the Town from 1700–1917.* Ipswich, MA: Ipswich Historical Society, 1917.

Watson, Harry. *Liberty and Power: The Politics of Jacksonian America.* New York: Hill and Wang, 1990.

Wentworth, William Edgar. *Vital Records, 1790–1829, from Dover, New Hampshire's First Newspaper.* Camden, ME: Picton, 1995.

White, M. J. "A Historical Study of Old Durham." Unpublished manuscript in the possession of the New Hampshire State Library, n.d.

Wilson, Lisa. *Ye Heart of a Man: The Domestic Life of Men in Colonial New England.* New Haven, CT: Yale University Press, 1999.

Wingate, Charles E. L. *History of the Wingate Family in England and America.* Exeter, NH: James D. P. Wingate, 1886.

Winiarski, Douglas L. "Souls Filled with Ravishing Transport: Heavenly Visions and the Radical Awakening in New England." *William and Mary Quarterly* 61 (January 2004): 3–46.

Wood, Gordon S. *The Creation of the American Republic, 1776–1787.* Chapel Hill: University of North Carolina Press, 1998.

Wood, Gordon S. *Empire of Liberty: A History of the Early Republic, 1789–1815.* New York: Oxford University Press, 2009.

Wood, Gordon S. *The Radicalism of the American Revolution.* New York: Alfred A. Knopf, 1992.

NEWSPAPERS

Boston Gazette, Boston, MA, 1811–12.
Daily Evening Times, Portsmouth, NH, 1883.
Essex Register, Salem, MA, 1812.
Greenfield Franklin Herald, Greenfield, MA, 1812.
Hallowell American Advocate, Hallowell, MA, 1812.
Merrimack Intelligencer, Haverhill, MA, 1812.
New Hampshire Gazette, Portsmouth, NH, 1795 and 1812.
New Hampshire Republican, Dover, NH, 1824.
Portland Eastern Argus, Portland, MA, 1812.
Portsmouth Daily Chronicle, Portsmouth, NH, 1883.
Portsmouth Journal, Portsmouth, NH, 1846.
Portsmouth Oracle, Portsmouth, NH, 1813–14.
Salem Gazette, Salem, MA, 1812–14.

ARCHIVAL AND GOVERNMENT SOURCES

BAKER LIBRARY HISTORICAL COLLECTIONS,
HARVARD UNIVERSITY, CAMBRIDGE, MA

Samuel and Ebenezer Joy Records, 1807–32.

BENTLEY HISTORICAL LIBRARY,
UNIVERSITY OF MICHIGAN, ANN ARBOR, MI

Diary of Timothy M. Joy (Written in Ipswich Prison, Salem, Massachusetts,
1812), box 7, Henry B. Joy Historical Research Record Group.

MAINE STATE ARCHIVES

Maine Court Records, 1696–1854.

MASSACHUSETTS SUPREME JUDICIAL COURT
ARCHIVES AND RECORDS PRESERVATION

Commonwealth v. Joy, Essex County Supreme Judicial Court, 1812 April term,
docket no. 183.

MILNE SPECIAL COLLECTIONS,
UNIVERSITY OF NEW HAMPSHIRE, DURHAM, NH

Durham (N.H.) Selectmen's Records.
Durham Town Records, 1732–1993.
Thompson Family Papers, 1703–1924.

NATIONAL ARCHIVES, WASHINGTON, DC

Bounty Land Grant Warrant Application of Mary Joy, dated October 21, 1850, "Bounty Land Files," can 306, bundle 97.
"Pension Application Files, War of 1812, Death or Disability," file 13557.
Third United States Artillery, Enlistment Register.

NEW HAMPSHIRE STATE ARCHIVES, CONCORD, NH

Inventories, Durham, 1811.
Inventories, Middleton, 1811.
Probate Records, vol. 18 (1750–54).
Provincial Court Records.
"Road and Highway Layouts, Durham," binder 14.
Rockingham County Deeds, vols. 25, 64, 70, 79, and 84.

PHILLIPS LIBRARY, PEABODY-ESSEX MUSEUM, SALEM, MA

Another Plot! The Heat of the Election Hatches a Brood of Plots and Falsehoods, n.d., ca. March 1812, "Broadsides."
Beware of Imposters or Slander Detected, n.d., ca. March 1812, "Broadsides."
Essex County Court of Common Pleas Docket (1812).
Essex County Court of Common Pleas Records (March 1812).
Ezra Northey Diaries, 1800, 1810–16.
Timothy Pickering Papers.

STRAFFORD COUNTY RECORDS, DOVER, NH

Grantee (Purchaser) Index, Register of Deeds.
Grantor (Seller) Index, Register of Deeds.
Strafford County Probate Records.

U.S. GOVERNMENT DOCUMENTS

Inter-university Consortium for Political and Social Research. UNITED STATES HISTORICAL ELECTION RETURNS, 1788–1823 [Computer file]. 5th ICPSR ed. Ann Arbor, MI: Inter-university Consortium for Political and Social Research [producer and distributor], 1995.
United States Federal Census, 1810, New Durham, Strafford County, New Hampshire.
United States Federal Census, 1820, Newmarket, Rockingham County, New Hampshire.
United States Federal Census, 1830, Newmarket, Rockingham County, New Hampshire.

United States Federal Census, 1840, Newmarket, Rockingham County, New
Hampshire.

United States Federal Census, 1850, Newmarket, Rockingham County, New
Hampshire.

United States Federal Census, 1860, Second Ward, Portsmouth, Rockingham
County, New Hampshire.

United States Federal Census, 1870, Newmarket, Rockingham County, New
Hampshire.

United States Federal Census, 1880, Durham, Strafford County, New Hampshire.

United States Federal Census, 1880, Newmarket, Rockingham County, New
Hampshire.

INDEX

Note: The abbreviation "TMJ" stands for Timothy Meader Joy. Names followed by family relations enclosed in parentheses apply primarily to their relationship to Timothy Meader Joy.

dismissal of Curtis Coe, 11–13
dismissal of Hugh Adams, 20–21
dismissal of John Adams, 21–22
Joy family purchase of pew 42, 11,
    186n1
TMJ death and burial, 2, 115–16,
    211n13
Corinthians 2, 97
credit system/instruments
    handshakes and promises as,
        49–50
    impact of war tensions on, 35–36,
        48
    politics, 78
    post-Revolutionary America, 47
    TMJ reliance on, 43–45, 199n18,
        201n24
    TMJ repayment of loans, 110–11
    TMJ views on, 77–79
    See also indebtedness
Crooker, Stephen, 37, 214n6
Crowninshield, John, 39
Cummings, David, 57, 59–60, 150,
    198n13, 205n28

Darby's Wharf. *See* Derby's Wharf
Davis, Susan, 69
Dearborn, Henry, 112
Defoe, Daniel, 209n30
Democratic-Republicans
    American foreign policy, 64–66
    gubernatorial campaign of 1812,
        37–38, 202n7
    Joy's political beliefs, 1
    Massachusetts politics, 72–74
    New Hampshire politics, 70–72
    post-Revolutionary politics, 8
    Salem election-day riot, 58–61
    TMJ Haverhill affair, 74–77
Demos, John, 126
Derby, Elias Hasket, 39, 214n9
Derby's Wharf (Salem), 3, 39–40,
    214n9
diary of TMJ

arraignment and setting bail,
    139–40
arrival in Salem and arrest, 138–39
assistance from outside the jail,
    142
cell mates, 141–43, 144–45, 152,
    170–71
confinement in Salem Jail, 140–44
departure from home and family,
    135–36
grand jury hearing, 166–68
Haverhill affair, 136–37
physical affliction in prison, 143,
    148–50, 157–61, 168
poetry, 156–57, 159, 162, 164, 165,
    175, 178, 181
about the reasons for journaling,
    135
release from prison, 183–84
strengthening of spiritual resolve,
    176–79
support from Eben, 146–47,
    165–66, 168–69, 184
transfer to Ipswich Prison, 144
visitors, 149–50, 158, 161–62, 168,
    171–72, 181
diary of TMJ as history
    author's discovery of, 125–26
    creating thematic focus, 131–32
    as journal of "situation," 130–31
    as microhistory, 126–28
    researching supporting evidence,
        132–34
    understanding the significance,
        128–30
disease. *See* illness, TMJ
disenfranchisement of voters, 58–60
Ditz, Toby, 47
Dover, N.H. (formerly Northam),
    14–15, 188n5
"Dr. Child's Memorial" petition,
    188n8
Dublin, Thomas, 126
Dummer's War (1722–25), 17

ect INDEX

Made in United States
North Haven, CT
21 June 2023

38026150R00157